A Course in
English
Language
Teaching

Penny Ur

CAMBRIDGE
UNIVERSITY PRESS

CAMBRIDGE UNIVERSITY PRESS
Cambridge, New York, Melbourne, Madrid, Cape Town,
Singapore, São Paulo, Delhi, Mexico City

Cambridge University Press
The Edinburgh Building, Cambridge CB2 8RU, UK

www.cambridge.org
Information on this title: www.cambridge.org/9781107684676

© Cambridge University Press 2012

A revised edition of *A Course in Language Teaching*
First edition 1996
Second edition 2012
Reprinted 2012

Printed and bound in the United Kingdom by the MPG Books Group

A catalogue record for this publication is available from the British Library

Library of Congress Cataloging in Publication Data

Ur, Penny.
  A course in English language teaching / Penny Ur. -- 2nd ed.
    p. cm.
  Rev. ed. of: A course in language teaching. 1996.
  Includes bibliographical references and index.
  ISBN 978-1-107-68467-6 (pbk.)
  1. Language and languages--Study and teaching.   I. Ur, Penny. Course in language
teaching. II. Title.
  P51.U7 2012
  428'.0071--dc23
                                                                    2012001484

ISBN 978-1-107-68467-6 Paperback

Contents

Acknowledgements

I should like to thank all those who have contributed in different ways to this book:

- To Barbara Górska, whose critical and constructive comments were based on her own hands-on experience using the first edition in teacher training and were of immense value at the early stages of writing;

- To Fran Disken and Nora McDonald from Cambridge University Press, who supported the writing of later drafts, with perceptive and creative suggestions for improving the content;

- To Jacque French, my painstaking copy-editor, who besides picking up and correcting inconsistencies and errors has been amazingly patient in her responses to my unending quibbles, uncertainties and changing demands;

- To the many teachers who contributed to the feedback on the first edition of this book, which furnished the basis for changes appearing in the second;

- To my teacher-trainer colleagues at Oranim Academic College of Education, who shared, discussed and tried out many of the practical procedures suggested in this book;

- To my BA and MA classes at the same college, who enabled me to develop as a teacher-trainer;

- And last but certainly not least, to all my school students: the children and teenagers to whom I have taught English and who have taught me to teach over the years.

The authors and publishers acknowledge the following sources of copyright material and are grateful for the permissions granted. While every effort has been made, it has not always been possible to identify the sources of all the material used, or to trace all copyright holders. If any omissions are brought to our notice, we will be happy to include the appropriate acknowledgements on reprinting.

p. 36 Screenshot from Lextutor vocabprofile website http://www.lextutor.ca/vp/bnc/ used with permission; p. 39 'The Purist' by Ogden Nash, published by Andre Deutsch, copyright © 1936 by Ogden Nash, reprinted by permission of Curtis Brown, Ltd; pp. 204–5 New Yorkers extract from *Effective Reading in a Changing World,* 3rd edition (companion website wps.prenhall.com/hss_wassman_effective_3/55/14085/3605849.cw/index.html) reading passage III, by Rose Wassman and Lee Ann Rinsky, published by Prentice Hall; p. 205 photo Morgan Creek/Warner Bros/Kobal Collection; pp. 206–7 'Emperor penguin makes epic detour to New Zealand beach' article published June 2011, used with permission of The Associated Press, copyright © 2011, all rights reserved; p. 294 photo by Mike Hogan.

The publisher has used its best endeavours to ensure that the URLs for external websites referred to in this book are correct and active at the time of going to press. However, the publisher has no responsibility for the websites and can make no guarantee that a site will remain live or that the content is or will remain appropriate.

Introduction

1 About the second edition

The first edition of this book, *A Course in Language Teaching*, was published in 1996, as part of the Cambridge Teacher Training and Development series. It related to language instruction in general, whereas this new edition focuses specifically on English teaching.

The second edition includes extracts from the previous one, but has been extensively rewritten. This is partly because my ideas on some subjects have developed and changed as a result of added experience, discussion with colleagues, and reading of the research literature. And it is partly because of feedback: teachers and trainers have told me which parts of the first edition were more helpful and which were less, and have provided suggestions for improvement.

2 Learning to teach

If you ask experienced English teachers how they became good at their job, the majority will tell you that most of their learning came from actual classroom experience. This is not very helpful to a new, or trainee, teacher, who does not yet have much experience but urgently needs to acquire the basic professional ability to walk into a classroom and teach a lesson.

This book provides the basis for professional learning both before and during classroom experience in the following ways:

1. It provides essential **information**, based on the experience of successful practitioners and up-to-date research-based theory. This includes topics such as what we know about how people learn additional languages, and what teaching strategies are likely to lead to successful learning.
2. It invites **reflection**, through inviting you to consider and criticize classroom activities or scenarios, relate theoretical ideas to your own experience as student or teacher, or to try out procedures.
3. It gives **practical guidelines** on how to teach particular aspects of language (e.g. grammar, or listening comprehension), run particular types of procedures (e.g. discussions, or tests), or improve lessons (e.g. how to add interest, or cope with discipline problems).

The aim is to equip you with the knowledge and skills needed to perform competently as an English teacher from the beginning: to plan and run interesting and learning-rich lessons, use texts and tasks effectively, and so on. Later, as you become more experienced, both your knowledge and your skill will increase. That is one of the nice things about teaching: you keep getting better at it as time goes on.

3 Using this book

Look through the contents page to get a general idea of the topics covered in this course. Then choose a unit whose subject particularly interests you, and glance through it in order to familiarize yourself with the layout, organization and different kinds of content.

The units

The first four units (a general introduction to issues in English teaching today, followed by units on lesson planning, the text and the task) provide enough preliminary knowledge to enable you to plan a lesson and teach it. The next seven units deal with the teaching of grammar and vocabulary and of the four skills. So the first eleven units can provide you with a short, fairly intensive training course in basic English-teaching skills and knowledge.

If you have more time, then it is up to you which of the later units you or the teacher trainer leading your course wish to study. If your top priority is practical teaching skills, then it is probably best to start with the units on assessment (12), materials (14) and teaching heterogeneous classes (19), as well as the relevant sections of the unit on teaching different age groups (18). If, however, you are aiming for longer-term professional awareness and knowledge as well as hands-on skills, then you will find the other units just as valuable.

Each unit consists primarily of informational content and critical discussion of selected practical examples. There are also occasional 'Practical tips': useful little teaching techniques or ideas about how to cope with specific problems.

At the beginning of each unit, you will find a list of the topics dealt with in the different sections. This will give you an overview of the content, and also enable you to decide which sections you want to spend more, or less, time studying.

The tasks

The tasks are optional: you can learn from the book without doing any of them. But I recommend doing as many as you can. They are interesting to do, will enrich your understanding, enable you to relate more thoughtfully and critically to the ideas provided in the main text, and ultimately result in better learning of the material.

There are two types of task. Those headed 'Task' are ones you can do without going outside the book. For example, you might be asked to relate critically to a recommendation in the light of your own experience learning a language, or to express your own opinion of a set of statements. These do not usually take very long, and can be done either on your own or in collaboration with colleagues. The ones headed 'Action task' demand some kind of action outside the book itself. For example, you might be asked to observe a lesson, or check out a particular aspect of a coursebook, or consult an experienced teacher. These demand more work, but they are also more rewarding in terms of their learning value.

Review

At the end of the unit is a set of questions which you can use to check whether you have understood the ideas given in the unit, and how much of the information you can remember. Doing these questions functions as a useful review of the content. If you are working alone, you might write down your answers, and then check back to see what you got right, correct yourself if necessary, and add anything you had forgotten. If you are working in a group, you could do the questions together, orally or in writing, pooling your knowledge. Then you can go back to the sections of the unit itself to check your answers.

Further reading
After the review at the end of each unit, you will find a short list of books, and sometimes websites, that are recommended if you wish to find more texts to read that will enrich your knowledge of the subject matter.

Glossary
The glossary, located at the end of the book before the bibliography, provides brief definitions of most terms associated with English language teaching that are used in the units. Usually such terms are explained where they first occur; but occasionally you may need to look up one that you find difficult to recall.

Bibliography
The bibliography at the end of the book provides a comprehensive list of all the books, articles and websites mentioned in the book. So if there is a brief reference to a research article in the course of a unit, you will find the full reference in the bibliography, not in the further reading section at the end of the unit.

4 For the trainer
Two components that are particularly useful for trainer-led courses are the tasks and reviews.

The tasks may well take up most of the time in your face-to-face sessions with trainees. They furnish the basis for hands-on experiment, sharing of previous learning experiences, and critical discussion. Although tasks are often worded as if they are addressing a single individual, they can in fact be done collaboratively. The action tasks based on actual teaching or observation are not always practicable, but they provide valuable learning experiences. In fact, if observation and (practice-) teaching are possible, you may want to add more such tasks: for example, to invite trainees to observe or try out particular procedures described in one of the units.

Tasks can also be used as the basis for written assignments, which can be checked and graded, and then used as one of the components of a final grade for the course.

The reviews can be used:

- as a basis for informal full-class review and discussion;
- as an individual homework assignment: students write their own answers and check themselves by referring back to the unit;
- as a test done in writing in class, followed by a full-class check of answers;
- as a written test at the end of the unit.

1 English teaching today: what do I need to know?

Overview

The sections in this unit are:

1.1 **Teaching priorities**. The importance of teaching for both accuracy and fluency; making learners aware of the variety of 'Englishes'; a focus on vocabulary; and the teaching of informal writing skills.

1.2 **English as an international language**. The increasing use of English for international communication and some of the implications for English language teaching worldwide.

1.3 **Language-acquisition theories and teaching methodologies**. A critical discussion of some of the most important language-teaching methodologies today and their roots in language-acquisition theories.

1.4 **Computerized teaching materials**. The increasing use of digital materials and internet-based texts and tasks to supplement coursebooks and other paper materials.

1.5 **Motivation**. Factors which motivate, or demotivate, learners in their learning of English, and what the teacher can do to increase learner motivation.

1.1 Teaching priorities

Teaching priorities in English language teaching have varied over the years: fashions are constantly changing. The summary below represents those that seem to me to be well established at the time of writing, and acceptable to most teachers and writers on methodology.

Fluency and accuracy

The balance between fluency and accuracy is a good example of something that has not changed very much, in spite of some temporary fluctuations in fashion. It is important for our students to learn to use English both fluently and correctly so that they can get their message across effectively while using standard grammatical, lexical, phonological and spelling conventions. However, something that has changed is that these conventions are no longer necessarily those of native speakers. They are, rather, those which are used by the majority of fluent, educated speakers of the language in international communication.

There will be situations where we are less fussy about absolute accuracy, because getting a message across is more important; and others (perhaps less frequent) where correctness is the priority. However, in general, we will do the best we can to make sure our students maintain a balance between the two (see, for example, Unit 6: Teaching grammar, and Unit 7: Error correction).

Task

Recall an occasion when you were reading or listening to English which had obvious mistakes in it. What effect did these mistakes have on you? Which of the items below best describes how you felt?

1. I had no problem at all with reading/listening and understanding. The mistakes didn't make any difference.
2. I felt slightly uncomfortable reading or listening. I would have felt more comfortable if there had been no mistakes.
3. I sometimes had to make an effort to understand.
4. I found it quite difficult to understand.
5. I actually misunderstood.

Inaccurate vocabulary, grammar, spelling and pronunciation very rarely produce misunderstandings. They may, however, interfere with the smoothness of the communication and result in a feeling of slight discomfort for both speaker/writer and listener/reader.

Different styles and Englishes

Since English is today being used for all sorts of purposes worldwide, it is important for our students to know that there is not just one 'English style'. There is, in fact, an enormous number of them. For example, students need to know the differences between informal speech and more formal written discourse; between the kind of text you can acceptably write in emails, or when chatting online, and the kind of text you should write in an academic essay. We therefore need to make sure that our teaching programmes include exposure to a range of styles in order to raise students' awareness of the differences between them. In some cases we may also want to get the students to try producing the different styles themselves.

There is also a large number of different varieties of English (Kirkpatrick, 2007), each associated with a particular local community (e.g. Singlish in Singapore), social group (e.g. teenage English in any native-speaking community) or profession (e.g. legal English).

Task

Make a list of the different kinds of English styles or genres you have heard, read, spoken or written over the last few days. For example: a shopping list, a telephone conversation, a text message (SMS) or a novel. How many different kinds of texts did you find?

Vocabulary

There has been a great deal of research on vocabulary teaching in recent years. A major finding has been the overall importance of vocabulary knowledge, particularly for reading comprehension. In order to read and understand an unsimplified text in English and guess the words they did not know before, learners probably need to know several thousand word families. Moreover, it appears that acquiring vocabulary simply by reading or listening during a language course will not provide learners with the amount of vocabulary they need. We have to supplement such incidental acquisition with deliberate teaching and review of lexical items (see Unit 5: Teaching vocabulary). This recommendation certainly matches the professional intuition of many experienced teachers, including myself. It contrasts with earlier methodologies which recommended spending most time teaching the grammar, assuming that the vocabulary would take care of itself. It also differs from an extreme communicative approach, according to which it is not necessary to teach vocabulary consciously because learners will acquire it through general communicative exposure to the language (see Section 1.3 below).

Task

What is your own experience of vocabulary learning when you learnt a new language in school? How did your teacher help you acquire vocabulary?

Writing

Writing is often – perhaps mainly – used in language teaching as a vehicle for language practice and testing, rather than for the sake of the writing skill itself. Until comparatively recently, it has been far less useful for communicative purposes than the other three skills of listening, reading or speaking. For this reason communicative writing activities are less common in teaching materials than ones which promote communication through the other three skills. However, the importance of informal writing for communication has increased immensely in the last generation (Crystal, 2006), mainly due to the widespread use of email, online chat, blogging, texting (SMS) and social networking tools such as *Facebook* and *Twitter*.

This means that we need to invest more effort in helping our students achieve written, as well as reading, fluency (see Unit 11: Teaching writing). They need to master basic spelling, common abbreviations typical of informal texts (e.g. *u* for 'you' and *r* for 'are'), the use of punctuation and so on. Perhaps even more important for written fluency is the promotion of fast typing. This does not mean that we need, as English teachers, to teach students how to type! But it does mean that we need to encourage them to practise doing so. (Note that the ability to type fast in another language does not immediately transfer to English, even if the L1 (mother tongue) uses the Latin alphabet, since fast typing – particularly touch-typing – involves the automatic production of typical letter combinations rather than individual letters.) This does not, of course, mean neglecting the teaching of clear and legible handwriting, which will continue to be a necessary skill for the foreseeable future. But the ability to type fast and accurately is at least as important, and in some cases more so.

> ### Task
>
> Have a look at your answers to the earlier task on p. 2 where you listed the different styles and genres you have encountered.
>
> Which of those you listed involved your own writing?
>
> How many of these, as far as you know, were being used before 1990?

1.2 English as an international language

Perhaps the most dramatic development that has taken place in the field of English language teaching in the last 50 years has been the shift in its primary function: from being mainly the native language of nations such as the UK or USA, to being mainly a global means of communication. The speakers of English whose L1 is another language already vastly outnumber native English speakers, and their number continues to grow. For most of its learners, English is therefore no longer a foreign language (i.e. one that is owned by a particular 'other' nation or ethnic group) but first and foremost an international language (one that has no particular national owner) (Rubdy & Saraceni, 2006). This development has brought with it a number of changes in the principles and practice of English language teaching.

> ### Task
>
> How many of the people you have spoken to in English recently were in fact native speakers of that language, and how many were native speakers of other languages, using English as a means of communication?
>
> The answer to this will depend of course on where you are living as you read this; but if you are not living in an English-speaking country, it is likely that most people you interact with in English are not native speakers.

Language standards

A question which many teachers in the previous generation had difficulty in answering was which of the major varieties of English to teach: British or American? This is no longer a relevant, or even an interesting, question. The question which needs to be asked is rather: which lexical, grammatical, phonological or orthographical (spelling) forms are most likely to be understood and used worldwide? These are the ones we should usually be teaching. For example, it is more useful to teach *two weeks* than *fortnight*, as *two weeks* is more universally used and understood. It is useful to encourage our students to pronounce the /r/ in words like *girl*, *teacher*, as this pronunciation is easier to understand and more 'transparent' for those who know the written form. And it is likely to be more useful to teach the spelling *organize* than *organise* – again for reasons of transparency, clarity and general acceptability. The same applies to choices we may need to make in the area of dialect, conventions of style and so on. The question should not be 'What does a Brit (or American, or Australian or whatever) say?' but rather 'What is likely to be most easily understood and accepted by other English speakers, native and non-native, around the world?'

Task

Can you think of any other vocabulary or grammatical forms which are specific to the variety of English you might use yourself with friends or family or in your local community, but that you would not use if you were communicating in English in a wider context?

The native and non-native English teacher

English teachers who speak the language as an additional rather than as a native language are, as implied above, the majority worldwide. The English spoken by such teachers, if they are (as they should be!) fully competent and fluent in the language, is also likely to be a better model of international English for their students than any 'native' variety. In addition, they have been through the same learning process as their students. They have insights into the kinds of problems that are likely to come up and how to deal with them. And they can function as role models: 'If I can do it, so can you!'

This is not to say that native English-speaker teachers cannot be effective teachers: of course they can. The point is that they are not necessarily superior to their non-native colleagues. Many teach very successfully in schools in non-English-speaking countries of the world (this is my own teaching background and that of many of my native-speaker colleagues). They are particularly in demand in some language schools whose students expect to be taught by 'native speakers', and in situations where the language is taught as a preparation for study or work in an English-speaking country.

The place of English literature and the culture of the English-speaking peoples

Methodology books of the twentieth century typically talk of the culture of the English-speaking peoples as the 'target culture' and assume that reading texts in course materials should be copied or adapted from 'authentic' texts from English-speaking countries. This also has changed. Courses today may include not only texts from English-speaking countries, but also those written in English, or translated into it, from anywhere in the world. And in most teaching contexts, it is inappropriate to talk about a 'target' culture, meaning a native-speaker one. Most learners need to become aware of a diverse, international, cosmopolitan set of cultural customs, literature, art forms and so on, rather than those of a single community (see Unit 15: Teaching content, pp. 218–19, 223).

It is, therefore, more important these days to foster multicultural awareness on the part of our students than to teach them particular codes of conduct or literary traditions (Byram, 1997). We cannot, obviously, teach them all the cultures of the world. However, we can expose them to a sample through our materials, make them sensitive to the kinds of differences from their own cultures that they may come across and foster intercultural competence (see Unit 15: Teaching content, pp. 219–20).

> ## Task
>
> Can you think of an example of how your own culture differs from that of speakers of English you have encountered from other backgrounds? Has this difference ever produced difficulties or embarrassments which, with hindsight, you could have avoided if you had known about it?

The place of the L1

It has been taken for granted in the past that the aim of an English course is to make the learners communicate like native speakers. This is for most learners an inaccessible goal; and these days it is not even an appropriate one. Even if the aim is to communicate with, among others, native speakers, this does not necessarily mean trying to be a 'native speaker' oneself. The appropriate model in most cases, as suggested above, is probably the non-native-speaker teacher. For most students today, English is a tool, like basic arithmetic, or literacy, or computer skills: an ability they need to master in order to function effectively in today's world. The L1 remains the learner's primary language and the one they identify with. What we as teachers are aiming for is functional English-knowing bilingualism (or, in many cases, multilingualism). There is, therefore, no particular reason to ban the use of the L1 in the classroom. On the contrary, the L1 is likely to play a valuable role in the acquisition of English, and translation – at least at word or sentence level – is a useful ability, to be promoted rather than discouraged.

> ## Task
>
> Thinking back to your own school lessons in English or another additional language: do you think the teacher used the L1 enough? Not enough? Too much?

1.3 Language-acquisition theories and teaching methodologies

Theories of language acquisition

The main ideas on how we acquire second or foreign languages in school can be summarized as follows:

- **Intuitive acquisition.** We learn another language the same way as we learnt our first: intuitive acquisition through lots of exposure to the language in authentic communicative situations (Krashen, 1982).

- **Habit-formation.** Language is a set of habits: we mimic and memorize and drill the patterns of the language until we learn to produce the correct forms automatically (based on an interpretation of Skinner, 1957).

- **Cognitive process.** Language involves the understanding of underlying rules: if we master these rules, we will be able to apply them in different contexts (based on an interpretation of Chomsky, 1957).

- **Skill-learning.** Language is a skill. We learn it in school just as we learn other skills: someone explains rules or words to us, we understand and practise them until we master them and use them fluently and skilfully (Johnson, 1996).

The main contrasting concepts underlying these four theories are *explicit* versus *implicit* teaching and learning. If you think that we learn languages through subconscious acquisition without actually working out rules or translating words, then you prefer an implicit model and would favour the first or second items above. If, however, you think that we need consciously to understand how the language works, then you would favour an explicit model, expressed in the third and fourth.

Probably all of these theories have some truth in them. None on its own can really cover the complexity of the second-language-learning process. They provide, in various combinations, the theoretical basis for the different methodologies summarized below.

Language teaching approaches and methodologies

An approach can be defined as a principled model of language teaching/learning, based on theories of language and language acquisition. A methodology is a collection of teaching procedures that accord with and apply a particular approach.

A wide variety of approaches and methodologies has been used for language teaching in the last century, and many continue to be used today (Richards & Rodgers, 2001). *Grammar-translation*, *audio-lingualism* and '*PPP*' were probably the dominant models of the early and middle twentieth century, and are still widely used. The *communicative approach*, expressed through various methodologies, dominated the late twentieth and early twenty-first centuries, though most people today would adopt what I have called, for want of a better term, the *post-communicative approach*.

Grammar-translation involves, as its name implies, explanation of grammar rules (by the teacher, in the L1) and translation of texts from and to the target language. It focuses on the written form of the language and more formal registers, and does not include very much oral or communicative work.

The direct method was largely based on a reaction against grammar-translation. It emphasizes oral communication more and bans the use of the L1 in the classroom: everything should be taught through the target language. It is still, to this day, the basic methodology of the Berlitz language schools.

Audio-lingualism is based on the idea that language is a set of habits and involves a lot of teacher-led drilling, learning by heart and repetition (Rivers, 1980). It is most important to learn the spoken form of the language, and most classroom procedures are speech-based. Like grammar-translation, its main aim is accuracy rather than fluency, and it focuses on grammar rather than vocabulary.

PPP stands for 'Presentation, Practice, Production'. This is a component of a methodology, or a description of suggested stages in a lesson, rather than a whole methodology. It is important because it is based on a skill-learning theory of language acquisition. Like the previous three items, it emphasizes grammatical accuracy and is very teacher-dominated.

The communicative approach gained increasing support from the late 1970s onwards (Widdowson,1978). It is based on the assumption that language is (for) communication and that we learn it best through naturalistic acquisition processes (i.e. processes similar to those used when learning a native language). The classroom is more learner-centred, and the conveying of meanings is seen as more important than accuracy. There are a number of methodologies based on this: perhaps the most widely used and written about ones today are task-based instruction and CLIL (content and language integrated learning). According to the first, learners perform communicative tasks such as problem-solving, conveying information to one another or filling in information on a map from instructions. They learn language in the course of these tasks naturalistically, by understanding and negotiating meanings. CLIL focuses on the use of English for the teaching of other school subjects or specific content (see Unit 15: Teaching content, pp. 220–3). As with task-based instruction, the assumption is that learners will absorb the language best through using it purposefully, and through understanding and creating meaningful texts.

The post-communicative approach maintains the position that the primary function of language is effective communication. Therefore any methodology based on it should include plenty of activities that involve meaningful use of the target language in communicative tasks. But it allows a much larger role for procedures such as explicit teaching of grammar, vocabulary, pronunciation and spelling, including form-focused (but usually meaningful) exercises. It also includes techniques associated with previous methodologies, such as translation and learning dialogues or texts by heart.

In fact very few teachers or textbooks have adopted the recommendations of the communicative approach to the letter and used them as a basis for all their teaching. Explicit language instruction in general, and grammar exercises in particular, have continued to play a major role in language teaching worldwide. The 'post-communicative approach' is one which most coursebooks and teachers today are using, and on which this book is based.

Task

Thinking back to your own learning of English or another additional language, do you think the methodology that your teacher used was similar to one or more of the models described above? How effective was it, and in what ways do you now think it could have been improved?

Action task

Observe two lessons in your school. How much of the lesson, more or less, was used for communicative language use? If you are working in a group, compare your results with those of colleagues.

1.4 Computerized teaching materials

The huge development that has taken place recently in the area of teaching materials is, of course, the dramatic increase in the use of computers and other digital resources. The acronym 'CALL', or computer-assisted language learning, started to be widely used in the 1990s and early 2000s, and there is already a large number of books and journals devoted to it: see, for example, Dudeney and Hockly, 2007, or the journal *ReCall* (www.eurocall-languages.org/recall/index.html).

However, it is important to remember that many students and teachers still prefer to do most of their learning and teaching through a coursebook. This is partly because books are cheaper, and in some places electronic facilities not easily available. It is also, perhaps mainly, because they can be quickly opened, used and navigated without dependence on technology, electricity or an internet connection. On the other hand, they lack the flexibility, adaptability to the individual, enormous range of informational sources and various interactive options of computer hard- and software. The main issue is, therefore, not *whether* to use computerized materials or not, but *how* and *where to use* them.

When personal computers and laptops became more widely available, they were at first used mainly for composing or editing texts and for doing self-check exercises. The production of new materials by teachers or of assignments by students could now be done more quickly and easily through word processing and presentation software like *Microsoft Word* or *Powerpoint*.

More recently, computerized hardware is being used in classrooms. The data projector enables presentations and teaching materials to be displayed on a screen. And the interactive whiteboard (IWB) combines the functions of data projector and conventional whiteboard, revolutionizing classroom teacher-led lessons. There are constant innovations in software as well. There are, for example, tools that enable you to hear what you are reading, or correct your pronunciation; and text-translation programs are developing fast, though at the time of writing they are still inferior to human translators.

The Internet was first used in the classroom for two main purposes, which are dominant to this day: communication through email, which enables teachers and students to interact outside the classroom; and information-gathering through the World Wide Web. More recently, interactive tools such as blogs, wikis, forums and Learning Management Systems (LMSs) have provided a range of possibilities for teaching different language content and skills (see Unit 14: Materials, pp. 212–14). And social networking tools like *Facebook* can be used for teacher–student and student–student interaction. All these are used in what has come to be called *blended learning* (see Unit 16: Classroom interaction, pp. 239–42).

1.5 Motivation

Motivation is a crucial factor in successful language learning; and a good deal of research has been carried out on how and why learners are motivated to learn, and what teachers can do to enhance such motivation.

Integrative and instrumental motivation

The terms *integrative motivation* and *instrumental motivation* are associated with the work of the Canadian researchers Lambert and Gardner (Gardner, 1991). Integrative motivation refers to the desire of the learner to learn the language in order to integrate into the community of speakers of that language. Instrumental motivation, in contrast, refers to the need to learn the language for material or educational benefit: to get a better job, for example, or to progress to advanced study. The original Canadian study found that integrative motivation was the more important of the two. More recent studies of learners of English in different countries, however, have found the opposite (e.g. Warden & Hsui, 2000). This is probably because of the changing role of English worldwide discussed earlier, and the fact that learners today need English for a variety of instrumental purposes rather than in order to join a particular English-speaking community.

Extrinsic and intrinsic motivation

These concepts represent a rather different, though overlapping, contrast. Extrinsic motivation is based on the perceived benefits of success in learning and penalties of failure. So instrumental motivation, as defined above, would be extrinsic, and so would the desire to pass exams or avoid getting bad grades at school. Intrinsic motivation is that associated with the activity of language learning itself: whether it is seen as interesting or boring, personally fulfilling or frustrating.

Self and personal identity

Another motivation-associated concept is that of the *self* and *personal identity*: how we see ourselves or wish to see ourselves in the future. A student who sees him- or herself as high-achieving, for example, will invest more effort in learning. A student who wishes to see him- or herself as a member of an international community will want to learn English in order to fulfil his or her own personal aspirations. This last type of motivation is perhaps a modern-day adaptation of 'integrative' motivation (for this and other aspects of identity and self-image in language-learning motivation, see Dörnyei & Ushioda, 2009).

> ### Task
>
> Can you define what factors influenced your own motivation, positively or negatively, when you were learning a new language? Can you relate these to the concepts discussed above?

Teachers – particularly those teaching young or adolescent learners within the education system of a non-English-speaking country – have a crucial role to play in increasing motivation to learn. We can influence learners' motivation in three main ways:

1. **By taking every opportunity to show them how important it is for them to know English.** In today's world English provides extensive opportunities for further study and possible employment, for leisure-time activities and entertainment, and – perhaps most significant for teenagers and young adults – social interaction with people from other cultures and languages, whether online or face to face. Most of this they will probably know already, but it does no harm to remind them!

2. **By fostering their self-image as successful language learners.** We can do our best to make sure they succeed in tasks (see Unit 4: The task, p. 44) and give them tests only when we are sure they will be able to perform well. And – particularly with younger learners – we need to be careful to provide negative or corrective feedback tactfully and supportively, and take every opportunity to praise and encourage. For more on motivating younger learners, see Unit 18: Learner differences (1): age, pp. 258–64.

3. **By ensuring that classroom activities are interesting.** It is not enough that tasks are 'communicative' or that texts are interesting. We need to employ a number of strategies in task design and administration that can help to create and, even more importantly, maintain student interest in doing them: the use of game-like activities, for example. For more detailed guidelines on this topic, see Unit 4: The task, pp. 51–5.

Review

Answer as many as you can of the following questions, and then check answers by referring back to the relevant passages in this unit.

If you are working in a group, note down your own answers first alone, and then share with the other members of the group. Finally, check the answers together.

Teaching priorities

1. What are two important findings of recent research into vocabulary learning?
2. Why has the importance of informal writing increased?

English as an international language

3. What is the difference between English as a 'foreign' language, and English as an 'international' language?
4. There has been a clear shift in recent years towards teaching English as an international language. List some of the differences this is making to the way English is taught.

Language-acquisition theories and teaching methodologies

5. What is the difference between 'intuitive acquisition' and 'skill-learning' as theories underlying the learning of a new language?
6. List some of the main features of the 'post-communicative' approach.

Computerized teaching materials

7. List some advantages of paper-based materials.
8. Can you think of at least five ways in which computerized materials are used today for English teaching?

Motivation

9. Can you give one example each of *integrative, instrumental, extrinsic* and *intrinsic* motivation?
10. Suggest some ways in which the teacher can help to raise student motivation.

Further reading

Byram, M. (1997) *Teaching and Assessing Intercultural Communicative Competence,* Clevedon: Multilingual Matters.
  (A clear presentation of what 'intercultural competence' involves and how to teach it)

Crystal, D. (2006) *Language and the Internet,* Cambridge: Cambridge University Press.
  (A discussion of the characteristics of the language used for written interpersonal communication through the Internet)

Dörnyei, Z. and Ushioda, E. (2009) *Teaching and Researching Motivation,* Harlow: Longman.
  (An overview of the main issues in motivation, research, theory and practice, with particular reference to language teaching and learning)

Dudeney, G. and Hockly, N. (2007) *How to Teach English with Technology*, London: Pearson Education.
>   (Various ways in which computer technology can be used to enhance English teaching and learning, with plenty of practical suggestions)

Lightbown, P. M. and Spada, N. A. (2006) *How Languages Are Learned* (3rd edn), Oxford: Oxford University Press.
>   (A clear, not too long, and readable account of the various theories about language acquisition)

Richards, J. C. and Rodgers, T. S. (2001) *Approaches and Methods in Language Teaching*, Cambridge: Cambridge University Press.
>   (A comprehensive and critical guide to the different methodologies and their underlying theory)

Rubdy, R. and Saraceni, M. (2006) *English in the World: Global Rules, Global Roles*, London: Continuum.
>   (A collection of articles on various aspects of the use of English as an international language)

Schmitt, N. (2008) Instructed second language vocabulary learning. *Language Teaching Research*, *12*(3), 329–63.
>   (A survey article, summarizing the findings of research on vocabulary teaching and learning, with references for further reading)

Widdowson, H. G. (1978) *Teaching Language as Communication*, Oxford: Oxford University Press.
>   (An early and perhaps the most influential explanation of the principles and practice of the communicative approach)

2 The lesson

2.1 The lesson: different perspectives

The lesson is a type of organized goal-oriented social event that occurs in most, if not all, cultures. And although lessons in different places may vary in topic, atmosphere, methodology and materials, they all have several basic elements in common. Their main objective is learning, they are attended by a predetermined population of learner(s) and teacher(s), and there is a pre-set schedule for where and when they take place.

There are additional aspects of a lesson which may be less obvious. These can be represented by metaphors such as the following.

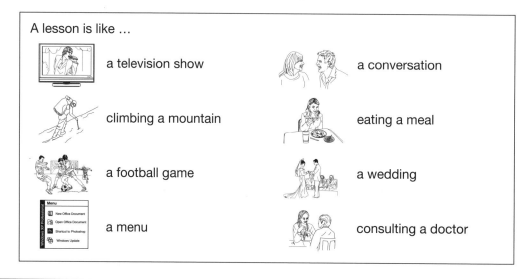

A lesson is like …

a television show

climbing a mountain

a football game

a menu

a conversation

eating a meal

a wedding

consulting a doctor

Task

Choose two or three of the metaphors above that seem to you to reflect the reality of an English lesson. Or suggest others that you think more appropriate. If you are working in a group, discuss your choices and the reasons for them with colleagues. Then read on.

The lesson: metaphors as reflecting reality

The lesson is a very complex construct, which fulfils a variety of functions and can be seen from a variety of perspectives by different people. A study of the metaphors listed above can reveal many of these functions and perspectives. Your own choice of metaphor, if you did the task, will show which you feel are most important, and what 'images' of the lesson are most real to you.

Cooperative interaction

This is most obvious in the metaphor of conversation but is also represented by the wedding, the television show and, in perhaps a rather different way, the football game. In this image of a lesson, the most important thing is the dynamic relationship among students, or between students and teacher. A lesson is something which primarily involves cooperative social interaction, and which promotes the participation of all members of the class.

Goal-oriented effort, involving hard work

Here, climbing a mountain might be an appropriate metaphor, or perhaps a football game. This image suggests the existence of a clear, worthwhile objective, the necessity of effort to attain it and a resulting sense of satisfaction and triumph if it is achieved, or of failure and disappointment if it is not.

An interesting or enjoyable experience

Enjoyment may be based on interest and entertainment (television show), challenge and fun (football game), or the satisfaction of a need or desire (eating a meal). The main point is that participants should enjoy it and therefore be motivated to attend while it is going on, as distinct from feeling pleased with the results.

A role-based culture

In a role-based culture, roles of participants are predetermined. If the lesson is perceived in this way, then the role of the teacher typically involves responsibility and activity, and that of the students responsiveness and receptivity. So the consultation with a doctor or the wedding would represent a role-based culture of this kind. Participants in such events know and accept in advance the demands that will be made on them and their expected behaviours. This often implies …

A social event with elements of ceremony

Examples here would be a wedding or a television show. Certain set behaviours occur every time: for example, there may be a certain kind of introduction or ending, and the other components of the overall event may be selected from a limited set of possibilities. In contrast, the lesson in some cases can also be …

A series of free choices

Occasionally it may happen that participants are free to do their own thing within a set of choices (a menu) or a relatively loose structure (a conversation). They construct the event as it progresses, by making their own decisions. The teacher is less of an authority figure than a facilitator, participating with the students in the teaching/learning process.

Summary

As you will have found if you did the task with colleagues, the lesson is seen quite differently by different people. But each of the interpretations described above – and you may well have discovered more – represents one aspect of the whole picture. It is important in your planning and teaching of specific lessons that you remain aware of these different possible perspectives: a lesson is not just a type of interaction, for example, or a goal-oriented process, or a ritual social event. It is all of these and more.

2.2 Functions of the teacher in the English language lesson

During the latter part of the twentieth century, there was a strong reaction against the old-fashioned image of the teacher as dictator and lecturer. As a result teachers have been encouraged to see themselves mainly as supporters of learning rather than enforcers of it, and as 'facilitators' who help students learn how to think rather than 'tellers' who teach facts. You may have heard condemnations of the 'mug and jug' method (the student as empty mug and the teacher as a jug pouring information into it) and may have been encouraged to elicit ideas from students, rather than instructing them.

In principle, of course, most teachers would like to see themselves as supportive rather than dictatorial, and to encourage learner independence and autonomy. But an extreme learner-centred approach, where learning is totally based on student initiative, can actually be counterproductive, particularly in language courses. Language is composed of a collection of arbitrary sounds, words and grammatical combinations: there is no way the students can discover or create them without an instructor. Effective language teaching, therefore, should arguably be based on a substantial amount of teacher-initiated instruction; though student-centred activation has an essential place as well.

Besides the two main functions of instructor and activator, the teacher also has several more functions during any lesson.

Task

How many different kinds of functions does the English teacher have during a lesson? Make a list, and then compare it with the list below. You've probably used different terminology, but will have some similar items. Check to see what your list has left out – or added.

Instructor

The teacher, together with the teaching materials, provides information about the language: its sounds, letters, words, grammar and communicative use. The most essential teaching skills are the ability to provide appropriate samples of spoken and written language and clear explanations.

Activator

Getting the students to use English themselves is essential for acquisition to take place. 'Using English' does not necessarily mean getting them to speak or write; it may involve only listening or reading. So you need to provide tasks that activate the students and get them to do something that involves engaging with the forms, meanings and uses of the language.

Model

The teacher normally represents the prototype of the English speaker during a lesson. It is your accent, writing and language usages that the students will use as their immediate model. So don't feel uneasy about taking lesson time to provide such a model: students need to hear and see you using the language.

Provider of feedback

The teacher provides feedback on student oral or written production. Exactly when and how much corrective feedback to supply is a tricky issue (see Unit 7: Error correction), but it is, along with the provision of approval and confirmation, an essential function. In order to progress, students need to know what they are doing right or well, what they are doing wrong or not so well, and how they can improve.

Supporter

The teacher encourages students, helps them understand and produce appropriate language, suggests learning strategies or resources that may be useful. This not only improves learning and raises motivation but also encourages the students to become independent learners who will continue to progress after and outside the lesson.

Assessor

Teachers occasionally have to spend some lesson time assessing students. This might be formally, through graded classroom tests, or informally, through quick quizzes or dictations. This is because in any process we need to know where we are now in order to know where to go next, and assessment provides vital information on students' present achievements (see Unit 12: Assessment and testing).

Manager

The management of classroom process includes activities such as bringing the class together at the beginning of a lesson and organizing group work, as well as making sure that individual members of the class are attending and responding appropriately. This may be more, or less, difficult to do, depending on the class population (see Unit 17: Classroom discipline and Unit 19: Learner differences (2): teaching heterogeneous (mixed) classes).

Motivator

The level of initial student motivation when they come to study English may vary, but whether the language-learning process in the course of the lesson is interesting and motivating or boring and demotivating is largely up to the teacher (for more on interesting tasks, see Unit 4: The task, pp. 51–5). Even students who are at first unwilling to participate can be motivated to do so if they are given appropriate and stimulating tasks together with the teacher encouragement and support mentioned above.

Task

Think about your own English (or other foreign language) lessons when you were a student. Which of the functions listed above was your teacher good or bad at?

2.3 Interaction patterns in the lesson

The most common type of classroom interaction is that known as 'IRF' – 'Initiation–Response–Feedback': the teacher *initiates* an exchange, usually in the form of a question, one of the students *responds*, the teacher gives *feedback* (assessment, correction, comment), initiates the next question – and so on.

However, there are alternative interaction patterns. The initiative does not always have to be in the hands of the teacher, and interaction may be between students, or between a student and the material. Here is a list of such patterns, ranging from the most teacher-centred at the beginning to the most student-centred at the end.

1. **Teacher talk.** This may involve some kind of silent response, such as writing something down, but there is no initiative on the part of the student.

2. **Choral responses.** The teacher gives a model which is repeated by all the class together; or gives a cue which is responded to in chorus.

3. **Closed-ended teacher questioning ('IRF').** The teacher invites response to a cue that has one right answer, nominates one student to respond, and approves or corrects the answer.

4. **Open-ended teacher questioning.** As above, but there are a number of possible 'right' answers, so that more students respond to each cue.

5. **Full-class interaction.** The students debate a topic or do a language task as a class. The teacher acts as discussion leader or 'chairperson'.

6. **Student initiates, teacher answers.** For example, in an interviewing simulation the students think of questions and the teacher responds as the 'interviewee'.

7. **Individual work.** Students work independently on an activity or task assigned by the teacher.

8. **Collaboration.** Students work in pairs or small groups on an exercise or task assigned by the teacher to try to achieve the best results they can by collaborating.

9. **Group work.** Students work in pairs or small groups on interaction-based tasks: conveying information to each other, for example, or decision-making. (This is different from 'Collaboration' because here the task itself requires interaction.)

10. **Self-access.** Students choose themselves what they want to do and work autonomously on paper-based or computer-based tasks.

Action task

Observe one or two English lessons, and note down the types of interaction you saw. After the observation, answer the following questions:

1. What was the main type of interaction you saw in this lesson?
2. Did teacher- or student-led interaction predominate? Or was there a balance?

Appropriate use of different interaction patterns

All the patterns above may be used at different times in the lesson and for different purposes. However, inappropriate choice for a particular teaching objective may lead to ineffective learning. We might, for example, consider which are the most appropriate interaction patterns for the following teaching goals.

Task

Look at the following teaching objectives, as expressed by the teacher, and suggest which of the interaction patterns listed above might facilitate their achievement most successfully. Then read on.

1. **Comprehension check:** 'We've just finished reading a story. I want to make sure the class has understood it, using the comprehension questions in the book.'
2. **Familiarization with text:** 'We've just finished reading a story. I'm fairly sure they've understood the basic plot, but I want them to get really familiar with the text through reading, as they're going to have to pass an exam on it.'
3. **Oral fluency:** 'I have a small [15] class of business people, who need more practice in talking. I want them to do a discussion task where they have to decide which qualities are most important for a manager.'
4. **Grammar check:** 'We've been working on the distinction between two similar verb tenses. I want to find out how far they've grasped it, using an exercise in the book where they have to choose the right tense for the context.'
5. **Writing:** 'They need to improve their writing. I want to ask them to write for a few minutes in class but am worried they might just make a lot of mistakes and not learn anything.'
6. **Grammar practice:** 'They need to practise asking questions. I thought of using an interview situation where they might interview me or each other.'
7. **New vocabulary:** 'I want to draw their attention to some new vocabulary we've met in a text.'

Comment

1. **Comprehension check.** Closed- or open-ended teacher questioning is the usual solution to this, but individual work is probably more effective. In full-class questioning, only a minority of the class answers: more students participate if you let all of them try to answer the question individually in writing, while you move around the class to help and monitor. You can always check their answers later by a quick full-class review or by taking in notebooks.

2. **Familiarization with text.** It is probably best to use individual work here, in the form of silent reading. Or, if the students have already read the text on their own, it can be helpful to read it aloud yourself (teacher talk) while they follow, in order to 'recycle' it in a slightly different way. Another possibility is to ask different students to study different sections of the story in depth, and then get together to teach each other what they have studied (individual and group work).

3. **Oral fluency.** Group work is best in this case: certainly much better than full-class interaction. A class of 15 may seem small, but even so, dividing it into five groups of three gives each participant, on average, five times as much speaking practice.

4. **Grammar check.** The teacher's clear objective is to test ('I want to find out how well they understand it'), though he or she does not actually use the word. Therefore, as with the comprehension check, it would be best to use individual work to ensure that each student has the chance to answer the questions.

5. **Writing.** Use individual work, supported by collaboration. Initially, most writing is done individually: the collaborative stage takes place later, as students help each other improve, correct and polish their texts. Teacher monitoring can take place during the writing, if there are not too many students in the class, or later.

6. **Grammar practice.** In order to make the interview produce as much practice in questions as possible, it is a good idea to let students prepare at least some of these in advance: individually, in collaborative pairs, or through full-class interaction (brainstorming suggestions). The interview may then be conducted with the teacher in the full class (student initiates, teacher answers) or with (volunteer) students in full-class or small-group interaction.

7. **New vocabulary.** In general, the most efficient way to deal with new vocabulary is just to present and explain it (teacher talk). If, however, you think that some of your class know some of the items, ask them, and give them the opportunity to teach them for you (closed- or open-ended teacher questioning). If you are fairly sure they do not know them, then such questioning is to be avoided: it is likely to result in silence or wrong answers and a feeling of frustration and failure.

For more in-depth discussion of teacher questioning, group work, individual work and blended learning, see Unit 16: Classroom interaction.

2.4 Lesson preparation

Most English lessons in schools are about 45 minutes long, though sometimes, particularly where the students are adults, they may be as much as 90 minutes. For the purposes of this unit, I am assuming that the lesson takes between 45 and 60 minutes.

An English lesson may include some or all of the following components:

- work on a listening or reading text, with associated comprehension tasks
- an oral communicative task, such as discussion of a controversial topic
- presentation and explanation of a grammatical point
- presentation and explanation of vocabulary
- exercises on linguistic usages, such as grammar, vocabulary, pronunciation, spelling or punctuation
- a writing task
- silent reading of simplified readers chosen by the students
- review of homework
- preparation for a test
- a test

Task

Can you think of any more lesson components that might be added to the list above?

Action task

Observe a lesson or, if you are a practising teacher, consider a recent lesson you taught. How many different components were included in the lesson? Do you think the lesson was sufficiently varied?

Lesson variation

In a lesson which is entirely taken up with one kind of activity, interest is likely to flag. Students will find it more difficult to concentrate and learn, and boredom may, in some classes, result in discipline problems. A varied lesson will be more orderly and produce better learning. It will also be more engaging and enjoyable for both teacher and students, and cater for a wider range of learning styles (see Unit 19: Learner differences (2): teaching heterogeneous (mixed) classes). It may also prolong energy levels by providing regular refreshing changes in the type of mental or physical activity demanded.

Lessons may vary in a number of ways:

- **Tempo.** Activities may be brisk and fast-moving (such as guessing games) or slow and reflective (such as reading literature and responding in writing).

- **Organization.** The students may work individually, in pairs, in groups, or as a full class interacting with the teacher.

- **Material.** A lot of your lesson may be based on the coursebook, but it is good to spend at least some of the time working on teacher- or student-initiated tasks or computer-based materials (see Unit 14: Materials).

- **Mode and skill.** Activities may be based on the written or the spoken language; and within these, they may vary as to whether the students are asked to produce (speak, write) or receive (listen, read).

- **Difficulty.** Activities may be easy and non-demanding, or difficult, requiring concentration and effort.

- **Topic.** Both the language-teaching point and the (non-linguistic) topic may change from one activity to another.

- **Mood.** Activities vary also in mood: light and fun-based versus serious and profound, tense versus relaxed and so on.

- **Stir-settle.** Some activities enliven and excite students (such as controversial discussions, or activities that involve physical movement). Others, like dictations, have the effect of calming them down (Maclennan, 1987).

- **Active-passive.** Students may be activated in a way that encourages their own initiative, or they may only be required to do as they are told.

Obviously when planning a lesson you cannot go through each of the items above and check out your plan to make sure you are covering them all! But hopefully reading through them will raise your general awareness of the various possibilities.

Note that lessons with younger learners should, on the whole, be made up of shorter and more varied components than those planned for older ones. But even adults in my experience dislike spending a whole period on the same task and appreciate a shift of focus and activity-type during the lesson.

All of this applies also to a sequence of lessons. Make sure you don't get into a dull routine of doing the same sort of thing every lesson, and that you cover, over time, a variety of tasks, texts and materials.

Practical tips

1. **Put the harder tasks earlier.** On the whole, students are fresher and more energetic earlier in the lesson and get progressively less so as it goes on, particularly if the lesson is a long one. So it makes sense to put the tasks that demand more effort and concentration earlier on (learning new material, or tackling a difficult text, for example) and the lighter ones later.

2. **Do quieter activities before lively ones.** It can be quite difficult to calm down a class – particularly of children or adolescents – who have been participating in a lively, exciting activity. So, if one of your lesson components is quiet and reflective, it is generally better to plan it before a lively one, not after. The exception to this is when you have a rather lethargic or tired class of adults. In such cases 'stirring' activities towards the beginning of the class can be refreshing and help students get into the right frame of mind for learning.

3. **Keep an eye on your watch!** Make sure that a particular activity doesn't run too long, and that you've left enough time to fit in all the components you wanted to include this lesson. See *Tip 7* below about having a reserve activity ready.

4. **Pull the class together at the beginning and end of the lesson.** We usually start with general greetings, attendance-taking and so on; but remember that it's a good idea to have some kind of rounding-off procedure at the end of the lesson as well (see the next tip). So activities which tend to fragment the class – group or pair work, or computer-based work, for example – are best done in the middle of the lesson, framed by full-class interaction before and after, which pulls the group together. Teachers of younger classes often find set rituals are useful for this: information about the date and weather at the beginning, for example, songs, greetings and goodbyes chanted in chorus.

5. **End on a positive note.** This does not necessarily mean ending with a joke or a fun activity. For some classes it could be something quite serious, like a summary of what we have achieved today, or a positive evaluation of something the class has done. Another possibility is to give a task which the class is very likely to succeed in and which will generate feelings of satisfaction. The point is to have students leave the classroom feeling good.

6. **Don't leave homework-giving to the end.** Give homework in the course of the lesson, and simply remind the students what it was at the end. If you leave it to the end, then you may find that you don't have enough time to explain it properly. In any case, it is better to round off the lesson with some kind of planned ending (see previous tip).

7. **Prepare a reserve.** Have an extra activity ready if you find you have time on your hands (see Ur & Wright, 1992, for some ideas for short activities). Similarly, note down in advance which components of your lesson you will cancel or postpone if you are running out of time.

2.5 Written lesson plans

It is essential to write down in advance what you plan to do in the lesson. It is not enough just to think about it and put a bookmark at the relevant page of the textbook! Even experienced teachers, including myself, prepare plans for every lesson, though they vary a lot in how they lay these out.

This is not just because you might want to refer to the plan during the lesson. In practice, I usually look through my lesson plan just before the lesson begins, and then rarely need to glance at it while teaching, except to check specific information like page or exercise numbers. A more important reason is that writing makes you think 'concretely' and practically. It ensures that you haven't forgotten anything and that you have planned and ordered all the components and materials appropriately. (For the value in general of writing things down to systematize and clarify thinking, see also Unit 20: Teacher development, pp. 289–90.)

A lesson-plan template

Date:	Time:	Place:	Class:
	Activity and aims	Materials	Time
Beginning			
Later comment			
Main activity 1			
Later comment			
Main activity 2			
Later comment			
Main activity 3			
Later comment			
Main activity 4			
Later comment			
Ending			
Reserve			
New language to be taught			
Language to be reviewed			
Later comment on the lesson as a whole			

To start with, it is useful to have a template such as the one above, since it:

- provides a framework for you to note systematically the various stages in the lesson and the order in which they will occur (beginning, main activities, ending);
- makes you think about and note down what your teaching aims are, as well as the content of what you plan to do;
- provides space to write down the particular language items (new words, grammar, spelling rules or whatever) that you plan to teach and/or review;
- reminds you also to prepare a reserve activity to use if needed;
- leaves space for later comment.

Note that you may plan fewer than four main activities, in which case you just leave the extra rows empty. If you plan more, then add them at the bottom. But try to make sure that the whole plan is only one page (or two at the most) so that you can lay it face up on your desk at the beginning of the lesson and glance at it quickly and easily when you need to.

Action task

Prepare a lesson for a class you know or are teaching, using the template given here. If you can, teach it and then fill in the 'later comment' section. If you are working in a group, compare your lesson plan with that of colleagues and discuss.

Using the lesson plan

Here are some ways you can use the lesson plan during or after the lesson.

Share with the class

At the beginning of a lesson, many teachers like to write up on the board the main 'agenda' – a shortened version of their lesson plan – so that the students are also aware of what the lesson is to include and have a sense of structure and direction. In general, sharing your plans and objectives with the students can contribute to a pleasant and cooperative relationship with the class, and this is one simple and practical way of doing so.

Adapt

You will find as you gain experience that you will change and adapt the template given here to suit your own teaching style and needs. Many experienced teachers, for example, stop writing in explicit 'aims', because they are aware of these intuitively. If asked, they can always tell you what their objectives are. They do, however, continue to note down what they are going to do, the materials and lists of language items they hope to cover.

Add later comment

Try to make a habit of filling in the 'later comment' section after the lesson. You don't have to comment on every single activity, of course, but it is useful to note down particular things that went well, or didn't, and what you need to remember to do, or not do, next time. You will also find that you need to make some changes to the 'language to be taught' and 'language to be reviewed' sections.

Almost inevitably there are some items you don't get round to, and others that need to be added during the lesson.

The 'later comment' sections can also be used for useful reflection and self-evaluation. You will not have time to fill in extensive, careful evaluations for every lesson (the place for these is in systematic teacher appraisal and development situations; see Unit 20: Teacher development, pp. 285–9), so here are suggestions for brief notes that you should have time for at the end of the day, and that will inform later lesson planning.

1. For each activity, write a ✓ if it went as expected, and a ✓✓ if it was particularly successful. If it did not work as well as you had hoped, note what went wrong, and add a suggestion about what you might do next time to improve it.

2. On the lesson as a whole, write down a ✓ or ✓✓ if you feel the students generally made good progress in the aspects of English that you were working on. After all, this is the main point of teaching a lesson! And add any note to remind yourself of practical things you need to remember to do differently next time, even if these are sometimes minor practical details like: 'Make sure I have enough time to explain homework!' or 'Don't let Johnny sit next to Sheila!'.

For a more systematic and extensive checklist for lesson evaluation, see Unit 20: Teacher development, pp. 287–8.

Review

Answer as many as you can of the following questions, and then check answers by referring back to the relevant passages in this unit.

If you are working in a group, note down your own answers first alone, and then share with the other members of the group. Finally, check the answers together.

The lesson: different perspectives
1. Can you define the concept 'lesson'?
2. Of all the ways of seeing the lesson described in this section ('cooperative interaction', etc.), which were the ones you yourself found most appropriate?

Functions of the teacher in the English language lesson
3. What are the two most important functions of the teacher in a lesson?
4. Can you remember at least four more?

Interaction patterns in the lesson
5. What is 'IRF'?
6. What is the difference between 'closed-ended' and 'open-ended' questions?
7. Why is group work appropriate for practising oral fluency?

Lesson preparation

8. Why should a lesson include a variety of different components?
9. In what ways may these components be varied?
10. Can you recall at least three practical tips about the planning or use of these components?

Written lesson plans

11. Why is it important to write down your lesson plans?
12. Why is it important to note comments on your lesson plans after the lesson itself is over?

Further reading

Maclennan S. (1987) Integrating lesson planning and class management. *ELT Journal*, 41(3): 193–7.

(An interesting distinction between 'stir' and 'settle' activities in the language classroom)

Ur, P. and Wright, A. (1992) *Five-Minute Activities*, Cambridge: Cambridge University Press.

(A collection of very short activities that can be used to bridge transitions, or as fillers or for lesson-closings)

Harmer, J. (2007b) Planning lessons. In *The Practice of English Language Teaching* (4th edn) (pp. 364–78), Harlow, Essex: Pearson Education.

(Some good, practical guidance on lesson planning)

Woodward, T. (2001). *Planning Lessons and Courses*, Cambridge: Cambridge University Press.

(A more extended treatment of various aspects of advance planning, both at lesson- and at full course level)

3 The text

Overview

The sections in this unit are:

3.1 **What is a text?** A definition of what we mean by *text* in the context of English language teaching; the distinction between 'intensive' and 'extensive' text study.

3.2 **Teaching the text: the goals.** What we want learners to get from text study: comprehension of content, language learning, discourse analysis and later enrichment, each of which is discussed more fully in the following sections.

3.3 **Comprehension of content.** Teaching procedures that can facilitate student comprehension of a text.

3.4 **Language learning.** Ways of selecting and teaching grammatical and vocabulary items from a text.

3.5 **Discourse analysis.** Aspects of discourse: genres, styles and structure, and how these can be taught.

3.6 **Follow-up tasks.** Some ideas for tasks that can be based on texts for later enrichment.

3.1 What is a text?

A *text* in the present context is a piece of writing or speech which we use for language learning. It can be studied as a complete and autonomous unit: the reader or listener can therefore understand it without necessarily knowing the context, even if it was originally an extract from a book, a conversation, etc. It is coherent, so it has a beginning, a middle and an end which make a clear sequence of thoughts or events. The term as it is used here does not therefore include things like lists of words to be learnt, or sentences that give samples of usage, or a grammar exercise.

Usually a coursebook text ranges from a paragraph to a page or more in length. It may, however, be longer or shorter: a whole book on the one hand, or a very short text, such as a proverb, quotation, joke or very short poem, on the other.

The text is normally used for *intensive* (see the following paragraph) language learning in various ways: for comprehension work, for learning the language items which appear in it, for analysis of content, genre or structure, and as a basis for further work on content or language.

We make a distinction between *intensive* and *extensive* text study. *Intensive* means that the text is not only understood, but also studied in detail, or 'milked', for the language that can be learnt from it. It is also possibly analysed or used as a springboard for further language work, as described later in this unit. *Extensive* means that the text is read or heard for pleasure and/or information, but not studied in detail. The main aim is to improve reading or listening fluency and any language learning is incidental.

Listening texts are often listened to repeatedly for the sake of detailed comprehension; however, they are not usually taught intensively, as defined above, since the fleeting nature of speech does not easily allow for repeated scanning and detailed study. Listening activities in the classroom are done essentially for the sake of improving comprehension in general.

This unit deals therefore mainly with texts used as the basis for intensive reading. For extensive reading and listening comprehension, whose aim is primarily to promote fluency in these skills rather than focused study of texts, see Unit 10: Teaching reading and Unit 8: Teaching listening, respectively.

3.2 Teaching the text: the goals

The main goals of teaching the text in a language course are comprehension of content, language learning, discourse analysis, and then enrichment through further tasks based on different aspects of the text.

Comprehension of content

1. **General gist.** First you need to make sure that the students understand the general content of the text: the plot, for example, if it is a narrative, or the argument or idea presented if it is an article which discusses a topic.

2. **Detailed understanding.** The next stage is more detailed comprehension of the different parts of the text. This usually means sentence-by-sentence study, providing explanations of new words or concepts where necessary.

3. **Reading between the lines.** You may invite students to infer meanings that are not stated explicitly. In a literary text that involves dialogue, for example, you may find it interesting to discuss the way the speech of different characters shows their personality or motives. Or in an article presenting an argument, learners may be able to elicit the underlying approach or prejudice of the writer, as revealed by his or her choice of 'emotive' words.

4. **Critical analysis.** The text may then be studied critically: students are invited to judge how truthful, consistent or logical a text is. This is particularly useful when reading texts that are designed to persuade: political speeches or commercial advertisements. For example, you might want to draw your students' attention to tautology (unnecessary repetition) in phrases like *a free gift*, or internal contradictions in phrases like *an objective opinion*.

Language learning
Vocabulary
The most important language-learning benefit of intensive study of a text is arguably vocabulary expansion or review. In such study, virtually all the words need to be understood by the students. By drawing attention to them and doing vocabulary-focused activities, you can help students to notice and learn new

items, and review ones they have met before (see Section 3.3 below and Unit 5: Teaching vocabulary).

Grammar

A secondary benefit is the learning of word- or sentence-grammar (morphology and syntax). Of course any text of more than a few lines will provide a large number of examples of different grammatical features. You will probably ignore the simpler ones that the students already know, but it is useful to draw attention to ones which the class has recently learnt. And you may sometimes pick out a new bit of grammar and spend a few minutes explaining and teaching it, providing further examples from outside the present text (see Unit 6: Teaching grammar).

See Section 3.4 below for guidelines on how to select language items to teach as well as some practical tips.

Discourse analysis

Discourse analysis is the discussion of the text as a whole, rather than particular linguistic features such as grammar or vocabulary; and it can only take place after students have thoroughly understood its content. It deals with questions of function, genre, style and structure, as well as meaning: see Section 3.5 below.

Follow-up tasks

Having finished comprehension, language and discourse-analysis work, you may find that many texts provide rich stimuli for further language-learning tasks which involve student production (speech or writing), such as discussions or creative writing or research projects. These may be based on the actual content of the text, or on aspects of the language, style or discourse genre: see Section 3.6 below.

Action task

Have a look at two different English language coursebooks. Compare the way that texts are dealt with. Which goals from the list above are included, and which are not? In your opinion, which book exploits texts better for language teaching?

3.3 Comprehension of content

The priority in dealing with a text is to get the students to understand it: first the gist, then in more detail.

Preparation

Preparatory work can be extremely helpful for comprehension. It can include discussing the topic, pre-teaching vocabulary, raising expectations and asking preliminary questions to which the text will provide the answers.

Presenting the topic

Previous knowledge of the topic is probably the factor which most helps text comprehension. So it is a good idea either to give students information about the content of the text in advance, or to elicit it from them by asking questions. In some cases, it may even be appropriate to provide a synopsis in their language in advance. Students do not necessarily have to discover for themselves what it is about, and they may get a pleasing sense of success as they recognize and understand known content through reading the English version.

Pre-teaching vocabulary

A lot of books and teachers do this routinely, but it may not actually be very helpful. Research on vocabulary pre-teaching by Chang and Read (2006) showed clearly that this was not very helpful for listening comprehension. Teaching too many words in advance overloads students' short-term memory, and they simply do not remember the meanings when they hear them in the text. It is true that when reading, the students can refer back to a list of vocabulary (if they wrote it down!). But, in that case, it is enough to provide a glossary, or translations/definitions of specific items in the margins rather than pre-teach. If you do pre-teach vocabulary, it is probably best to limit this to a small number of vital items (the ones likely to come up anyway during an introductory discussion of content) that are likely to be more easily remembered, and to supply explanations of the rest through a glossary or margin notes.

If the text is not too difficult, it may not be necessary either to pre-teach vocabulary or to supply a glossary. The new vocabulary can be guessed or simply ignored at first reading, and explained when re-reading.

Raising expectations and curiosity

It is important to motivate students to read the text. A useful strategy is to arouse their curiosity by giving them questions to discuss, to which the text will provide the answers. Alternatively, let them glance at the title, headings and any illustrations, and make guesses or ask questions about the content of the text.

Another way of doing this that students enjoy is to use the post-text comprehension questions. Ask students to guess the answers to these in advance without reading the text. Present it as a kind of guessing game: tell them frankly that of course there's no way they can know the right answers, it's a kind of gamble. They just guess what the answers might be, and find out later if they have managed by chance to hit on the right ones. Then they read the text in order to find out if they were right or not (try it yourself in the task below). These types of preliminary questions make comprehension easier when students read the text, as well as raising their motivation to read.

Task

Look at the comprehension questions below, and guess what the answers might be. Then look at the text on which they were based (shown at the end of this unit) and see how many you got right!
1. Where was Jane walking?
2. What did she hear behind her?
3. What was her necklace made of?
4. What did the thief steal (two things)?
5. What did he do next?

Reading for understanding

There are three main ways a new text is actually read in class: the teacher reads aloud while students read along; students read it silently; students read sections aloud, in turn.

> ### Task
>
> Which of these three ways, in your experience as a student learning a language (not as a teacher!), helped you best to understand a new text? Answer, and then read on.

In many cases, a difficult reading text encountered for the first time will be best understood by students if you yourself read it aloud at an appropriate speed while they read along. There is some research showing that this can be an effective strategy (see, for example, Fitzgerald & Milner, 2007). Keep occasional eye contact with your students, and allow yourself to stop now and then to clarify or check comprehension.

A more challenging alternative is to allow silent reading, provided there has been some preparation of content and there are glosses of new words readily available (see *Practical tip 3* below). If successful, this will have the added bonus that the students can feel satisfied that they have read and understood the text on their own.

Asking students to take turns reading aloud a new text may not help comprehension very much. This is partly because a student reading aloud focuses on the decoding and pronunciation of words and does not have much attention to spare for understanding meanings. It is also because a student often cannot read well enough to communicate the meanings to other members of the class who are listening: certainly not as well as you can. However, in some learning cultures it is routinely done: students actually expect to be asked to read aloud and are disappointed if you don't let them! In that case, try to postpone the reading aloud to the second or third time you read the text, when students already understand most of it and are likely to be able to read it more fluently and meaningfully.

> ### Task
>
> Try reading aloud a text in a language which you learnt in school. How well did you do so? How well did you understand the content? Would you have felt more comfortable reading it silently?

Comprehension tasks

Comprehension questions

The most common type of text comprehension task is comprehension questions following the reading. But these may not always be very effective, as the following example makes clear.

Selection

We cannot normally teach every single word and all the grammatical features in the text: how do we select?

Vocabulary

It is important to look carefully at the selection of vocabulary to be taught from texts in the coursebooks you are using. Of course, most coursebook authors are now aware of the importance of focusing on the most useful and common vocabulary. However, some materials still either do not provide enough vocabulary work on texts, or list every new item, as if these were all equally important – which, of course, they are not. At least for beginner or intermediate classes, we need to make a distinction between two types of vocabulary items: some are really important and common, and students need to know them; others will only be needed for one particular text and are less important for students' own production. So it is essential when starting to work on a text to choose and list those items you want to teach thoroughly. You might, for example, tell students to note the text-specific but not-so-useful vocabulary items in the margins, while listing the more important ones in their notebooks for later review.

The main basis for deciding which items to teach more thoroughly has to be frequency: we want students to learn the most common and useful items before the rarer ones. On the whole, you yourself are likely to be a competent judge of which these are, but some published works and websites also provide guidance on relative frequency of items (see Unit 5: Teaching vocabulary, pp. 63–4, and also *Practical tip 1* below).

You may, of course, sometimes want to select items for a reason other than overall frequency: for example, student interests or needs.

Grammar, spelling, punctuation

Again, you usually need to note for yourself in advance which features you want to teach or review. The selection here is simpler than that of vocabulary. As in the case of vocabulary, however, you should prioritize features that are more important and frequent, and not worry too much about infrequent ones, or ones that are too advanced for your students' level. The items you focus on might be ones you have recently taught, minor ones which students might not notice on their own, or usages which are noticeably different from parallel ones in the students' L1. An alternative is to select features spontaneously during the session: perhaps in response to a student question or error, or because you notice something interesting as you work through the text.

Teaching selected items

Once you have selected which items from the text you are going to teach, you need to think about how to do it. There is some discussion, as we have seen in Unit 1, about whether it is better to learn language implicitly (absorbing it intuitively, through hearing or reading it in a communicative context) or explicitly (receiving explanations about the new language and deliberately practising it). The answer is that you probably need both. When reading a text, students encounter the language first within a meaningful context and need to understand it in order to understand the text as a whole. However, once the content is understood, it is useful to take time to focus on specific language points to ensure good learning.

With relatively minor, easily explained items – a spelling peculiarity, for example, or a word you think they probably know and just want to check – it may be enough simply to draw students' attention to them during a second or third reading. In many cases, however, you will need at some stage to take the target items out of context and spend time focusing on them individually. So you might make a separate list of new words that occur in the text and that you want to teach. Then you can deal with each one in turn, explaining it and perhaps adding information which is not provided by the context, including any other meanings, words with which it collocates and other derivatives from the same root. Or you might take time to explain a grammatical point and perhaps provide an exercise to practise it.

Practical tips

1. **Use online sites to check vocabulary frequency.** At the time of writing, the most useful one I know is *Lextutor Vocabprofile* (www.lextutor.ca/vp/bnc/), through which you can double-check your own intuitions in deciding which words are more, or less, frequent and useful and therefore worth teaching. You type, or copy-paste, your text into a window, click on 'submit' and immediately receive information on the frequency of the different words.

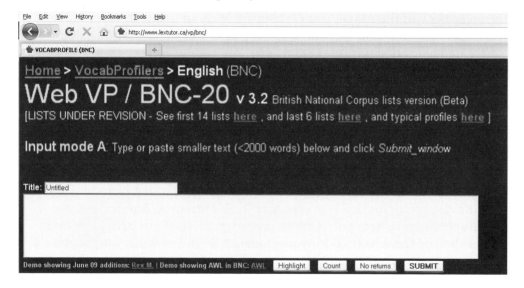

2. **Ask students to underline words they know rather than ones they don't.** When checking which words may need teaching, it's a good idea to ask them to underline or highlight all the words they do know rather than the ones they don't. Then they can compare and help each other reduce the number of non-underlined ones. This achieves the objective of identifying unknown items but is more encouraging and morale-boosting for the students.

3. **Note what you've taught.** Make sure you note down for yourself which language items you have taught from a text so that you can come back and review them later.

4. **Include whole expressions, not just single words,** in the vocabulary items you select to teach more thoroughly (see Unit 5: Teaching vocabulary).

Task

Choose a text from a coursebook, a newspaper or a website, and imagine you are going to use it with an intermediate class. Identify:

- the items you think are very common and probably already known by students (leave unmarked)
- the items which are not so common but would probably be useful to teach (underline)
- the items which are much more advanced and do not need to be taught in an intermediate class, but might be appropriate for an advanced one (double underline).

Optionally, check how your intuitions compare with a corpus-based analysis, by using a website such as the Lextutor Vocabprofile mentioned earlier, or a dictionary that provides indications of frequency levels for its headwords, such as the Longman Language Activator.

3.5 Discourse analysis

Genre

There is an enormous number of different genres of text, written and spoken, that can be used for language learning. Below is a sample.

Task

Look through the lists below of shorter and longer text genres. Can you add at least five more genres to each list?

Longer texts

television commercials	telephone conversations	academic papers
stories	recipes	radio or television news items
newspaper reports	lectures	plays, instructions (manuals)
poems	interviews	
advertisements	blogs	

Shorter texts

sayings or proverbs	short poems (haikus or limericks, for example)	book or movie titles
advice or tips	micro-blogging, e.g. 'tweets'	newspaper headlines
one-liner jokes		cartoon captions

It will usually be quite clear to which genre any particular text belongs. But it is useful with an advanced class to discuss this aspect of any text you are studying. You could explore its typical content, structure and style, and perhaps compare it with another text of a similar genre. (For some discussion of the teaching of literary texts, see Unit 15: Teaching content, pp. 223–5.)

If you are teaching English for Specific Purposes (ESP), the texts you focus on will be from a limited range of genres, depending on the professional field you are focusing on. If, on the other hand, you are teaching in a primary or secondary school, you are interested in preparing your students to deal with English for general international communication and will wish to provide texts from as wide a range of genres as possible.

> ## Task
>
> Look at the list of genres provided above, including your own additions. Write a ✓ by all those you feel are important to include. Now check out a coursebook that you are familiar with. How many of the items you ticked did you find?

A lot of coursebooks contain a surprisingly limited range of text genres: mostly dialogues, informative articles and narrative (stories). This means that we often need to supplement by providing some of the missing genres ourselves. It is fairly easy these days to find suitable material on the Internet, though we may find it necessary to simplify or shorten the text.

Style
Style refers to the choices a writer/speaker makes to clarify his or her message, attitude or identity and to impress his or her reader. These choices can include features such as: grammatical structure(s) and choice of vocabulary; punctuation or use of capitals, spacing, different fonts in written texts; use of voice quality, volume, intonation, pause in spoken texts; and use of literary devices such as repetition, alliteration or assonance, and imagery.

Even with less advanced classes, it is worth drawing students' attention to basic stylistic features. For example, you might look at the way the use of contractions such as *can't* shows informality. With more advanced classes, work can be done on the link between genre and style: what stylistic characteristics are shown, for example, in an email text we are studying that do not appear in academic writing, and vice versa? What sorts of language use are typical of newspaper headlines, but rare elsewhere?

Structure, coherence and cohesion
Drawing students' attention to how a good text is carefully structured with a beginning, middle and end can help when they come to write their own compositions, or prepare oral presentations. A diagram, table or list can be a way to represent clearly the components and the way they are ordered. For example, you might summarize the description of the process of an experiment by a flowchart, or list the main events in a story.

A related topic is coherence and cohesion: the way the text 'hangs together'. Coherence is the 'macro': the text as a whole unit of meaning whose parts combine to make sense. Cohesion is the 'micro': the way individual paragraphs, sentences or phrases are linked to each other. To achieve cohesion, we use cohesive devices: grammar and lexis which refer backwards and forwards. Some cohesive devices are:

- repetition
- paraphrase
- conjunctions such as *and, but, yet, because, although, if*
- sentence adverbs or adverbial phrases such as *however, on the one hand, in addition*
- pronouns or possessives with antecedents such as *the one, she, their*.

Students can be encouraged to identify cohesive devices within the text.

Task

Have a look at the short text below, or choose one of your own. What might you draw students' attention to with regard to genre, style, structure, coherence and cohesion?

The Purist
I give you now Professor Twist
The conscientious scientist.
Trustees exclaimed: 'He never bungles!'
And sent him off to distant jungles.
Camped on a tropic riverside
One day he missed his loving bride.
She had, the guide informed him later,
Been eaten by an alligator.
Professor Twist could not but smile.
'You mean,' he said, 'a crocodile.'

Ogden Nash

3.6 Follow-up tasks

Once your class has finished studying a text, learning its language and perhaps analysing some aspects of its genre, they can now go on to do follow-up tasks. These use the text as a 'trigger' for further language enrichment work. Below are some examples of text-based follow-up tasks (adapted from Maley, 1993) addressed to the learner. They are designed to be used after studying a text of one to three paragraphs. If the text is very much shorter or longer, then adapt as necessary.

Shorten the text
- Delete as many words and sentences in the text as you can, but the result has to be a grammatical and coherent text!
- Take out all the adjectives and/or adverbs. What difference did this make to the overall meaning or 'feel' of the text?

Extend the text
- Add adjectives and adverbs wherever you can.

- Add at least three extra sentences within each paragraph, without destroying its coherence.
- Insert 'linking' words wherever these might be appropriate: words like *unfortunately, probably* expressing the writer's or speaker's attitude, and words or phrases like *finally, on the other hand* expressing the relationship with previous sentences.

- Add an introductory paragraph or an extra paragraph at the end.

Change the text

- Insert synonyms of words in the text wherever you can. What difference did this make to the overall impression of the text?
- Change the tense throughout. Or change active to passive, or vice versa.
- Change the style of the text. Change formal English to informal; or change formal or informal into online chat, email or text message (SMS); or change an informal text into formal academic style.
- Change the genre of the text. For example, if it is written as a poem, rewrite as a letter.
- (For a monolingual class) Translate the text into L1. Discuss with the class any interesting translation problems that came up.

Compare

- Compare the content and style with another text you have studied previously, or with a new one provided by the teacher.

Create your own text

- Write your own text based on the genre and structure of the text you have just studied, but on a topic of your own choosing.
- Write a personal response to the text. This could be in the form of a letter to the writer, responding to his or her ideas, or it could be in the form of an essay. In either case, you should make clear your own opinion or interpretation of the ideas brought up in the original text.

Expanding knowledge

- Discuss the issues raised in the text: either through a class discussion, or online (a forum, an exchange of emails, a blog, a wiki).
- Conduct a survey on issues raised in the text.
- Find out more about the content of the text by searching for information from the Internet, books, or people you know. Create a presentation displaying the results.

Evaluation and reflection

- Evaluate the text: did it achieve its objective? What was good or bad about it? How did you personally respond to it? Did you enjoy studying it?
- Reflect on your own learning: what have you learnt, in terms of information, new ways of thinking about things and language?

Some of the suggestions above are quite challenging, but a lot of them are enjoyable tasks that provide a pleasing 'rounding off' to the study of a text. However, you should not use too many of them. One or two each time are probably plenty. If you see that students were not interested in a particular text, you may choose not to do any follow-up work at all on it, but move immediately on to the next.

Review

Answer as many as you can of the following questions, and then check answers by referring back to the relevant passages in this unit.

If you are working in a group, note down your own answers first alone, and then share with the other members of the group. Finally, check the answers together.

What is a text?
1. What is meant by 'intensive' study of a text?

Teaching the text: the goals
2. What are the main goals of teaching a text?
3. What different levels of comprehension of content may be required from students?

Comprehension of content
4. What can we do before reading or listening to a text to help students understand it?
5. What are some common problems with comprehension questions on texts? How can they be overcome?
6. Can you recall at least three other types of comprehension tasks that you could use?

Language learning
7. How might you decide which lexical items from a text to teach and which not?
8. Should you teach the new lexical or grammatical features explicitly, or just let students absorb them intuitively through understanding the text?

Discourse analysis
9. Can you recall at least seven different genres of text that we might use with a class?
10. What aspects of style might you want to draw your students' attention to?
11. What is the difference between *coherence* and *cohesion*?

Follow-up tasks
12. How many types of follow-up tasks can you remember (e.g. 'Shorten the text')? Can you give an example for each of those you remember?

Further reading

Driscoll, L. (2004) *Reading Extra*, Cambridge: Cambridge University Press.
(A variety of different reading texts of varying lengths, with some ideas of how to teach them)

Maley, A. (1993) *Short and Sweet: Short Texts and How to Use Them*, London: Penguin.
(A useful collection of short texts of varied genres, with some very imaginative but practical ideas on how to teach them in the English classroom)

Schmitt, N. (2008) Instructed second language vocabulary learning. *Language Teaching Research,12*(3), 329–63.
(Various aspects of the teaching of vocabulary: look in particular at the passage on the provision of glosses in a reading text)

Thornbury, S. (2005) *Beyond the Sentence: Introducing Discourse Analysis*, Oxford: Macmillan Education.
(A discussion of how written and spoken texts are structured, and how a knowledge of this structure can help us teach a text)

Websites

Vocabprofile, accessible from www.lextutor.ca/vp/bnc/
(Enables you to find out which words in a specific text are more, or less, common, according to the British National Corpus. However, it does not distinguish between different meanings of the same word, or provide information on multi-word expressions.)

TESL/TEFL/TESOL/ESL/EFL/ESOL Links – ESL: Reading, accessible from http://iteslj.org/links/ESL/Reading/
(A useful list of sources from which you can download a variety of texts)

Reading text referred to in the task on p. 31:
As Jane was walking down the street, she heard someone walking quietly behind her. She began to feel afraid. Suddenly a large hand touched her neck: her gold necklace broke and disappeared. In another moment, her bag too was gone, and the thief was running away.

4 The task

4.1 The language-learning task

A *task* is defined in this book as a learner activity that has two objectives: learning of some aspect of the language; and an outcome that can be discussed or evaluated. It could be a grammar exercise, a problem-solving activity or a writing assignment. This definition excludes tests, which are designed to assess, not necessarily produce, learning. It applies also to the tasks you have been doing in this book: they also are aimed at bringing about learning (in this case, about language teaching) and have clear outcomes. (Note that this is a wider definition of the word *task* than is used in the methodology called 'task-based instruction' (Skehan, 1998), where it refers to communicative tasks only and excludes language exercises.)

A good task produces good learning: from the teacher's point of view, this is the major criterion for its evaluation. The following are some underlying practical principles of task design that are conducive to good learning.

Validity

The task should activate students primarily in the language items or skills it is meant to teach or practise. This is an obvious principle that is surprisingly often violated. For example, oral fluency tasks based on full-class discussions actually allow for very little oral fluency practice by most of the class. Discussions in pairs or small groups are likely to provide far more speaking practice and are therefore more valid as a vehicle for achieving this aim.

The principle of validity does not necessarily imply that the language should be used for some kind of replication of real-life communication. Pronunciation drills and vocabulary exercises, for example, may also be valid if they in fact serve primarily to rehearse and improve the items to be practised.

Quantity

Roughly speaking, the more English the students actually engage with during the activity, the more they are likely to learn. If the time available for the activity is seen as a container, then this should be filled with as much 'volume' of language and language activity as possible. So we need to make sure that if, for example, we are practising a particular grammatical form, then students engage with it repeatedly in different contexts; or if we are doing an activity aimed at improving listening, then the students actually do a lot of listening. And we should try to activate as many students as possible simultaneously rather than one by one, and to minimize time spent on classroom management or organization, or on fruitless puzzling out or 'not knowing'. Many word games and puzzles, such as sorting out scrambled words or wordsearch puzzles, involve the students spending most of their time looking for, rather than finding, the answers. In other words, they are wasting a lot of potential learning time on 'not knowing', when they could have been using it for engaging with, and improving their knowledge of, language they understand.

Success-orientation

On the whole, we learn by doing things right. Continued inaccurate use of language items tends to result in 'fossilization' of mistakes, and unsuccessful communication impedes progress in fluency. This is not to say that there is no place for errors and error correction; there is, of course. However, error corrections by the teacher and explanations of what caused communication problems are a transitional stage whose function is to make students aware of what they have done wrong in order to raise their consciousness of how to do it right. They then need plenty of opportunities to perform sucessfully in order to consolidate learning of the target item or communicative skill.

It is therefore important to select, design and administer tasks in such a way that students are likely to succeed in doing them most of the time: they should not be too difficult, require mostly known language and involve simple and easily explained processes. Repeated successful performance is likely to result in automatization of vocabulary and grammar, as well as reinforcing the students' self-image as successful language learners and encouraging them to take up further challenges.

Heterogeneity (of demand and level)

A good task is heterogeneous: that is to say it provides opportunities for students to engage with it at all, or most, of the different levels of proficiency within a class. If you give a learning task which (like most grammar exercises in coursebooks) invites single predetermined 'right answers', then a large proportion of your class will not benefit very much.

For example, here is an item in an exercise on *can/can't*:

Jenny is a baby. Jenny (can/can't) ride a bicycle.

Students who do not know *can* or the words *ride, bicycle* may not be able to do the item at all. Those who are more advanced and could make far more complex and interesting statements with *can/can't* have no opportunity to do so and get no useful practice at a level appropriate to them.

However, if you redesign the text and task as follows:

> Jenny is a baby. Jenny can smile, but she can't ride a bicycle. What else can, or can't, Jenny do?

… then the activity becomes heterogeneous. You have provided weaker students with support in the form of sample responses, and you have given everyone the opportunity to answer at a level appropriate to him or her, from the simple (*Jenny can drink milk*, for example) to the relatively complex (*Jenny can't open a bank account*). A much larger proportion of the class is therefore able to participate and benefit (for more ideas about heterogeneity see Unit 19: Learner differences (2): teaching heterogeneous (mixed) classes).

Interest

If the task is relatively easy because of its success-orientation, and if there is a lot of repetition of target forms resulting from the principle of 'quantity', then there is obviously a danger that the task might be boring. And not only is boredom an unpleasant feeling in itself, it also leads to student inattention, low motivation and ultimately less learning.

However, if interest is not based on the challenge of getting the answers right, it has to come from other aspects of the activity: an interesting topic, the need to convey meaningful information, a game-like 'fun' task, attention-catching materials, appeal to students' feelings or a challenge to their intellect or creativity. See Section 4.4 below for more ideas on how to make tasks interesting.

4.2 Task evaluation

The principles presented in the previous section can serve as a useful set of criteria for evaluating the effectiveness of classroom tasks such as those illustrated in the scenarios below.

Task

Have a look at the scenarios described below. How effective do you think the learning tasks are? How might you improve them? Then read the following comments.

Scenario 1: Spelling
(This is based on the game 'Hangman'.)

The teacher writes seven dashes on the board and invites the students to guess what letters they represent. They start guessing letters:

Student 1:	E.	
Teacher:	No. (writes *E* on the board, and a baseline indicating the foot of a gallows)	
Student 2:	A.	
Teacher:	Right. (fills in *A* on the second-to-last dash)	

Student 3:   S.
Teacher: No. (writes up *S*, draws in a vertical line in the gallows drawing)

… And so on. After a minute or so of guessing, the class arrives at the word *JOURNAL*, which is written up in full on the board. It is then erased, and the teacher, or a student, thinks of another word, marks up the corresponding number of dashes, and then the guessing process is repeated.

Scenario 2: Listening comprehension
The class listen to the following recorded text:

> Ozone is a gas composed of molecules possessing three oxygen atoms each (as distinct from oxygen, which has two atoms per molecule). It exists in large quantities in one of the upper layers of the atmosphere, known as the stratosphere, between 20 and 50 kilometres above the surface of the earth.
>
> The ozone layer filters out a large proportion of the sun's ultra-violet rays and thus protects us from the harmful effects of excessive exposure to such radiation.

The teacher then tells the students to open their books and answer the multiple-choice questions on a certain page. The multiple-choice questions are:

> 1. The passage is discussing the topic of
>   a) radiation.   b) oxygen.   c) ozone.   d) molecules.
> 2. Ozone molecules are different from oxygen molecules in that they
>   a) have three atoms of oxygen.
>   b) exist in large quantities.
>   c) may have one or two atoms.
>   d) have one atom of oxygen.
> 3. The stratosphere is
>   a) above the atmosphere.
>   b) below the atmosphere.
>   c) more than 20 kilometres above the surface of the earth.
>   d) more than 50 kilometres above the surface of the earth.
> 4. The ozone layer
>   a) prevents some harmful radiation from reaching the earth.
>   b) stops all ultra-violet rays from reaching the earth.
>   c) protects us from the light of the sun.
>   d) involves excessive exposure to ultra-violet rays.

When the students have finished, the teacher asks volunteers for their answers, accepting or correcting as appropriate.

Scenario 3: Grammar exercise
The exercise is intended to practise the present perfect.

> 1. Lina is looking in her bag, but she cannot find her keys. (*lose*)
> 2. The Browns live in that house on the corner, but they are not there at the moment. (*go away*)
> 3. Mark and Dan are delighted. (*pass the test*)
> 4. Becky won't be playing today. (*break her leg*)
> 5. Sam will be late. (*have an accident*)
> 6. We aren't going on holiday after all. (*change plans*)

The teacher asks the students to suggest a sentence in the present perfect that describes what has happened to produce this situation, using the verb in brackets at the end. A student volunteers: 'Lina has lost her keys.'

The teacher approves this answer and asks for a volunteer to answer the second item. This time the student answers wrongly. The teacher asks for another student to provide a more correct response. The process continues until the exercise is finished.

Scenario 4: Vocabulary

Teacher:	Who knows the meaning of the word *disappointment*? (puzzled looks; a student hesitantly puts up his hand) Yes?
Student 1:	Write a point?
Teacher:	No … anyone else? (silence) Come on, think everybody, try again!
Student 2:	Lose a point?
Teacher:	No, it has nothing to do with points. Try again. It has something to do with feelings.

(After another few guesses, the last of which, after broad hints from the teacher, comes fairly near, the teacher finally gives the correct definition.)

Comment

In fact, none of the tasks shown here is very effective. Some reasons are given below, with suggestions for improvement.

Scenario 1: Spelling. The task as described here is apparently designed to practise the spelling of the word *journal*. But out of the minute or so spent by the students on the guessing process, they engage with the actual spelling of the target word for only a few seconds at the end. The rest of the time is spent on more or less random calling out of letters, or on mistaken guesses. In other words, we have an activity at least nine-tenths of which contributes little or nothing to engagement with the target language form: it lacks both validity and quantity.

This is an interesting example of a task which is superficially attractive – motivating and fun for both students and teacher, as well as demanding little preparation – but which, when carefully analysed, proves to have very little learning value.

If we wish to practise the spelling of a set of words, then it is better to display the words from the beginning and think of a procedure that will induce students to engage with their spelling (see, for example, *Recall and share* in Unit 11: Teaching writing, p. 164).

Scenario 2: Listening comprehension. This is a listening activity which in fact provides little opportunity to listen: it lacks validity. There is more reading than listening: the written text (the questions) is longer than the listening, and more time is spent dealing with it during the procedure as a whole. The task relies heavily on memory rather than on ongoing comprehension: students need to recall accurately a set of facts presented very densely and quickly. This may be extremely difficult for those who do not have the underlying knowledge in advance, since it is based on a subject which may be unfamiliar to them. If, on the other hand, they did know the information, then they will probably be able to answer most of the questions without listening at all! The task also scores low on quantity (the listening text is very short) and on heterogeneity (there are no opportunities for giving responses at different levels).

The text would be improved if it were longer, with the information given less densely. A better task might be to ask students to take notes on the text as they hear it, and then compare with each other or with a replay of the original text. Alternatively, brief questions might be given in advance, so that students can listen out for the answers and note them down as they hear them. (See Unit 8: Teaching listening.)

Scenario 3: Grammar. A lot of the students' time and energy is spent reading the cue sentences, which do not include the target feature at all. This means that the task is of dubious validity. Moreover, the whole exercise produces only six responses using the target structure, so there is little quantity. And, since each response is limited to one right answer, the task lacks heterogeneity. Finally, it is not very interesting!

The exercise could be improved by deleting the verb in parenthesis at the end of the 'cue' items, and inviting students to account for the given situation each time by various statements using the present perfect. The first sentence, for example, might elicit a number of sentences like *She has forgotten them at home, She has left them on the bus, She has dropped them, Her brother has taken them, Someone has stolen them, The dog has buried them* and so on. The validity and quantity of the exercise thus increases, and it is also more heterogeneous and interesting. (For more on this adaptation, see Unit 19: Learner differences (2): teaching heterogeneous (mixed) classes, p. 279.)

Scenario 4: Vocabulary. This may look like a caricature of a vocabulary-teaching procedure; but I have seen it happen. The task is based on elicitation of information from students: but it is information which they simply do not have, so they cannot do the task. It is obviously failure-oriented, and most of the time is spent 'not knowing': a waste of time – no validity, and very little quantity – as well as increasing students' feelings of frustration and inferiority.

If the teacher wished to base a task on elicitation of meanings of vocabulary, he or she should immediately have provided contexts or hints that would help students to succeed, or allowed them to refer to dictionaries. But it might be better in this case to abandon the 'elicitation' aspect altogether: simply provide an explanation or translation of the target vocabulary, and then use the time saved for a task which gives opportunities to use it purposefully and interestingly in context. For example, he or she could invite a number of students to describe situations when they or someone they know experienced 'disappointment'. (See Unit 5: Teaching vocabulary.)

4.3 Organizing tasks

The success of a task in bringing about learning and engaging students depends not only on good initial task design but also on how you actually run it. It is worth thinking carefully about the way you give instructions, provide ongoing support during the task process and give feedback at the end.

Instructions
Class attention
Everyone has to be listening when you are giving instructions; otherwise students may do the task wrong, or waste time consulting each other or getting you to repeat yourself. It is worth waiting an extra minute or two before you start giving instructions to make sure that everyone is attending. This is particularly true if the task involves getting into small groups or pairs. Once they are in groups, students' attention will be naturally directed to each other rather than to you. And if they have written or graphic material in their hands, the temptation will be to look at it, which may also distract them (see *Practical tip 1* below).

Repetition
A repetition or added paraphrase of the instructions may make all the difference. Students' attention may wander occasionally, and it is important to give them more than one chance to understand what they have to do. Also, it helps to present the information again in a different mode: if it's not too long, both say it and write it up on the board, and/or ask students themselves to recap the main points.

Brevity
Students – in fact, all of us – have only a limited attention span; they cannot listen to you for very long at maximum concentration. Make your instruction as brief as you can. This means thinking fairly carefully about what you can omit, as much as about what you should include! In some situations it may also mean using students' L1, as a more accessible and shorter alternative to a long and difficult English explanation.

Examples
Very often an instruction only 'comes together' for an audience when illustrated by an example, or preferably more than one. If it is a textbook exercise, do the first one or two items with the students. If it is a communicative task, perform a 'rehearsal' with a volunteer student or two, to show how it is done.

Checking understanding

It is not enough just to ask 'Do you understand?'; students will sometimes say they did, even if they did not, out of politeness or unwillingness to lose face, or because they think they know what they have to do when in fact they have completely misunderstood! It is useful to ask them to do something that will show their understanding: to paraphrase in their own words or, if you have given the instruction in English, to translate into their L1. This also functions as an extra repetition for those who missed something earlier.

Ongoing support

One of the basic functions of a teacher is to help the students succeed in doing the learning tasks: it therefore makes sense to provide support in the course of the task itself. In a teacher-led interactive process, this involves such things as allowing plenty of time to think, making the answers easier through giving hints and guiding questions, or confirming beginnings of responses in order to encourage continuations. In group or individual work, it means being 'there' for the students, available to answer questions or provide help where needed.

On the other hand, we also want to encourage students to manage on their own, and not to be too teacher-dependent. So this means treading a narrow line between providing help when students really could not do the task successfully without it, and holding back or challenging them when you know they could, with a bit more effort, manage on their own.

In either case, it needs to be clear to the students throughout that you are involved and aware of what is going on.

Feedback

It is important to provide a feedback stage whose main aim is to 'round off' the task: by evaluating results, commenting on the work done and signalling an end to this activity as preparation for moving on to the next one.

Showing appreciation for the results

Usually a task based on group and individual work has a clear outcome which can be used as the basis for a full-class feedback stage. If it is problem-solving, elicit and discuss the solutions that different groups have come up with. If it is a brainstorming activity, pool their ideas on the board. If it is discussion, comment on their suggestions and ideas. Such procedures may not be absolutely necessary for language learning, but they show that you relate to and appreciate what the students have achieved.

Summarizing and evaluating

In some cases, there are no obvious final results you can relate to in full class – for example, if you have been doing a teacher-led exercise and providing feedback as it was going on, or if the students have been doing writing assignments which need to be checked individually. However, even in such cases there is still a need for a brief full-class feedback session. This may review the main learning points which have been the focus of the task, and may provide evaluative comment: appreciation for the work accomplished, mention of aspects that need further work or singling out particular students for praise.

Practical tips

1. **Give instructions before materials.** If you are doing group work based on particular task sheets or other written or graphic materials, explain the task before you give out the materials. Otherwise students often start looking at the materials and don't listen to what you are explaining.

2. **Tell them during the preliminary instructions how and when the task will end.** Use the initial instructions to prepare students for ending: give information about how much time they have (particularly if there is a strict time limit), how you intend to stop them, and more or less how much you expect them to have achieved by the end.

3. **Give advance warning when you are going to stop group or individual work.** Tell the class a few minutes before ending how much time they have left to work – perhaps even twice: an advance ten-minute warning, and then a final two- or three-minute one. This makes it much easier to stop them when the time comes, and forestalls protests.

4. **Have a reserve activity ready.** Sometimes groups or pairs finish early. If you want other students to continue work, then you need to be ready with something for the faster workers to do while the others are finishing: an extension or variation of the original activity, reading, something from the coursebook or a short further task.

Action task

Observe a lesson. It doesn't necessarily have to be an English lesson, and could be one you are attending yourself as a student. Make notes on how the teacher instructs the class to do a task. How clear were the instructions? Could they have been improved by one or more of the suggestions provided in this unit?

4.4 Interest

Probably the best way to explore the reasons why some tasks arouse and maintain student interest, and others don't, is to try to analyse the differences in interest between pairs of tasks that have similar teaching aims.

Action task

Try doing some or all of the pairs of tasks described below, together with colleagues ('peer teaching'), or with a real class, if you are teaching one of the appropriate level. All the tasks will probably have useful language-learning outcomes – none are really 'bad' tasks – but there are differences from the point of view of interest. Think about which of each pair was the more interesting to do and why.

1. **Spelling: the spelling and pronunciation rule of the suffix -*tion***
The teacher explains the rule, and then ...

Task 1
Students are given a dictation as follows:

prevention	intervention	instruction
intention	conception	nation
reaction	eviction	
distraction	direction	

Task 2

Students are asked to brainstorm in groups as many words as they can that end in *-tion*, and make sure everyone in the group knows what they mean. They can check their ideas in a dictionary. The teacher then 'pools' all their ideas on the board.

2. **Vocabulary: reviewing a set of words learnt from a text**
   The words are written on the board.

Task 1

The teacher invites students to take any one word of their choice, and compose a sentence that contextualizes it.

Task 2

The teacher invites students to take any two words of their choice, and compose a single sentence that contextualizes both of them.

3. **Vocabulary: learning and understanding a set of words describing emotions and moods**

Task 1

Students complete the following sentences on their own to describe experiences they have had, and then share with partners.

I was *angry* because …	_____
I was *sad* although …	_____
I felt *jealous* when …	_____
I was *confident* so …	_____
I was *tense* although …	_____
I was *doubtful* because …	_____
I felt *apathetic* so …	_____
I was *delighted* when …	_____

Task 2

Students do the following matching exercise on their own, and then check with partners.

1.	angry	a.	unhappy and angry because someone has something you want
2.	sad	b.	feeling pleasure or satisfaction
3.	jealous	c.	lacking interest or energy
4.	tense	d.	sure or trusting
5.	confident	e.	unhappy or sorry
6.	doubtful	f.	nervous, anxious, unable to relax
7.	apathetic	g.	uncertain about something
8.	happy	h.	having a strong feeling against someone or something that makes you want to shout or hurt them

4. **Grammar: there is / there are**

The teacher displays a picture that shows a lot of different people, things and activities.

Task 1

In small groups, the students suggest and write down sentences using *there is / there are* that apply to the picture. Later, the teacher elicits from each group the sentences they had thought of.

Task 2

In small groups, the students suggest sentences using *there is / there are* that apply to the picture. They are told they have one minute to think of and say as many as they can. They do not write anything down: a 'secretary' notes a tick (✓) for each sentence anyone produces. The teacher stops them after exactly one minute and asks the groups how many ticks they have.

Comment

1. **Spelling: the spelling and pronunciation rule of the suffix *-tion*.** The second activity is more interesting to do, because there is some initiative on the part of the students. All things being equal, an activity which calls on students to **initiate ideas** themselves rather than repeat or be tested on a set of given items is likely to be more interesting. Connected to this is the fact that the task is **open-ended** (there are a number of 'right' answers): it is almost always more interesting to produce or hear a response that is not predetermined or predictable, as we shall see with other examples below. Finally there is the aspect of **collaboration**: the students are working in a team, which means not only that they can enjoy working together, but also that the result is likely to be more **successful**.

2. **Vocabulary: reviewing a set of words learnt from a text.** Both tasks here are open-ended and allow for student creativity and initiative; but the second is significantly more interesting to do. The difference in this case is produced by the added challenge of connecting two items, which implies the use of **higher-order thinking** skills: looking for connections between two concepts and expressing these in a statement. Other higher-order thinking challenges can be used to review the same set of words: asking students to make false statements, for example, or to work on classification, sorting the words into different groups.

3. **Vocabulary: learning and understanding a set of words describing emotions and moods.** In this case it is the first task which is the more interesting to do. Like the previous ones, it requires student initiative and is open-ended; here, however, we have the added dimension of **personalization** and real **interpersonal communication**. The students are relating the target items to their own experiences and sharing these experiences with one another. Finally, there is the less obvious aspect of the use of higher-order thinking skills: in this case, logical or temporal relations, demanded by the conjunctions *when, because, although*, etc., which make the students think a bit more deeply about the logical structure of their sentences.

4. **Grammar: there is / there are.** The second task is based on the first, but if you have done it you will have found that it is far more interesting and feels a bit like a game. You feel a slight rise in adrenalin, produced by the rush to produce as many sentences as you can before the teacher stops you. The **game-like** effect is produced by the combination between a clear and easily achievable objective (making simple sentences), combined with a constraint, or rule, which makes it a bit more tricky: in this case, the **time limit**. Other interest-producing factors here are the collaboration, and the use of the **visual focus** of a picture.

Summary

The main practical principles contributing to interest in the design of classroom tasks can be summarized as follows:

- **Initiative**: students initiate their own ideas in response to the task.

- **Open-ending**: students produce a number of different ideas, all of which may be 'right'.

- **Collaboration**: students work together to produce a better result than they could have done on their own.

- **Success**: students succeed in achieving the task objective.

- **Higher-order thinking**: students are challenged to think about causes and effects, categories, connections, priorities and so on, rather than just recalling or saying simple sentences.

- **Personalization**: students express their own experiences, opinions, tastes or feelings.

- **Interpersonal communication**: students interact with one another to share or discuss ideas.

- **Game-like activity**: students experience a feeling of playing a game, produced by the combination of a clear and easily achieved objective, together with 'rules': constraints that limit how they can achieve it (a **time limit** is one of the easiest to implement).

- **Visual focus**: students use a picture or other visual stimulus which functions as a basis for the task.

4.5 Homework

Homework becomes an increasingly important factor in learning as students get older and/or more advanced. In younger beginner classes, most of the learning takes place in the classroom, and homework is given to extend and reinforce what has been done there, or just to get students into the routine of doing it. For example, students might be asked to finish an exercise they started in class, or to reread a text. Later, more substantial learning takes place out of the classroom: students might write essays; or they might do projects using internet-based research; or they might read their own simplified books. Eventually, after students leave school, their continued learning of the language will depend largely or entirely on their own ability to study outside classroom lessons: reading books or internet texts, for example, or conversing with other English speakers.

So homework is not only a way to provide extra opportunities for language study outside the lesson, but also an investment in the future, in that it fosters students' ability to work on their own as autonomous learners and to progress independently of the teacher.

> **Task**
>
> Recall from your own schooldays one homework assignment, or type of assignment, that you remember as being a waste of time, and another that you feel was worthwhile and learning-rich. What were the factors that made the difference?

Types of homework tasks

Routine review

Not all homework tasks have necessarily to be interesting. A lot of language learning depends on repetition for its success (few language items, whether lexical or grammatical, are learnt through one-off exposure), and homework is one way of ensuring that the necessary review takes place. So use homework to get students to re-read texts, to learn lists of lexical items or to do grammar exercises. They may groan, but they will do it – particularly if you explain why it is important (see *Practical tip 2* below). But don't do it all the time: use the other types suggested below as well.

Previews and preparation

Homework is rarely used to anticipate upcoming lessons, but it can be usefully exploited to do so. For example, students can be asked to find out all they can from the Internet about the subject of a text you intend to work on with them, or to read through a new text and look up words they did not know in a dictionary.

Creative assignments

Give occasional assignments that demand some kind of creative response, however brief, on the part of the students. They are more interesting to do and also make students more willing to do the routine homework types described above. These can be as simple as creating two or three more similar questions to add to an exercise you have already done; or suggesting multiple answers to a 'brainstorming' cue ('How many ... can you think of that ...'); or suggesting alternative answers to questions given in the book (see, for example, the suggestions for improving the exercise shown in *Scenario 3* in Section 4.2 above).

Preparing presentations

Students can be asked to prepare presentations to give in class. This is an important aspect of oral fluency (see Unit 9: Teaching speaking), but one which needs preparation time in order to be done effectively. Presentations can be as short as presenting a new lexical item (see Unit 5: Teaching vocabulary) or three- or five-minute talks on a pre-selected topic, or as long as full presentations of projects (see next item).

Projects

Projects are done largely at home, as a series of homework assignments, and can take varied forms. They could be research on famous people or historical events; information about a topic, hobby or profession; metalinguistic work on aspects of the language itself. If the projects are done in pairs or small groups, then working on them outside the classroom may mean dividing up the fact-finding or composition responsibilities between the different students, using class time to coordinate. Such assignments usually culminate in presentations (sometimes with *PowerPoint* slides) given in class and booklets or posters displayed in the classroom.

Giving feedback on homework tasks

Often teachers use the first part of the lesson to go through the homework students have just done, eliciting answers from different members of the class, checking and correcting. The problem with this is that it is very time-consuming: it substantially cuts down the amount of time you have for all the other things you want to get through in a lesson. Also, most of the answers are probably right (if they are not, then this exercise should not have been given as homework in the first place!) – so you will not be teaching them very much by going through them again.

It is much more learning-productive for the students, and saving of lesson time, to take in notebooks and check homework assignments at home ... but then the amount of homework for you can get unmanageable! Some things that can help are the use of electronic communication and selective checking (see *Practical tips* below). Alternative strategies are simply to provide the right answers (if the exercise produces single answers to each item), either written up on the board or dictated by you so that students can self-check. Or give five minutes in the course of the lesson for students to check each other's homework in small groups, calling on you only if they have any questions.

If homework has involved the preparation of presentations (see *Preparing presentations* and *Projects* above), then obviously these will need to be presented in class; but the feedback can be given later, through email.

Practical tips

1. **Take time to explain.** Don't just tell students briefly at the end of the lesson what the homework is: take time during the lesson (see *Practical tip 6* on lesson planning in Unit 2: The lesson, p. 23) to explain what it involves, how it will be checked, what options there are, and to answer any questions. Linked to this, it is important to ...

2. **Say why.** Tell students why they are doing this homework assignment: its importance for learning, or its place in the general programme of studies, or relevance to an upcoming exam.

3. **Make homework a component of the grade.** When allotting an end-of-term grade, include the regular completion of homework assignments as a component: say, 10%. This encourages students to do their homework and enables less proficient, but hardworking, students to raise their grade.

4. **Limit homework by time rather than quantity.** Tell students to spend 20 minutes (or whatever you think appropriate) on Exercise D and do as much as they can, rather than just to 'do Exercise D'. This means that slower-working students will not have to take hours doing something that other students finished in a few minutes: each will work according to his or her own speed and ability.

5. **Provide extras.** Add extra, optional homework assignments that students may do if they finish the compulsory ones early, or if they wish to do more (see Unit

19: Learner differences (2): teaching heterogeneous (mixed) classes). If students are encouraged to read simplified books or stories (extensive reading, see Unit 10: Teaching reading), then they can be told to spend time getting on with these as the extra assignment.

6. **Don't worry too much about students 'copying' from one another.** It is true that copying homework may mean that one student is not learning anything, but it might also mean that one is helping the other, which may well promote learning and therefore should not be condemned. And the alternative may be that the weaker student wouldn't do it at all! Encourage students to tell you if they worked together so that you know about it, but don't ban it completely.

7. **Use email or a Language Management System (LMS)** (see Unit 16: Classroom interaction, p. 241). If they have computers at home, send students their homework, and get the completed assignments back, through email or through an LMS such as Moodle. Correcting and commenting is also much easier and quicker this way than doing it on paper. Even if some students do not have computers, using email with those who do will still save time.

8. **Selective checking.** If you have a large class and cannot possibly check all their homework every week, take in, say, one-third of the class's notebooks each week to check, and then the others in later weeks. Keep lists of when you check each student so you do not find yourself neglecting some of them. If you are using an LMS, selective checking and record-keeping is fairly simple.

Review

Answer as many as you can of the following questions, and then check answers by referring back to the relevant passages in this unit.

If you are working in a group, note down your own answers first alone, and then share with the other members of the group. Finally, check the answers together.

The language-learning task

1. What are the two objectives of a 'task' as defined here?
2. What are the main characteristics of a good task? Can you recall all five of the ones listed in this section?
3. What is a 'heterogeneous' task?

Task evaluation

4. Suggest two problems with a listening comprehension task based on an informative spoken text followed by written multiple-choice questions.
5. What's wrong with 'Hangman' as a spelling task?

Organizing tasks

6. Give at least three good tips for making sure that task instructions are understood.
7. In what ways can a teacher provide ongoing support for students as they perform tasks.

8. Suggest some reasons for giving feedback at the end of a task, other than telling the students if they have succeeded or not.

Interest

9. What is 'higher-order thinking'?
10. Can you recall at least four other features that are important when designing interesting tasks?

Homework

11. Suggest some reasons why it is important to give homework.
12. What are some problems for the teacher when providing feedback on homework? And some possible solutions?

Further reading

Hallam, S. (2004) *Homework: The Evidence*, London: Institute of Education, London University.

(A summary of research-based information on homework and its effectiveness in promoting learning)

Nunan, D. (2004) *Task-Based Language Teaching*, Cambridge: Cambridge University Press.

(This book uses a rather narrower definition of 'task' than that given here but provides a useful range of types of tasks and some guidelines on their design and use)

5 Teaching vocabulary

Overview

The sections in this unit are:

5.1 **What is vocabulary?** A definition of the word *vocabulary* in the context of English language teaching.

5.2 **What students need to learn: aspects of vocabulary knowledge**. Aspects of lexical items that learners need to learn, associated with their form, meaning and use in context.

5.3 **How best to teach vocabulary: some facts and figures**. Research-based information about how vocabulary is most effectively learnt and taught.

5.4 **Presenting new vocabulary: selection and presentation**. The selection and initial presentation of new lexical items.

5.5 **Vocabulary review: consolidating and extending lexical knowledge**. Later practice and enrichment activities to enhance vocabulary learning.

5.6 **Vocabulary assessment**. Different methods of testing the various aspects of vocabulary knowledge.

5.1 What is vocabulary?

Vocabulary can be defined, roughly, as the words in the language. However, it may include items that are more than a single word: for example, *post office* and *mother-in-law*. There are also longer multi-word expressions such as *call it a day, in any case, How are you?* which express a single concept and are stored in the memory as a whole 'chunk'. A useful convention is to cover all such cases by talking about vocabulary 'items' rather than 'words'.

The term *vocabulary* is also sometimes taken to include *grammatical items*: pronouns such as *she, someone*, or determiners such as *the, that, any*. These are contrasted with *lexical items* (nouns, verbs, adjectives, adverbs). Grammatical items do not have much meaning on their own but are used to show the relationships with other words within meaningful utterances. They are 'closed sets' (it is unlikely that the language will acquire a new pronoun, or another demonstrative to add to *this/that*), whereas lexical items are an 'open set': items are constantly being added, lost or changed.

In this book the word *vocabulary* usually refers to the lexical items of the language.

5.2 What students need to learn: aspects of vocabulary knowledge

The most important things the students need to know about a lexical item are its written and spoken form and its most usual meaning. However, there are additional aspects which also need to be learnt: its grammar, collocational links, connotations, appropriateness of use, and relationships with other items in English and in the students' L1.

Form: pronunciation and spelling

The learner has to know what a word sounds like (its pronunciation) and what it looks like (its spelling). Many people assume that meaning is more important than form: but remember that knowing a meaning is pretty useless without knowing the form it is attached to. In most cases the learners will encounter a form before they know its meaning, not vice versa – which is why it is put first here. You may stress either pronunciation or spelling when teaching a particular item, depending on where it was found: ultimately, students will need to know both. Most English words are pronounced and spelt according to regular rules (see Unit 11: Teaching writing, pp. 163–4), but where they are not, you will need to teach the irregular form.

Meaning: denotation

The meaning of a word or expression is what it refers to, or denotes, in the real world. This is given in dictionaries as its definition. Occasionally a lexical item in English has no parallel in the learners' L1, and you will find yourself explaining an actual concept as well as the item that represents it.

Sometimes a word may have various meanings: most often these are metaphorical extensions of the meaning of the original word (for example, the 'foot' of a mountain, deriving from *foot* as part of the body). But sometimes a word such as *bear* has multiple meanings (*bear* the animal and *bear* meaning 'tolerate') because they are derived from two different words which happen to have developed into the same form (*homonyms*).

Grammar

The grammar of a new item will need to be taught if this is not obviously covered by general grammatical rules. An item may have an unpredictable change of form in certain grammatical contexts (for example, the past tense of irregular verbs), or may have some particular way of connecting with other words in sentences (for example, the verbs which take *-ing* forms after them rather than the *to* infinitive). It is important to provide students with this information when, or soon after, introducing the item itself.

Collocation

Collocation refers to the way words tend to co-occur with other words or expressions. For example, we normally say *tell + the truth* but not *say + the truth*.

A specific phrase may be grammatically correct and yet sound wrong simply because of inappropriate collocation. For example, you can *do* your homework, but you cannot *make* it. Similarly, you *throw a ball* but *toss a coin*; you may talk about *a tall man*, but not **a tall mountain*.

Collocations are often, but not always, shown in dictionaries under the headword of one of the collocating items.

for-eign /£'for-ən, $'f□:r-/ *adj* (not gradable) belonging or connected to a country which is not your own ● *Spain was the first foreign country she had visited.* ● *I wish I had learned more foreign languages at school.* ● *His work provided him with the opportunity for a lot of foreign travel.* ● *She's a former foreign correspondent for the Financial Times newspaper.* ● (*literary*) Something can be described as foreign to a particular person if it is unknown to them or not within their experience: *The whole concept of democracy, she claimed was utterly foreign to the present government.* ● An object or substance which has entered something else, possibly by accident, and does not belong there is sometimes described as foreign: *a foreign object/substance* ○ *foreign matter* ○ *At the hospital they cleaned the cut thoroughly to stop any foreign bodies from getting into my arm.* ● **Foreign affairs** are matters that are connected with other countries: *the minister of foreign affairs* ● **Foreign aid** is the help that is given by esp. a richer country to esp. a poorer one, usually in the form of money. ● **Foreign exchange** is the system by which the type of money used in one country is exchanged for another country's money, making international trade easier: *On the foreign-exchange markets the pound remained firm.* ● In Britain, **the Foreign Office**

Connotation

The connotations of a word are the emotional or positive–negative associations that it implies. The words *moist* and *damp*, for example, have the same basic meaning (slightly wet); but *moist* has favourable connotations while *damp* has slightly unfavourable ones. So you could talk about a *moist chocolate cake*, which sounds appetising; but a *damp cake* would imply that something had gone wrong with the recipe! Many words have only weak connotations or do not have them at all; however, where the connotation is marked, as in the above example, it does need to be taught. The dictionary does not always specify connotations in its definitions, though where these exist they may often be understood from the examples or collocations provided.

Appropriateness

In order to know how to use an item, the student needs to know about its appropriateness for use in a certain context. Thus, it is useful for a student to know, for a particular item, if it is very common or relatively rare; or if it is usually used in writing or in speech, in formal or informal discourse. Some items may be 'taboo' in most social interactions; others may belong to certain varieties of English. For example, learners need to know that the word *weep* is virtually synonymous with *cry*, but it is more formal, tends to be used in writing more than in speech, and is in general much less common.

Task

How would you present the meanings (denotations) of the words *swim*, *fame*, *childish*, *political*, *impertinence*, *kid*? For which would you mention their connotations? Collocations? Appropriate contexts?

Suggested answers are provided in the *Key to task* on p. 75.

Meaning relationships

It can also be useful to look at how the meaning of one item relates to the meaning of others, though this is perhaps less essential for students than the aspects discussed above. There are various such relationships: here are some of the main ones.

- **Synonyms:** items that mean the same, or nearly the same
  Example: *bright, clever, smart* may serve as synonyms of *intelligent*.
- **Antonyms:** items that mean the opposite
  Example: *rich* is an antonym of *poor*.
- **Hyponyms:** items that serve as specific examples of a general concept
  Example: *dog, lion, mouse* are hyponyms of *animal*.
- **Co-hyponyms** or **coordinates:** other items that are the 'same kind of thing'
  Example: *red, blue, green* and *brown* are co-hyponyms or coordinates.
- **Superordinates:** general concepts that 'cover' specific items
  Example: *animal* is the superordinate of *dog, lion, mouse*.
- **Translation:** words or expressions in the students' L1 that are similar in meaning to the item being taught but may have slightly different connotations or contexts of use that it is interesting to explore.

Besides these, there are other, perhaps looser, ways of associating meaning that are useful in teaching. You can, for instance, relate parts to a whole (the relationship between *arm* and *body*); or associate items that are part of the same real-world context (*tractor, farmer, milking* and *irrigate* are all associated with *agriculture*).

All these can be exploited in teaching to clarify the meaning of a new item, or for practice or test materials.

Word formation

Words can be broken down into *morphemes*: for example, *unkindly* is composed of the prefix *un-*, the root word *kind* and the suffix *-ly*. Exactly how these components are put together is another piece of useful information, though mainly for more advanced learners.

You may wish to teach the common prefixes and suffixes: for example, if students know the meaning of the prefixes *sub-, un-* and the suffix *-able*, this will help them guess the meanings of words like *substandard, ungrateful* and *untranslatable*. They should, however, be warned that in many common words the meaning of the prefix or suffix has got lost and knowing it may not help them understand the meaning (*subject, refine*). New combinations using prefixes and suffixes are not unusual, their meaning usually 'transparent' from an understanding of their component morphemes (*ultra-modern, watchable*).

Another way vocabulary items are built is by combining two (occasionally three) words to make one item, sometimes hyphenated (*bookcase, follow-up, swimming pool, four-wheel drive*). Again, new coinages using this kind of combination are very common.

5.3 How best to teach vocabulary: some facts and figures

The importance of vocabulary teaching and learning (as compared, for example, with the teaching of grammar or pronunciation) for second or foreign language acquisition has been discussed briefly in Unit 1 (pp. 2–3). Various aspects of the topic have been researched, resulting in a number of interesting findings. Some of these are summarized below.

How many of its words do you need to know in order to understand a text?

Many people think that if you understand 80–85% of the words of a text, then you can probably guess the rest and understand the text as a whole. This is now known to be an underestimate (try the task below if you don't believe me!). It is generally agreed by researchers today that in order to understand a text, you need to be able to understand between 95% and 98% of its words (Schmitt, 2008). Roughly speaking, this means that if there is more than one word every two lines that you do not understand, you may have trouble understanding the text and may not be able to guess successfully the meanings of unknown items.

Task

Have a look at this extract from a speech by President Obama in 2010. I have deleted slightly fewer than 15% of the more advanced words. You can understand that he is talking about terrorism, but can you understand what he is saying he has done about it? Can you guess the words that should fill the gaps?

> That is the work we began last year. Since the day I took office, we renewed our focus on the terrorists who _____ our nation. We have made _____ _____ in our homeland _____ and _____ _____ that threatened to take American lives.

Now have a look at a version with only about 4% of the words deleted. This time you probably have a better idea of the sort of things Obama is talking about. But can you guess the missing words?

> That is the work we began last year. Since the day I took office, we renewed our focus on the terrorists who threaten our nation. We have made substantial _____ in our homeland _____ and disrupted plots that threatened to take American lives.

Here is the final version below: how accurate were your guesses?

> That is the work we began last year. Since the day I took office, we renewed our focus on the terrorists who threaten our nation. We have made substantial investments in our homeland security and disrupted plots that threatened to take American lives.

Knowing about 98% of an unsimplified text means knowing a huge number of word families: the number estimated by different researchers ranges between 5,000 and 8,000 (Schmitt, 2008). The term *word families* means groups of words which are based on a common root (for example, *nation, nationalize, national, international*); so the number of single words to be learnt is even larger. It will be larger still if we include idiomatic expressions such as *call it a day* and *on the other hand*, whose meaning cannot necessarily be worked out from the component words.

The challenge facing the teacher is how to help students achieve such a huge vocabulary. Schoolchildren learning English in a country where English is not spoken as an L1 receive English instruction during the 30 to 40 weeks of the school year for about three or four hours a week for eight years or so. If you add it up, that means that they need to learn about 20–30 word families a week. There will be fewer, of course, in the younger classes and more in the older; but however you divide it, it is a lot of words.

In addition, it is not enough for learners just to read or hear and understand a new item once. They need also to review it. Researchers claim that we need at least 6, maybe as many as 16, re-encounters with an item in order for it to be properly learnt (Zahar et al., 2001).

Incidental and deliberate teaching and learning

An important question is: Can you acquire a large vocabulary incidentally, only through listening, reading and conversation? This is the way we learn vocabulary in our L1. However, in second language learning in the context of a formal school course, this does not work so well. It is simply inefficient (Laufer, 2003): very slow and rather unreliable. Most researchers agree that we need to include some deliberate, focused vocabulary-teaching procedures as a supplement to – though not a substitute for – incidental acquisition through extensive reading and listening.

Deliberate vocabulary-teaching procedures can be divided into two groups: those that are aimed to teach new items for the first time in order to expand the students' vocabulary; and those that are designed to provide opportunities for review in order to consolidate and deepen students' knowledge of the new items. The next two sections will deal with these.

5.4 Presenting new vocabulary: selection and presentation
Selection and sources of new vocabulary

The most important criterion for the selection of which vocabulary items to teach has to be its usefulness for our students' own needs. One helpful measure of the usefulness of an item is *frequency*, i.e. how often a word, or expression, is used in conversation or writing (often measured by the survey of a corpus[1]). There are vocabulary lists based on frequency available to teachers online: for example Oxford 3000 (www.oxfordadvancedlearnersdictionary.com/oxford3000/) shows the 3,000 most frequent words, and English Profile (http://wordlistspreview. englishprofile.org/staticfiles/about.html) provides lists of words and phrases appropriate to the various levels of the Common European Framework of Reference for Languages (CEFR). Good learner dictionaries will also indicate the frequency level of each headword: for example, *Cambridge Advanced Learner's Dictionary*, or *The Longman Active Study Dictionary*. For academic students, a useful additional list is the Academic Word List (Coxhead, 2000; see also the website http://intra.collegebourget.qc.ca/spip/IMG/doc/AWL_complete_list-2.doc).

However, frequency is not the only criterion. We might want to teach new items because they are important for the students' own present situation or culture; or because they are easy to learn (short, easily pronounceable, perhaps similar to a word in the L1); or simply because they are fun or interesting items in themselves. In any case, when we come across a long list of new vocabulary items in a text, we do need to differentiate between which items are important to teach and review so that our students remember and can use them, and which only need to be explained so that they can understand the particular text being studied.

However, text study may not supply all the vocabulary our students need. It is also important to provide activities whose focus is simply vocabulary expansion. For example, we might have a 'spot' in the lesson, perhaps at the beginning, called 'word of the day' or 'expression of the day' where we teach a new item. Or we might have students themselves 'show and tell': find out about new items and teach the rest of the class. For more ideas for vocabulary expansion activities, see Ur (2012).

---

[1] A corpus is a large database of authentic texts in the language, usually including both spoken and written discourse.

Presenting new vocabulary

Once we have selected the items to teach, we then have to get students to perceive their form and understand their meaning(s). We want to do this as emphatically and interestingly as we can so that the students pay attention and take the items into short-term memory. Some key practical principles are:

Include both written and spoken form, both receptive and productive. Usually the new items have to be written up on the board, and said as they are being written. Some students find it easier to perceive new items through seeing them, others through hearing; but for all of them providing both written and spoken forms will make the target item more memorable.

Similarly, if students say and write down the item, they will be more likely to remember it than if they only hear or see it, particularly if they write it down together with its meaning (most usually in the form of an L1 translation).

Ensure understanding of meanings. As we have seen in Section 5.3, guessing meanings of words from context can be quite difficult, and students often guess wrongly. Even looking words up in the dictionary is not reliable: the student may choose the wrong meaning. Both these strategies can be used to access meanings, but they will need to be checked and supplemented by you.

If you yourself are presenting the meaning of a new item, there are various ways you can do this. At beginner or elementary level, where the meanings of new vocabulary tend to be more concrete, you can use pictures, realia (actual objects or toy models), gesture and mime. Later, you are more likely to use translation, definition or description, giving examples or hints, and sample uses of the item in context. Probably the most effective in most cases is translation (if you have a monolingual class and are fluent in your students' L1). Translation is at least as accurate as any of the other options, quick and easy, and likely to be the most easily understood by students (see Unit 1: English teaching today, p. 6 for a discussion of the increasing acceptability of the use of L1 in English teaching). Pictures are sometimes misleading, and English definitions and synonyms may not be clear enough. Once you have provided the students with the L1 equivalent so that they know more or less what it means, the more precise meaning(s) and use of the target item can be clarified through multiple examples and contexts, and/or through the other tools (pictures, etc.) suggested above.

Optimize impact. The more impact your presentation of new items makes, the more likely students are to remember it. A memorable first presentation does not make review unnecessary, but it does make learning easier and faster. This is one good reason for using pictures, mime and gesture (particularly if you are a good artist and/or actor!) instead of, or to back up, translation and explanation. The use of realia (actual objects), where possible, is also effective: I have found that real objects make more impact than pictures, particularly (but not only) in younger classes.

Another useful strategy to increase impact is to use mnemonic devices, in particular the technique called 'keywords': students link the target word with an image involving a similar word in their own language. For example, supposing you were teaching the word *shelf* to a group of German speakers: tell them to imagine a cat (or any animal they like) sleeping (*schläft*) on a shelf. The next time they come across the word, or need to use it, the image of a cat asleep on a shelf will help them remember it.

What helps students remember individual items?

Some interesting insights on how memory works are gained through an experiment where subjects are asked to memorize contrasting lists of vocabulary: all with three letters, but of varying difficulty and meaning-value. Examples are shown below.

A	B
WHO	ARM
DOT	LEG
COM	FAT
LAR	PIG
SEX	PEG
OCT	FOX
PED	DOG
AWE	CAT
ION	MAN
NUB	BOY
OWN	SON
DIG	MUM
OBI	DAD
STA	BAD
THE	SAD

Task

Try this yourself. Give yourself a minute to learn List A. Then close the book and see how many you can remember and write down. Do the same with List B. If you are working in a group, then compute the average scores of the group.

Then think about or discuss the results. Which list was remembered better? Which individual words? Can you explain why? And what particular strategies did you, or others, use to help you remember?

List B often produces near-perfect scores; List A noticeably less. There are two main reasons for this: the uniform (fairly low) level of difficulty of the items in List B in contrast to the rather more advanced and varied level of List A; and the fact that the words in List B are grouped according to meaning- or sound-association, whereas in List A there is no such grouping. When faced with the challenge of learning such lists, people often use these links to help them recall individual items. The results would indicate not only that we learn words better when they are easier (i.e. we can easily assign meaning to them, and/or their spelling and pronunciation are transparent, but also that it is helpful to learn words in pairs or small groups, where one word can be associated with another: because they are naturally associated in our minds (*dog + cat*) or because they would go together in a natural phrase (*fat + pig*) (but see second bullet point below). Words with emotional associations (*mum, dad, sex*) are remembered better. Words at the beginning of a list also tend to be remembered better.

The implications for the teaching of new vocabulary can be summarized as follows:
- The easier a word is to say and spell, the more quickly it will be remembered: so we will find it easier to get our students to remember, for example, *sky* than *earth*: the teaching of *earth* will demand more attention and effort.
- It is useful to link words together when teaching and reviewing them. Several studies have shown, however, that teaching a larger set of isolated items for the first time which are co-hyponyms, or the same 'sort of thing' (e.g. *dog, cat, horse, mouse, sheep*), can be confusing and lead to less effective memorizing (e.g. Papathanasiou, 2009). Better results can be obtained if you select and present them in pairs rather than large sets, as they would combine naturally in a phrase or sentence, e.g. *fat + pig*.
- Learners remember words better if they have some personal significance or emotional connection. So when presenting them, try to link them to students' own lives, feelings and experiences, or to your own.
- Words taught earlier are on the whole learnt better: if you are teaching a whole set of words in a lesson, put the more important ones first.

Practical tips

1. **Get students to use vocabulary notebooks.** Students should write down the new vocabulary they have learnt. The best way to do this is to have a vocabulary notebook, which can then be used for later review (see next section). They can also list the items in a file on their laptops, cellphones or tablet computers of course, but a paper notebook is probably more convenient and accessible for most people. They should note down the meaning of each item beside it (usually in L1). Later, they can cross out items they are sure they know. Usually, students will simply write down the items in the order they came across them, but you could encourage them to organize their notebooks so that they will find it easier to refer to them later, for example by having different pages for different topics or parts of speech.

2. **Don't insist on students writing detailed entries for each item.** It is sometimes suggested that students add to each item an English definition as

well as an L1 one, a sentence contextualizing it, a note as to the part of speech, maybe a drawing, but experience shows that students rarely keep this up over time and find it more tedious than helpful.

3. **Encourage students to think up their own 'keyword' devices for remembering words.** Students are more likely to remember keywords that they have devised themselves rather than those suggested to them.

4. **Don't teach more than ten new items at a time in intermediate classes;** and even fewer for younger classes. There's a limit to how many items can be taken on board in one lesson. Highly motivated classes of adult learners can, however, cope with more.

5. **Teach new items early in the lesson.** Students are fresher and better at learning new material at the beginning of lessons than they are later.

5.5 Vocabulary review: consolidating and extending lexical knowledge

It has already been noted that a learner needs to re-encounter a new item several times in order to remember it permanently. Very common items like *go, put, person, day* are likely to be met again in the course of texts or interpersonal communication anyway. But as soon as you start expanding taught vocabulary to include even slightly less common items like *business* or *cook*, this becomes less and less likely, and we need to create opportunities for review. This means using effective learning tasks (see Unit 4: The task) whose focus is multiple, meaningful encounters with the target items. Probably every lesson should include some vocabulary review work.

A useful principle here is that of 'expanding rehearsal' (Baddeley, 1997). The most effective review takes place when students still remember the item but need a slight effort to recall it. So do the first review very soon after students have learnt the item – in the next lesson, for example. The next review can be after a longer gap – perhaps a week. Then two weeks, then a month and so on. As students learn the item better and better, the length of time they can remember it without a reminder grows, as does the speed at which they can retrieve it when needed, until they get to the point at which the item is part of their permanent vocabulary.

Reviewing, not testing

It is important to ensure that review tasks are not just tests. Essentially, tasks that review vocabulary aim to consolidate and deepen students' basic knowledge. In other words, their aim is to teach. Tests aim to find out what students know; they may not result in much learning.

The aim of a vocabulary review activity is that students should engage successfully, meaningfully and accurately with the target items (see Unit 4: The task, pp. 43–5 for a discussion of what makes a good task). So there is plenty of room for peer-teaching and collaboration, for creative and original responses. But there is no particular need for assessment or the giving of grades. It is the process of doing the task, not the product, which is important.

Some procedures may be used for either testing or review: dictations, for example. But if dictations are used for review, then you are likely to do various things to make sure they get the answers right: go over the items in advance to remind students how they are spelt and what they mean, give hints and help while they are writing, let them work in pairs. Immediately afterwards, show them the right answers so that they can self-check.

Types of review tasks

Single-item

Review of single words or expressions does not have to be done through encountering them in full sentences. Reminding students themselves of the meaning or form of individual items is also very useful, and a lot quicker than working on full contexts.

Very quick reviews can take the form of simply going through the target items and reminding students of what they mean, or giving a few minutes for students to look through their vocabulary notebooks during lesson time, or writing up the items on the board and asking students to identify those they do not remember so that you can re-teach them.

Here are some examples of slightly longer activities that review single item:

- Dictations (see above); but check that your students understand the items they write.
- How many can you remember? Students 'brainstorm' all the new items they remember learning recently, reminding each other, if necessary, what they mean.
- Quick Bingo. Each student writes down his or her choice of 5 of a set of 15 items you put on the board; you call out each one (or a hint or translation) in turn, and students cross it off if they have it. The first and last students to finish are the winners.
- Guessing. Tell the students you are thinking of an item they have learnt this year, and give a hint or rough definition. Students guess it. The successful guesser then thinks of another item and gives a hint for the rest of the class to guess … and so on, until you have covered 10 or 15 recently learnt items.

Items in context

Asking students to engage with (understand or produce) items within a sentence or longer text takes longer. However, it provides for review and deeper learning of aspects of the way the word is used (grammar, collocation, appropriateness, etc.), which cannot be provided in single-item work.

Here are some examples:

- Compose sentences. Students compose sentences that contextualize items. This is fairly boring: it is better to ask them to compose sentences that link two words, or compose personalized or clearly false sentences – strategies that add extra challenge and interest (see Unit 4: The task, pp. 51–5).
- Compose a story. In groups, students make up stories that contextualize as many as possible of a random set of items from those you have recently taught.

- Find collocations. Students are given single words and find other words or expressions that collocate with them either from their own previous knowledge or using reference sources such as dictionaries or websites like ForBetterEnglish (http://forbetterenglish.com/) or JustTheWord (www.just-the-word.com/).

More activities for reviewing and enriching vocabulary knowledge can be found in Ur (2012).

Practical tips

1. **Get students to review on their own.** Explain to students the importance of vocabulary review and urge them to use their vocabulary notebooks to remind themselves of items regularly at home. Even better is to …

2. **Use word cards.** Word cards are slips of stiff paper with the target item on one side and the L1 translation on the other. If students make one of these for each new item they are taught and keep a pack of them in their pockets or bags, they can take them out and check through them at odd moments: on the bus or in a doctor's waiting room, for example. They can throw away (or put aside for the moment, perhaps retrieving later for review) any cards showing items they are sure they know.

3. **List new items on mobile phones.** Tell students to note the new items either on their mobile phones or on any other mobile electronic equipment, such as tablet computers, that they carry around with them. They can then check through them at odd moments, as with word cards.

4. **Display the new vocabulary (semi-)permanently.** New vocabulary can be displayed on the classroom wall or on the board so that students see it often and can easily refer to it.

5. **Recall at the end of the lesson.** Use your lesson summary time (see Unit 2: The lesson, p. 23) to remind students of the new items they have learnt this lesson.

6. **Go back to earlier items.** Remember to review occasionally items you taught a month or two ago, or even before, as well as those taught more recently.

5.6 Vocabulary assessment

We need every now and again to check how much of the vocabulary we have taught students has in fact been mastered by them, either receptively or productively. It is also useful to do an assessment of how much vocabulary students know overall, including both what we have deliberately taught and what they have learnt on their own. This is most conveniently done through a variety of vocabulary tests.

Tests of target vocabulary

Most vocabulary tests target specific sets of items, but how and what they test often varies. For any particular test you need to ask yourself:

- Does this test only check understanding (receptive knowledge) of the target items, or does it find out if students can actually say or write them when needed (productive knowledge)?
- Does it test spoken or written knowledge of the item, or both?
- Does it require students to contextualize the item or just understand or produce it in isolation?
- Does it provide for objective assessment (such as multiple-choice), or does it need some measure of subjective judgement (such as open sentence writing)?
- Does it assess aspects other than meaning and form, such as the connotation or collocational links of an item?
- How convenient, practical or easy is it to design and administer? Multiple-choice items, for example, though easy to check, are really difficult to design (see Unit 12: Assessment and testing, p. 176 for more discussion of this point). Tests of vocabulary based on interviews are effective in checking spoken knowledge, but very time-consuming to administer.

Here are some common vocabulary test formats:

- **Multiple-choice.** Students mark the right option of several possibilities.
- **Gapfills.** Students fill in a single gap in a sentence with the right word. This can be expanded to …
- **Focused cloze.**[2] A full, coherent text is supplied with the target items missing; students fill in the appropriate items.
- **One-to-one matching.** Students match appropriate items from parallel lists: these could be, for example, matching a word to its definition, or matching opposites.
- **Dictation.** Students write down items from the teacher's dictation. A variation of this is translation-dictation, where the teacher says the word in L1 and the student writes down the English translation – or vice versa.
- **Sentence completion.** Students are given the beginning of sentences that include the target item, and complete them to demonstrate understanding.
- **Say if you know it.** Students simply state whether they know the given item or not. If they say they do, they may be asked to demonstrate by contextualizing it in a sentence.
- **Translate.** Students translate the item, isolated or in a sentence context, to or from the L1.
- **Read aloud.** Students read aloud the items, showing they can pronounce them properly.
- **What's in the picture?** Students tell you orally what items they can see in the picture.
- **What more do you know about this word?** Students tell you the meaning of the target item and any further knowledge they have about it: what it collocates with, what would be an appropriate or inappropriate context of use, what other words they know from the same family and so on. This would be appropriate for higher-level classes.

---

[2] Traditional 'cloze' tests are texts with words deleted at regular intervals; for example, every seventh word. For vocabulary-testing purposes, however, the target words are deleted, wherever they occur.

Task

Choose one or more of the vocabulary test formats listed above, and consider with regard to each:

- What aspect(s) of the target item is it testing?
- What aspects of the target item is it not testing?
- How easy is it to design and administer?
- How easy is it to check and grade?

See Unit 12: Assessment and testing, pp. 173–7 for a critical analysis of some of the test items shown above.

Tests of overall vocabulary knowledge

Two tests that assess the overall vocabulary knowledge of learners are the **Vocabulary Levels Test** and the **Lexical Frequency Profile**.

The Vocabulary Levels Test was developed by Paul Nation (2001) and can be found in the Appendix to his book and on the Lextutor website (www.lextutor.ca/tests/). It is composed of test items at different levels, based on multiple matching of words to meanings, as in the following example:

> 1. business   _____ part of a house
> 2. clock   _____ animal with four legs
> 3. horse   _____ something used for writing
> 4. pencil
> 5. shoe
> 6. wall

Such test items are grouped according to frequency, at five levels.

- Level 1: items that fall between the 1,000–2,000 most frequent words
- Level 2: items between 2,000 and 3,000
- Level 3: items between 3,000 and 5,000
- Level 4: items in the Academic Word List
- Level 5: items up to the 10,000 frequency level

Results of these tests will therefore show clearly more or less how much vocabulary the students have: for example, if they get almost all the Level 1 items right but only about half of Level 2, then their vocabulary consists probably of somewhere between 2,000 and 3,000 word families.

The Lexical Frequency Profile was devised by Batia Laufer and Paul Nation (1995). Students submit compositions, which are then copied and pasted into an internet tool (Lextutor: Vocabprofilers: www.lextutor.ca/vp/eng/). This immediately assesses how many of the words they used are at the different levels of frequency, expressed as percentages. An advanced text can be expected to show about 90% of its lexis up to the 3,000 frequency level and 10% beyond; whereas an intermediate text will have about 95% up to the 3,000 frequency level and 5% beyond.

Review

Answer as many as you can of the following questions, and then check answers by referring back to the relevant passages in this unit.

If you are working in a group, note down your own answers first alone, and then share with the other members of the group. Finally, check the answers together.

What is vocabulary?

1. What does the term *lexical item* include?

What students need to learn: aspects of vocabulary knowledge

2. What aspects of the meaning, form and use of a word does a learner need to know?
3. Why is it important to know the common collocations of a newly learnt word?
4. Can you give some examples of the kinds of connotations a word might have?

How best to teach vocabulary: some facts and figures

5. How much (%) of the vocabulary of a given text does the reader need to know in order to be reasonably sure of understanding it?
6. How many times (approximately) do you need to re-encounter a new item in order to be sure of remembering it?

Presenting new vocabulary: selection and presentation

7. What are two important criteria for selection of the vocabulary to teach a class?
8. What are some ways of making sure that the initial presentation of new items has impact?

Vocabulary review: consolidating and extending lexical knowledge

9. What is 'expanding rehearsal'?
10. Can you recall at least four different activities shown here that can be used to review or deepen vocabulary knowledge?

Vocabulary assessment

11. What are some of the questions you need to ask yourself when designing or selecting vocabulary testing items for your class? Can you recall at least three?
12. How might you get an idea of how much vocabulary overall your students know?

Further reading

Academic Word List. Available from: http://intra.collegebourget.qc.ca/spip/IMG/doc/AWL_complete_list-2.doc.

> (The actual list of words in the academic word list can be used as the basis of vocabulary-teaching exercises for more advanced classes. See Coxhead, 2000 for details on its design)

Baddeley, A. (1997) *Human Memory*, Hove: Psychology Press.
(Some interesting and relevant information on how we remember – and forget – items. See particularly Chapter 7: 'When practice makes perfect')

Bogaards, P. and Laufer-Dvorkin, B. (2004) *Vocabulary in a Second Language: Selection, Acquisition and Testing*, Amsterdam/Philadelphia: John Benjamins.
(Articles summarizing research on various aspects of vocabulary learning and teaching)

Hinkel, E. (2004) *Teaching Academic ESL Writing: Practical Techniques in Vocabulary and Grammar*, Mahwah, NJ: Lawrence Erlbaum Associates.
(Some excellent practical techniques for getting advanced classes to extend and consolidate their vocabulary)

Nation, I. S. P. (2001) *Learning Vocabulary in Another Language*, Cambridge: Cambridge University Press.
(A classic, comprehensive book on various aspects of vocabulary teaching and learning. Rather long: you probably need to read it selectively)

Read, J. (2000) *Assessing Vocabulary*, Cambridge: Cambridge University Press.
(A summary of relevant research findings, followed by coverage of the main methods of assessing vocabulary, including future directions in computer-based assessment)

Ur, P. (2012) *Vocabulary Activities*, Cambridge: Cambridge University Press.
(A range of practical activities for vocabulary expansion, enrichment, review and assessment)

Key to task on p. 62

swim *means to move oneself through the water by moving parts of the body: you might clarify by using pictures or mime. It has no particular connotations and collocations, and is neutral as regards context of use.*

fame *means the state of being well known. It has a positive connotation; you would not use the word about someone who is well known because they have done something bad. It has no particular collocations and is neutral as regards context of use.*

childish *means like a child, but it has a strong negative connotation: it would be used to insult, or criticize behaviour. It often collocates with* games, silly, stupid. *It is neutral as regards context of use.*

political *means associated with politics. It can have a negative connotation in some contexts: where, for example, political motives are contrasted with motives of justice or morality. It commonly collocates with* party, prisoner, decision. *It is neutral.*

impertinence *means being rude or cheeky. It has no particular connotation or collocation but is used only in formal speech or writing.*

kid *means a child, of either gender. It has slight connotations of affection (though it can also be used with negative adjectives) and commonly collocates with* sister, brother. *It is normally used only in informal conversation or writing.*

6 Teaching grammar

Overview

The sections in this unit are:

6.1 **What is grammar?** A brief definition.

6.2 **What students need to learn: standards of grammatical acceptability.** What grammatical forms are acceptable, or unacceptable, in the different contexts in which English is used today.

6.3 **How best to teach grammar: explicit and implicit processes.** The pros and cons of explicit grammar teaching (explanations, practice) as contrasted with implicit (intuitive acquisition through communicative activity).

6.4 **Presenting grammar: explanations.** Some practical guidelines on the provision of grammatical explanations in the classroom.

6.5. **Grammar practice: consolidating and automatizing grammatical knowledge.** Different types of grammar practice and the importance of meaningful, communicative practice of grammar in context.

6.6 **Grammar assessment.** A set of test items that can be used to assess grammatical knowledge, divided into closed-ended (one right answer) and open-ended (a number of possible right responses).

6.1 What is grammar?

Grammar is sometimes defined as 'the way words are put together to make correct sentences'. So in English *I am a teacher* is grammatical, **I a teacher*, and **I are a teacher* are not. This is a good starting point, but the definition needs expanding to include all the aspects that the term *grammar* covers and that we need to teach.

First, it is not just a question of correctness. Grammatical forms nearly always carry meaning: the meaning of a particular message in a communicative situation is created by a combination of vocabulary and grammar. We use grammatical items and constructions to express, for example, time (using tenses) or place (using prepositions) or possibility (using modals or conditional clauses). It is often the meanings that create problems for our students and need careful teaching, rather than the forms (for example, when contrasting present perfect simple *I have done my homework* with present perfect progressive *I have been doing my homework*).

Second, we can apply the term *grammatical* to units smaller or larger than sentences. A brief phrase said or written on its own can be grammatically acceptable or unacceptable in its own right: *a tall woman* sounds right;**a woman tall* does not. The grammatical components may not be whole words; for example, the *-ed* suffix indicating the past tense of a regular verb in English, or the *-s* plural of nouns. And sometimes it is not even a question of just arranging and combining words or parts of words; some items may actually change their spelling and pronunciation as a result of a change in grammatical form (for example, *go* becomes *went* in the past tense). At the other extreme, the term *grammar* can be used to relate to passages longer than sentences; we can talk about a 'story grammar' for example.

Grammar may involve grammatical words or affixes (*morphology*), or their combination in phrases or sentences (*syntax*). Morphology includes words like *she, that, our* and suffixes such as the plural *-s*, and syntax includes things like the formation of the negative, or relative clauses.

6.2 What students need to learn: standards of grammatical acceptability

One of the points discussed in Unit 1 was the importance of both accuracy and fluency in language teaching. There is, however, some debate as to whether we should worry about grammatical accuracy when it does not interfere with effective communication of a message. For example, should we correct a student who drops the third person *-s* suffix in the present simple (saying *she like* instead of *she likes*)? And should we correct a student who uses *which* instead of *who* in relative clauses (saying *the person which* instead of *the person who*)? Or should we insist on accuracy only when it affects meaning, for example correcting a student who uses a present tense verb where a past tense is needed?

In practice, of course, most of us teach the conventional grammatical forms and meanings of English because that is what the coursebooks we are using do, or because that is what the exams test, or because that is what the school policy, the parents or the students themselves demand.

However, you sometimes do have some measure of flexibility, and in any case it is important to clarify your own professional approach to the teaching of grammatical rules. So you need to ask yourself: All things being equal, and if the decision depends only on my own judgement, will I in principle insist on forms like the third person *-s*, or will I not?

Task

What is your own opinion on this? Where would you insist on correct forms and where would you not? And what are your arguments in support of your position?

Teaching standard grammar

Although the use of the variant forms mentioned above (such as *she like* and *the person which*) does not affect meaning and will not cause a breakdown in communication, it is arguable that we should mostly treat them as errors and encourage our students to use standard grammar (for exceptions see below). I use the term *standard* here to mean the usages which are seen by most speakers of English as internationally acceptable, not necessarily the usages associated with the 'native' varieties of English.

The main reasons for this are as follows:

- These forms are preferred and actually used by the majority of competent speakers of English, including those for whom English is not their L1 (Seidlhofer, Breiteneder & Pitzl, 2006). This group obviously includes most teachers, who are often the main English-speaker model for their students.
- Even if the variant forms are sometimes used in informal speech, they are rarely used in writing.
- As a matter of professional standards, most teachers feel they should aim to have their students achieve internationally accepted levels of accuracy and fluency in their speech and writing.
- Students also on the whole wish to be accurate, in the sense of using standard forms, and to be corrected if they make errors (see Unit 7: Error correction, pp. 91–4).
- Most high-stakes English exams require responses from candidates that use standard forms, and may penalize errors.

Task

What is your own opinion about the desirability of teaching standard grammatical forms? Do you agree with the arguments above? Are there any you have reservations about? If you are with a group, exchange opinions with others.

We need to be aware, however, that there are situations where grammatical accuracy matters more, or less. It obviously matters much more if errors actually result in miscommunication than if they do not (as with the examples given at the beginning of this section). They matter more in formal written communication, and less in informal chat. For example, if we are teaching a course in conversational English with the aim of improving oral fluency, we may well ignore grammatical errors which do not affect meaning, and not let them affect our assessment of students' performance. This would not be appropriate, however, if our course is aiming for improvement of academic English for participants who are planning to apply to a university.

The bottom line is, I suggest, that all things being equal, we shall continue to teach our students to observe the conventional grammatical rules as laid out in our textbooks, while remaining sensitive to the need for flexibility: where we need to be more, or less, fussy about how these are applied.

6.3 How best to teach grammar: explicit and implicit processes

Having decided which grammatical features we are going to teach, how should we do this? Should we allow our students plenty of opportunity to hear, read and use the correct forms, but not explain them ('implicit' teaching)? Or should we provide explanations ('explicit')? Or should we use a combination of the two?

Stephen Krashen (1999) claims that grammar is best acquired implicitly, through plenty of comprehensible input (listening and reading). But he has been outvoted:

the research literature provides a large amount of evidence against this view. For example Norris and Ortega (2001), in a survey covering a large number of studies, came to the conclusion that on the whole students who receive some explicit instruction in grammar perform better than those who do not. Teachers and students also generally feel that grammar instruction is helpful.

However, there is still a place for communicative input and output, and the possibility of acquiring some grammatical features through intuitive acquisition. As with vocabulary, we need both kinds of procedures, implicit and explicit, for effective teaching and learning.

Task

If you learnt English, or another foreign language, in school, how was grammar taught? What kinds of things were helpful/unhelpful in getting you to use the grammar of the language correctly?

There is some discussion of the place of explicit grammar practice in the form of drills or exercises. Again, this is something that most teachers and coursebooks provide, and that students expect. But all experienced teachers are familiar with the phenomenon that students continue to make mistakes in the target grammar even after extensive practice. So practice does not necessarily make perfect. Should it therefore be abandoned?

One of the explanations for the phenomenon just described is Pienemann's (1984) *teachability hypothesis*. Pienemann observed that learners of German acquire German grammatical structures in a fixed order, regardless of the order in which they were taught. And there is some evidence that this is true for the acquisition of other languages as well. From this he hypothesized that the teaching of a grammatical item or construction for which the learner is not developmentally ready will not result in learning. Ellis (2001) proposes the solution of *consciousness-raising*. He suggests that perhaps it is enough to raise learners' awareness of what a rule is, without demanding immediate implementation in learners' own speech and writing. Then, when they are developmentally ready, they will notice the occurrence of the grammatical features in input and gradually start using them themselves. Ellis suggests that practice exercises are, therefore, pointless. If the learner is ready to acquire the grammar, they will do so anyway, without practice; if they are not, then practice won't help.

However, there is evidence that practice does substantially improve performance and has an important place in formal, course-based language learning (Dekeyser, 2007). It seems that most learners do, indeed, go through a fairly stable order of acquisition of grammatical features, but that explanation combined with practice may speed up this process. We need to abandon the exaggerated claim that 'practice makes perfect' and content ourselves with the expectation that practice, like explanations of rules, can make a significant contribution to good learning and is therefore worth including in our teaching.

The practical guidelines in the following sections are based on the premise that there is value in explicit explanation and practice of grammar in English courses, as well as in providing our students with opportunities to use it for communication.

6.4 Presenting grammar: explanations

Grammar explanations may be initiated by you because they are indicated in your syllabus or course materials. Or you may be responding to a learning need; you may have noticed that students are making mistakes in a particular feature and might benefit from some focused explanation. In any case, below are some guidelines on how to explain. See also Swan (1994) for some useful practical principles for presenting grammar rules in the classroom.

Presenting and explaining grammar

Provide students with examples of the target feature in meaningful contexts before explaining it. This sounds obvious, but I have seen teachers start by writing up an isolated phrase on the board and then analysing it immediately, when the students had little or no idea what it might mean in context.

Both say and write examples of the target form. This is important, not only because students might need to use the grammar in both speech and writing, but also because students vary in their learning styles and preferences. Many find it difficult to grasp a sequence of language if they only hear it; others have similar problems if they only see it. In either case, both spoken and written forms are needed.

Teach both form and meaning. Which of these you emphasize depends on what the target feature is. Some grammatical constructions have fairly easy forms, but rather complex meanings that may have no parallel in the student's L1 and need careful explanation and lots of examples (the present progressive, for example). Others may have very simple meanings, and you need to focus on teaching the forms (the comparative of adjectives, for example).

You may or may not use grammatical terminology. This will depend on your situation and students. On the whole, older or more analytically minded students will benefit more from the use of terminology. With younger students, try to manage without it.

Explain the grammar in the students' L1, unless they are proficient enough to cope with English explanations. The level of English needed to understand a grammatical explanation in that language is quite high, so it may be difficult to understand for many classes. Using L1 can save time which can then be used for practice or communicative use of the target grammar. Only use English for explanations with relatively advanced classes who can easily understand them.

Compare the English structure with an L1 parallel if you can. Where there are substantial differences between English and the L1, it can be very helpful to compare and contrast the meanings of the English structure with an L1 parallel. Awareness of such differences can help to prevent mistakes. For example, you might point out that the use of the present perfect in a sentence with *for* or *since* (*I have worked here for six years*) is likely to correspond to the use of the present tense in the students' L1.

It is often useful to provide an explicit rule. But you have to think about striking the right balance between accuracy and simplicity. The explanation should cover the great majority of instances students are likely to encounter. Obvious exceptions should be noted, but too much detail may confuse and mislead. As a rule, a simple generalization, even if not entirely accurate, is more helpful to students than a detailed grammar-book definition.

You can ask students to work out rules for themselves, based on a set of examples (*inductive* process), or you can give the rules yourself, and they later work on examples (*deductive*). The deductive process is more common in both textbooks and classroom teaching. However, if the students can work out the rule for themselves, then they are more likely to remember it. The problem with inductive teaching is that if the rule is really difficult, students may waste a lot of time on frustrating guessing or on misleading suggestions. In such cases it is better simply to provide the information yourself. A compromise might be to provide very obvious examples, and then lead the students towards the formulation of a rule by guiding questions and hints.

Action task

> Watch an experienced teacher explain a grammatical point to a class, perhaps using the items above as a checklist. In what ways did the teacher's explanation follow, or differ from, these recommendations? Were there any other interesting ways, not mentioned here, in which he or she helped the students understand the explanation?

Practical tips

1. **Use pictures.** If appropriate, use pictures to help your explanation; or, even better, realia. They help make the explanation memorable.

2. **Don't just say 'Do you understand?'** Students will often say 'yes' out of politeness or unwillingness to admit they haven't really understood. Ask them to demonstrate their understanding by giving examples or explaining in their own words. Or try using the next tip.

3. **Get feedback.** When you have finished explaining, delete everything from the board, tell students to close their textbooks, and to write down in their own words what the rule was, in English or L1. Then ask them to read out what they have written, or share with one another. This will give you a good idea of how well they have understood the explanation.

4. **Teach early in the lesson.** As with the teaching of new vocabulary, it's a good idea to plan grammatical explanations to take place towards the beginning of the lesson when students are fresher and more willing to engage with new material.

6.5 Grammar practice: consolidating and automatizing grammatical knowledge

I have already mentioned (in Section 6.3) the phenomenon of students who do all the grammar exercises perfectly, but then make mistakes in the same items when they are composing their own free speech or writing. The problem here is that the structures have not been thoroughly mastered. The student still depends on a certain amount of conscious monitoring in order to produce them correctly. And when students are concentrating mainly on communicating, they do not have enough attention to spare for this monitoring. If students have not mastered the grammatical point to the degree that they can produce it automatically, then in communicative situations they will make mistakes, usually based on L1 interference.

What we can do as teachers is to help our students make the leap from form-focused grammar exercises to fluent production by providing tasks that encourage them to combine the two. At the beginning it can be useful to give the traditional gapfills and matching exercises, with definite right and wrong answers. However, if this is all the grammar practice the students get, they will not be able to transfer their knowledge to their own output. Therefore, such conventional grammar exercises need to be supplemented by activities that prompt students to use the target features to produce their own sentences, while keeping an eye on grammatical accuracy.

Below is a description of a number of grammar tasks that provide practice in a range of grammatical features. They move from the very controlled and accuracy-oriented exercise at the beginning to a fluency activity giving opportunities for the free use of the grammar in context at the end. The aim of most of them is to get students to use the grammar in order to 'say their own thing', paying attention to both communicative purpose and linguistic form.

It is not suggested that this sequence should be strictly followed in classroom teaching, though on the whole the more controlled exercises tend to come earlier. But it is important that our lessons should overall include a combination of tasks, providing both form-focused and meaning-focused practice.

Type 1: Awareness
After the students have been introduced to the grammatical point, they are given opportunities to encounter it within some kind of discourse, and then do a task that focuses their attention on its form and/or meaning.

> Past tense. Look at the extract from the newspaper article and underline all the examples of the past tense you can find.

Type 2: Controlled drills
Students produce examples of the structure. These examples are predetermined by the teacher or materials and have to conform to very clear, closed-ended cues. They can often be done without understanding.

> Present simple tense. Write or say statements about Eva, modelled on the following example:
>
> Eva *drinks tea* but she *doesn't drink coffee*.
>
> a) like: ice cream / cake b) speak: English/Italian
>
> c) enjoy: playing football / playing chess

Type 3: Controlled responses through sentence completion, rewrites or translation

Students produce examples of the structure that are predetermined by the teacher or materials by being required to rewrite according to a set cue, or to translate a sentence from L1. (For the benefits in principle of the use of L1 in grammar teaching, see the discussion at the end of Section 6.6.) In either case they will need to understand in order to respond correctly.

> Passive. Rewrite the sentence so that it means more or less the same, but using a form of the word in parenthesis.
>
> I received a lovely present. *(give)*

Type 4: Meaningful drills

Again the responses are very controlled, but the student can make a limited choice and needs to understand in order to answer.

> Present simple tense. Choose someone you know very well, and write down their name. Now compose true statements about them according to the following model:
>
> He/She *likes ice cream*; or He/She *doesn't like ice cream*.
>
> a) enjoy: playing tennis b) drink: wine c) speak: Polish

Type 5: Guided, meaningful practice

The students form sentences of their own according to a set pattern, but exactly what vocabulary they use is up to them.

> Conditional clauses. Look at the following cue: *If I had a million dollars*. Suggest, in speech or writing, what you *would* do.

Type 6: (Structure-based) free sentence composition

Students are provided with a visual or situational cue (for example a picture showing various people engaged in different activities) and invited to compose their own responses. They are directed to use the structure.

> Present progressive. Look at the picture and describe what is going on.

Type 7: (Structure-based) discourse composition

Students hold a discussion or write a passage according to a given task. They are directed to use at least some examples of the structure within the discourse.

> Modals. Recommend solutions to a social or ethical dilemma. For example: You see a good friend of yours cheating in an exam. What might you do? Your recommendations should include the modals (*might, should, must, can, could*, etc.).

Type 8: Free discourse

As in Type 7, but the students are given no specific direction to use the structure. However, the task situation is designed so that instances of it are likely to appear.

> Modals. As above, but without the final direction.

Task

> Have a look at a locally used coursebook or its workbook component, find ten grammar tasks, and classify them roughly according to the types above. Is there a reasonable balance of types, or are there some missing? Do you think the teacher would need to introduce or change tasks in order to make up for any missing types?

For more ideas for meaningful or communicative grammar practice, see Ur (2009).

6.6 Grammar assessment

Grammar assessment, as with vocabulary, is done in most classrooms primarily through written tests. Many of the actual task formats used as the basis for grammar tests can be used also for practice: for the differences between a learning or practice task on the one hand and a test on the other, see Unit 5: Teaching vocabulary, pp. 69–70.

Grammar-test items require students to respond to cues in order to prove that they have understood and can apply a grammatical rule, and they should be designed to be quickly and easily assessed and graded. They are very often 'closed-ended': require one predetermined right answer. But a similar problem arises in grammar testing as that discussed above with regard to practice: if a student fills in all the right answers in such a test, this does not necessarily mean that they are able to produce the target grammar in their own unguided output. It just means that they can get the grammar right *when they are thinking about it.*

If we give tasks that ask students to invent their own phrases, sentences or longer passages ('open-ended' items), this will give a truer picture of how well they know the grammar. But it will be more time-consuming and sometimes difficult to assess. There is a payoff between how valid the test is in providing reliable information on how much the learner knows, and how practical it is to administer and check.

Closed-ended test items

Closed-ended test items include the following, some of which are similar to those described in the section on vocabulary testing (see Unit 5: Teaching vocabulary, pp. 71–3).

Multiple- (or dual-) choice

> Have you (1)_____ heard of Aconcagua? (*never, sometimes, ever, often*)
>
> How *do you pronounce / are you pronouncing* this word correctly?

Guided gapfills

> If I _____ (know) the answer, I _____ (tell) you.

Transformation

> They sell mobile phones in that shop.
>
> Mobile phones _____.

Matching

> I've never played   computer games recently.
>
> I haven't been playing   a computer game like that before.

Rewrite

> Katia began to learn English about three years ago.
>
> *learning*
>
> Katia _____ three years.

Correct the mistake

> *I saw the girl which I used to know.

(Examples from *Active Grammar*, Levels 1 and 2, W. Rimmer and F. Davis, Cambridge University Press; *Active Grammar*, Level 3, M. Lloyd and J. Day, Cambridge University Press.)

Open-ended test items

Test items of this type, as illustrated below, require less predictable responses and are more difficult to check, but they arguably give a clearer picture of how well the student can communicate using the target grammar.

Open-ended sentence completion

If I could fly _____

Sentence-composition

Compose three sentences comparing these two people, using comparative adjectives.

Ella   Max

Translation

Translation is a little-used testing technique, but an interesting one which merits a more extended discussion. It is open-ended up to a point: there is usually a limited range of correct responses. The reason it is rarely exploited is the widespread but mistaken assumption that students should be encouraged to think in English only, and discouraged from relating English to their L1.

Very often, errors in English grammar are rooted in the L1. Students naturally think first in their L1, and when trying to express something in English are likely to be influenced by the way their L1 expresses the same idea. Paradoxically, the best way to combat such interference is by using deliberate contrast to make students aware how it occurs. This makes it very useful during explanations and is why I have included it in the previous section as the basis for a practice item. Similarly, a good way to test whether students have overcome the temptation to imitate L1 and can express ideas through acceptable English grammar is to require them to translate something from L1 into English.

For more on the topic of assessment and tests, see Unit 12: Assessment and testing.

Review

Answer as many as you can of the following questions, and then check answers by referring back to the relevant passages in this unit.

If you are working in a group, note down your own answers first alone, and then share with the other members of the group. Finally, check the answers together.

What is grammar?

1. Why is 'the way words are put together to make sentences' an inadequate way to define *grammar*?
2. What is the difference between *syntax* and *morphology*?

What students need to learn: standards of grammatical acceptability

3. Give some reasons for insisting on standard grammatical forms in our teaching, even if non-standard variants would not affect meaning.
4. When, or why, might we wish to ignore such non-standard variants/errors?

How best to teach grammar: explicit and implicit processes

5. What are some reasons for including explicit grammar teaching (explanations and focused practice) in our teaching?
6. What is the *teachability hypothesis*?

Presenting grammar: explanations

7. Can you recall at least four useful guidelines when explaining a new grammar point to the class?
8. What is the difference between *deductive* and *inductive* teaching of a rule?

Grammar practice: consolidating and automatizing grammatical knowledge

9. What kind of practice can help students transfer knowledge of a grammatical rule so that they can use it fluently in their own production?
10. Can you give two or three examples of exercises that get students to use the grammar to express meanings, rather than just to get the form right?

Grammar assessment

11. What is the difference between closed-ended and open-ended tests?
12. Why might we design test items based on translation from L1 to English?

Further reading

Swan, M. (1994) Design criteria for pedagogic language rules. In M. Bygate, A. Tonkyn and E.Williams (eds.), *Grammar and the Language Teacher* (pp. 45–55), Hemel Hempstead: Prentice Hall International.
> (A useful set of guidelines for the explanation of grammatical rules to a class)

Swan, M. (2005) *Practical English Usage*, Oxford: Oxford University Press.
> (A very accessible and user-friendly guide to English grammatical usage, with plenty of examples, including common learner errors)

Ur, P. (2009) *Grammar Practice Activities* (2nd edn), Cambridge: Cambridge University Press.
> (A collection of game-like or communicative activities that provide meaningful practice in the different grammatical features of English)

7 Error correction

7.1 Error correction: for and against

Error[1] correction by the teacher (sometimes referred to as 'corrective feedback') is another much-discussed topic. Most teachers and students assume that it is a natural and necessary component of the language teaching/learning process; however, it has some disadvantages and limitations that need to be taken into account.

Goals of error correction

In a first language, learners have no 'competing' language, and their mistakes therefore will be a result of what they know, or don't know, of the language so far. For example, they may over-generalize rules (e.g. *goed instead of went). As they hear the correct forms more and more, these will naturally take over, and conscious correction is not absolutely necessary (although it is sometimes supplied by, for example, a mother talking to her child). However, second-language learners are already fluent in one language. So, unless they are aware of the differences, they may sometimes unconsciously apply a usage which is not appropriate for the second language ('interference'). For example, a French speaker may say something like *We drink every day coffee*. This word order is perfectly acceptable in French, but not in English; and some learners never notice that English orders the words differently unless their attention is drawn to it.

---

[1] A theoretical distinction is sometimes made between an 'error' – an unacceptable form which the student regularly makes because he or she does not know a rule, or has internalized it wrongly – and a 'mistake' – a slip, which the student could in fact have avoided with a little more thought. But the two are almost impossible to distinguish when they actually occur, and the difference does not help us very much in practice. I use the two terms here interchangeably.

This is the main function of error correction: to prevent mistakes from becoming permanent (or 'fossilizing'), whether they are rooted in interference from the first language or in some difficult feature within English itself.

So when we correct a student's error, our goal is to make him or her aware of what was wrong and what the correct form should have been so that the same error can be avoided in future. The process is a very conscious one: it involves explicit thinking 'about' the language rather than just using it for communication.

Sometimes the goal may be wider: to use one student's mistake as a basis for teaching the whole class a tricky language point, and thus to anticipate and possibly prevent similar mistakes by others.

Limitations and problems

The main problem with error correction is that it does not produce either immediate or consistent results. Many teachers are familiar with the situation that they correct a student in one lesson – and then see them making precisely the same mistake in the next! Were they not listening? Did they not understand? Why don't they remember?

Some writers have been led by this phenomenon to suggest that correction does not work at all (e.g Truscott, 1996, 1999), or is even counterproductive because it may hurt students' feelings (see Section 7.2 below) or distract from communication (see Section 7.3 below).

However, the evidence from research is that error correction does produce improvement (Sheen & Ellis, 2011), although not necessarily immediately. The delay may be because the influence from the student's L1 is too strong, or he or she may have got into the habit of using the inaccurate feature and find it difficult to change. But in most cases, error correction does lead to a raising of awareness of the mistake, which is likely, eventually, to help students avoid it. The effectiveness of a particular correction depends on a number of factors, which will be dealt with in the sections on oral and written correction below.

We should not, therefore, expect every correction of every error to produce clear and immediate improvement in students' performance. However, this does not mean that we should not correct: we just need to be patient, and willing to re-correct the same errors as necessary.

Other problems have to do with attitudes of both teachers and students towards error correction in general, which will be treated in the next two sections.

7.2 Attitudes to error correction

Error correction means, basically, that you are telling someone else that they have done something wrong and should do it differently. This has clear implications – possibly negative – for the relationship between the person who corrects and the person who is corrected. And it means that we need to be very sensitive in the way we do it.

Some specific implications are suggested in the statements shown in the statements below. If you do not wish to do the task yourself, read the statements and then go on to the following discussion.

Task

Write an 'x' on the 'Agree .... Disagree' lines, to show how far you agree with the statements above them. If you are working in a group, then compare your answers with those of your colleagues. Then read on.

Statements: agree or disagree?

1. The fact that the teacher assesses and corrects students' language implies a power hierarchy: the teacher above, the student below.
   Very much agree ←---→ *Totally disagree*

2. Receiving corrective feedback from the teacher is potentially humiliating to the student.
   Very much agree ←---→ *Totally disagree*

3. Teachers should try not to correct very much, in order not to demoralize students.
   Very much agree ←---→ *Totally disagree*

4. It is also important to draw attention to when students get things right, not just when they get them wrong.
   Very much agree←---→ *Totally disagree*

5. Teachers should not let students correct each other's work, as this is harmful to their relationships.
   Very much agree←---→ *Totally disagree*

6. Oral corrective feedback should be given privately, not publicly.
   Very much agree←---→ *Totally disagree*

Comment

1. **Power hierarchy.** My own answer here would tend towards the 'Agree' end of the line, which may surprise you. In order to understand, you need to free yourself from the negative connotations often associated with the phrase 'power hierarchy'. Power hierarchies may in some circumstances be necessary, productive and fully compatible with good human relationships. In the classroom, the fact that the teacher is an authority with the power to assess and correct student errors undeniably gives him or her a position of power. It is important to be aware of this in order to be careful not to exploit such a position ... which leads us to the next item.

2. **Potentially humiliating.** Note the crucial word *potentially*! The issue here is not whether assessment humiliates, but if there is or is not such a **potential:**

and again, I would tend to agree. As with the previous item, this is a question of awareness: we need to be aware that we have the power to humiliate a student in order to take care not to do so!

3. **Correction may demoralize.** It is true that a lot of corrective feedback with no compensating praise (see next item) may result in demoralization and even antagonize; however, too little may lead to frustration or even irritation on the part of the students. Most students expect the teacher to correct them as part of the normal classroom process (see Section 7.3 below).

4. **Notice things that are right.** Very true. Many teachers simply do not think of drawing attention to students getting things right. It is seen as a sort of 'default' situation, not needing to be noticed. But surely getting it right should not be taken for granted: a student who produces an accurate bit of language (particularly if he or she is avoiding a very common mistake) deserves to be noticed and praised. Moreover, other students are likely not only to learn from the language item to which their attention has been drawn, but also to be motivated by the hope of similar notice for themselves in the future and therefore be more accepting of the correction of their mistakes.

5. **Correcting each other.** It is true that students do not really like being corrected by one another (see Section 7.3 below); this is not so much because of embarrassment or distress, but because they do not rely on one another to provide the appropriate correction and prefer to get it from the teacher. In some situations, however, helping each other to get things right can be a positive experience for all.

6. **Public correction.** In general, it is important to provide oral corrective feedback publicly, in order for the whole class to benefit. But obviously it is essential for the teacher to provide such feedback in a clearly objective and supportive way, making it clear that the criticism is aimed at the mistake, not at the student personally.

7.3 Student preferences

With regard to an issue as sensitive as error correction, it makes sense to ask our students what their own preferences are. We are not necessarily obliged to do exactly as they want – our own professional judgement also counts for something! – but we can certainly gain insights and awareness that can inform classroom decisions. (For a suggested student feedback questionnaire on our teaching in general, see Unit 20: Teacher development, pp. 291–2.)

This section reports a previously unpublished survey of student preferences with regard to error correction which I carried out first a few years ago, and then replicated four times with other groups. The exact numbers varied, but the overall results in terms of majority/minority opinions were consistent throughout the replications. The target population was a mixed group of primary and secondary school students studying English in Israel: their L1 was either Hebrew or Arabic (about half-and-half). In the survey I am showing here (2007), the total number of respondents was about 500, of whom the majority were from secondary school.

The students were asked to fill in a questionnaire which is shown below.

Oral correction

When you make a mistake in class, you think it's … if the teacher	very good	good	not very good	bad
1. … ignores it, doesn't correct at all.				
2. … indicates there's a mistake but doesn't actually tell you what's wrong, so you have to work it out for yourself.				
3. … says what was wrong *and* tells you what the right version is.				
4. … says what was wrong and gets you to say the correct version yourself.				
5. … says what was wrong and gets someone else to say the correct version.				
6. … explains *why* it was wrong, what the rule is.				

Written correction

When you make a mistake in a written assignment, you think it's … if the teacher	very good	good	not very good	bad
1. … ignores it, doesn't correct at all.				
2. … indicates there's a mistake (e.g. underlines it) but doesn't actually tell you what's wrong, so you have to work it out.				
3. … tells you what's wrong (e.g. 'spelling') but doesn't actually give you the correct version, so you have to work it out yourself.				
4. … writes in what it ought to be.				
5. … corrects (any of the ways 2–4 above) but doesn't make you write out the correct version.				
6. … corrects (any of the ways 2–4 above) and makes you rewrite correctly.				

Task

Fill in the questionnaire yourself with your own preferences as a student learning another language. Then, if you are teaching, fill in the answers you guess your students would write, using another colour.

Compare your entries with my results as shown below.

Results

The histograms below contrast the positive and negative responses, showing the sums of 'very good' + 'good', as against the sums of 'not very good' and 'bad'.

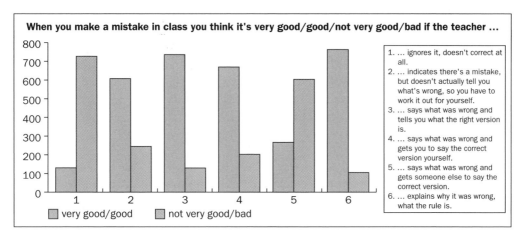

When you make a mistake in class you think it's very good/good/not very good/bad if the teacher ...

■ very good/good   ■ not very good/bad

1. ... ignores it, doesn't correct at all.
2. ... indicates there's a mistake, but doesn't actually tell you what's wrong, so you have to work it out for yourself.
3. ... says what was wrong and tells you what the right version is.
4. ... says what was wrong and gets you to say the correct version yourself.
5. ... says what was wrong and gets someone else to say the correct version.
6. ... explains why it was wrong, what the rule is.

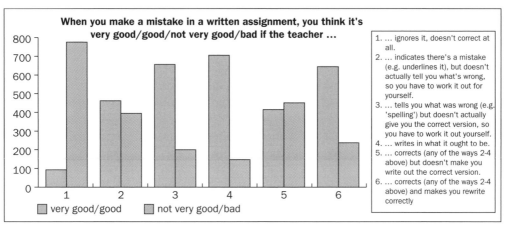

When you make a mistake in a written assignment, you think it's very good/good/not very good/bad if the teacher ...

■ very good/good   ■ not very good/bad

1. ... ignores it, doesn't correct at all.
2. ... indicates there's a mistake (e.g. underlines it), but doesn't actually tell you what's wrong, so you have to work it out for yourself.
3. ... tells you what was wrong (e.g. 'spelling') but doesn't actually give you the correct version, so you have to work it out yourself.
4. ... writes in what it ought to be.
5. ... corrects (any of the ways 2-4 above) but doesn't make you write out the correct version.
6. ... corrects (any of the ways 2-4 above) and makes you rewrite correctly

Discussion of results

Students want to be corrected. The large majority of students do want to be corrected, and this was true of both primary and secondary students. Perhaps some would rather not be corrected when they are in the middle of fluent speech: I didn't ask about this. However, I strongly suspect that if we did, many of them would ask to be corrected even in such situations (as in Harmer, 2005). Note that these results were more noticeable for written correction than for oral.

Students want to be told what the correct form is. In both writing and speech, students prefer to be told what the mistake was and what the right form should be, rather than to have to work it out for themselves. In oral work, this is in fact what happens: teachers tend to provide the correct form as a 'recast' (see Section 7.4). However, in writing many teachers either just underline, or write a code such as 'sp' for 'spelling', and ask the students to work out what was wrong. Most students, in contrast, prefer to be told explicitly what the right form is.

One's immediate suspicion is that the students are just looking for the easy way out. However, later on they are actually asking for more work for themselves by saying that they should rewrite assignments, incorporating corrections (see point 4 below). So, I think we can believe the students here: it is genuinely more helpful for them to be told what the right form is than to have to look for it themselves (and maybe not find it, or not be sure they are right). This also corresponds to some other research, e.g. Chandler (2003).

Another objection would be that surely it is better for learning if the learners have to make the effort to work out what's wrong. There is, indeed, evidence from the research (see Section 7.4) that it is important for students to invest some work in clarifying what's wrong in negotiation with the teacher. But the teacher does need to confirm the right version.

Most students don't like to be corrected by other students. We have to guess the reasons for this. Maybe it is because they feel embarrassed or uncomfortable being corrected by peers. However, it is more likely that they simply don't rely on each other to be right, and prefer the more reliable source of the teacher. Whatever the reason, it seems to be a fairly clear majority opinion, and one that we should take into account.

Students think they should rewrite. Students say that in writing it is not enough for them to be told that something is wrong, or even for them to be shown the right answer: they should be asked to rewrite the corrected text. This was the answer which convinced me that the students are not just looking for easy answers (see point 2 above) and also confirmed my own intuitions. They are right, of course: learning is much better if they rewrite, implementing the corrections from the first draft (see Section 7.5 below).

Conclusion

The results of the questionnaires are interesting and thought-provoking, and probably reliable. They do not, as mentioned at the beginning of this section, necessarily oblige us to change our practice in order to provide exactly what students say they want: but it is important to listen to the students and respect their opinions. If we decide to do things otherwise, we need to have convincing research-based, pedagogical, educational or practical reasons for doing so.

> **Action task**
>
> Administer the questionnaire to a group of students and see if the results are similar to mine. If there are significant differences, can you explain or comment on them?
>
> You may, of course, wish to change individual items to make them more appropriate to your own teaching situation, or even create a new questionnaire.

7.4 Oral correction

The main methods of oral correction used in most classes are as follows:

1. Recast. The teacher simply says the correct version of the student's erroneous utterance, without any further comment:

> Student: I reading a book
> Teacher: I **am** reading a book.

2. **Elicitation.** The teacher elicits the correct form from the student (assuming that the student can in fact produce it!):

> Student: I reading a book.
> Teacher: Can you correct that?
> Student: I am reading a book.

3. **Clarification request.** The teacher asks for a clarification of the meaning:

> Student: I reading a book.
> Teacher: I didn't understand, can you tell me more clearly?

4. **Metalinguistic feedback.** The teacher explains using grammatical or other linguistics terminology:

> Student: I reading a book.
> Teacher: In the present continuous you need the verb *be* before the *-ing* form of the verb …

5. **Explicit correction.** The teacher says explicitly that there has been a mistake, and what the right form is:

> Student: I reading a book.
> Teacher: No, that is incorrect. You should have said …

6. **Repetition.** The teacher repeats the incorrect utterance, with a rising intonation and a doubting expression, implying that there's something wrong with it:

> Student: I reading a book.
> Teacher: I *reading* a book??

Task

Before reading on, which of the above would you guess would be the most effective in getting the student to learn from the correction and stop making the error in future? Which would you expect to be the least effective?

Effectiveness of the different techniques

The 'recast' is by far the most common of all the techniques listed above. Teachers use it because it is quick and easy and causes minimum disruption of a student's speech. However, it is also the least effective in producing 'uptake' (i.e. in getting the student to understand and produce the correct form in response to the correction), and therefore the least likely to result in lasting learning. This may be partly because the student sometimes does not realise it is a correction at all; he or she may not notice that the teacher's utterance was different from his or her own and understand it merely as an 'echo' or confirmation.

Various studies carried out by Lyster (e.g. Lyster, 2004) indicate that the most effective oral correction involves some kind of negotiation and active contribution from the student. So elicitations, repetitions or metalinguistic feedback, which get the student to rethink what he or she has said and produce the correct form, are significantly better than recasts.

Should we correct during fluent speech?

The above conclusion produces a dilemma. On the one hand, we do not want to interrupt a student as they are speaking, which might disrupt the flow of speech, discourage and harm communication. On the other hand, no correction at all might lead to the mistakes being confirmed or 'fossilized'. So many teachers correct during student talk using a quick 'recast', hoping to disrupt the speech as little as possible. But then, as we have seen, the correction might be totally ineffective: they might as well not have bothered. If you are going to correct effectively, you need to stop the student, and correct in a way that ensures that he or she has noticed and accepted the correction – which will inevitably involve some disruption of communication. There is always the possibility of noting the mistake and coming back to it later, but this is probably less effective than 'online' correction.

So we have the following dilemma: are you going to correct effectively and risk disturbing the flow of communication, or are you going to refrain from correcting and risk the error being reinforced?

The answer to this question is that it is up to your own professional judgement, taking into account a number of factors, such as the level and confidence of the student, the goals of the course, the frequency or gravity of the error, the willingness of the students to tolerate interruption and so on. The main point to be remembered here is that even if generally you prefer not to interrupt communicative interaction, there may be times where such interruption for the purposes of error correction may be useful and productive. It is up to you to identify when this is so: one of the many 'on your feet' decisions that you gradually learn how to make as you gain experience.

7.5 Written correction

This section relates to the correction of language errors in short writing assignments, such as language exercises, answers to comprehension questions, or brief compositions, in response to communicative tasks. (For guidance on giving feedback on longer written assignments, including corrections, aimed at the rewriting and improvement of the composition as a whole, see Unit 11: Teaching writing, pp. 158–62.) Below are some samples of uncorrected student work, followed by some Frequently Asked Questions (FAQs) which relate to the correction of such assignments.

Task

Imagine that the written assignments shown below are ones submitted by your own (intermediate-level) students.

The first sample is a grammar exercise on the present perfect tense, which the students did for homework. The second is a test on vocabulary, which is also intended to check students' mastery of the use of relative clauses in definitions.

The third is a short piece of writing done in class as an individual summary of a group discussion, and given in to the teacher at the end of the lesson.

Write in your corrections and other feedback. If you are in a group, compare your response with other participants. You could work in pairs, reading each other's corrections and discussing differences. Then read on to the FAQs and their answers, and (re-)consider your corrections in the light of these.

1. Grammar exercises on the present perfect, given as homework

8.1 You are asking people questions about things they have done. Make questions with **ever** using the words in brackets.
1. (ride / horse?) _Have you ever ridden a horse?_
2. (be / California?) Have _you been in California?_
3. (run / marathon?) _have you ever ran the marathon?_
4. (speak / famous person?) _have you ever spraken with famous person_
5. (most beautiful place / visit?) What's _you have most beaufify/ place evervisited?_

14.2 *Complete the answers to these questions. Use the verb in brackets.*
Example: Is it a beautiful painting? (see) Yes, _it's the most beautiful painting I've ever seen._
1. Is it a good film? (see) Yes, it's the best _film I'ev ever seen_
2. Is it a long book? (read) . Yes, it's the _longer book I'ev ever read_
3. Is she an interesting person? (meet) Yes, she's the most _interested gril I have ever met._

2. Test on vocabulary and relative clauses

Define the following words, using who/which/that/whose/when/where.

For example: a deserted house = a house where nobody lives

1. a temple: _a house where religious people lives in._
2. a motionless tree: _a tree which not moving at all._
3. an illusion: _a false sight._
4. courage: _a man who not have any fear._
5. sweat: _it's like terrible but more then this._
6. a PR man: _a man who work on a public relations._
7. a virus: _a thing which make people sick._
8. an antibody: _a thing which help the man get over the sickness_
9. a host: _a man who takes visitors to his house_
10. a paw: _a proke of a animal._

3. Writing following a discussion

Dear Helpful Harriet,

I have a problem with this teacher at school. He is always shouting at me, though I don't disturb more than lots of other pupils in the class. It's true that I sometimes don't do my homework, but I know his subject very well, always get high marks on the tests, so there is no point doing silly homework. He gave me a much lower mark than I deserve at the end of the term. It's not fair. And it's no good saying go to the class teacher, she always backs him up. What can I do?
        Yours,
        FRUSTRATED STUDENT

My advice to you is to talk with the problematic teacher and trying to expline him what do you fill and think about her and what do you think that you can do together to solve your problem together please tet me know what happend with your case

Action task

If you are teaching, you might prefer to use your own students' work as a basis for this task rather than using the material shown here. Alternatively, ask a practising teacher if they would be willing to let you work on some of their students' assignments.

FAQs

1   Should I use a red pen (or red insertions, if the responses are in digital form) for my comments? Or another colour?

A: It's probably best to use a colour for corrections, simply in order to make them clear and visible to the student. Some teachers feel that red is an aggressive colour and prefer green or another colour. If you are using digital editing tools like 'track changes' – these are automatically in a different colour from the original document. The advantage of 'track changes' is that the corrections are very clear and and user-friendly: the student can immediately implement your suggestions and easily produce a corrected version.

2   Is it necessary to give an evaluative comment at the end such as 'Well done'?

A: Students really like to know what your overall assessment was of the assignment: so let them know what it was in an evaluative note such as 'Excellent'. Even more helpful are specific comments aiming to help the student in future similar assignments: 'Remember next time to start sentences with capital letters!'

3   Should I correct all the mistakes? If not, how do I decide what to correct and what not?

A: A general guideline might be that if there are not many mistakes, correct them all, but if there are a lot, allow yourself to ignore some of them. Correcting everything in an exercise full of mistakes is not only demoralizing for the student, it is also inefficient. The student will be overloaded and cannot possibly pay attention to and learn from them all. You certainly need to correct mistakes that are associated with the goal of the exercise (for example, in an exercise on the past tense you will correct mistaken past forms). Of the others you need to decide for yourself which are the most important ones to correct and which can be ignored for the moment. Of course, there are exceptions to this: some adult academic classes expect you to correct absolutely everything!

4   Should I write the mistakes I correct in the correct form? Give a hint what it should be ('sp', for example, for 'spelling')? Simply underline to indicate it was wrong, without any hint?

A: It is clear that students on the whole like you to tell them exactly what the mistake was and to write in the correct version (see Section 7.3 above). This is not because they are lazy, but because the correction then is more quickly accessed and more reliable. On the other hand, we simply don't have the time to write in all the correct forms in all our students' compositions if we are to provide feedback on their writing on a regular basis. Probably the answer is a compromise: write in the corrections if you think the student would find it difficult to work them out on their own, and otherwise just underline, cross out or put in an 'insertion' mark ⌃. Whether you use a code such as 'sp' for 'spelling' is a matter of personal preference; there is some evidence that students prefer simple underlining (Chandler, 2003).

5   **Should I only correct, or also note things that were good, e.g. particularly effective use of language by a student?**

A: It is important to remind yourself to note positive things, where appropriate: ticks, double ticks, complimentary comments in the margin. These responses can draw students' attention to their successes, boosting morale and reinforcing learning.

6   **When or why should I require the student to redo some or all of the assignment?**

A: If your students are working on computers, then they can very easily implement your corrections and rewrite. On paper, however, rewriting of the items of a grammar exercise can be mechanical and rather tedious and does not benefit students so much. You might, instead, give the class the same, or similar, exercises a few days later to see if there has been progress in eliminating errors. Full written compositions, in contrast, should usually be redrafted, whether on paper or digital, correcting mistakes of language, style, content and organization. For more discussion of this topic, see Unit 11: Teaching writing.

Review

Answer as many as you can of the following questions, and then check answers by referring back to the relevant passages in this unit.

If you are working in a group, note down your own answers first alone, and then share with the other members of the group. Finally, check the answers together.

Error correction: for and against
1. Can you define one primary function of error correction in the classroom?
2. What is the main problem with error correction as a means of helping students improve accuracy?

Attitudes to error correction
3. Why is it important to understand that the teacher, when correcting student errors, is in a position of power?
4. Why do teachers often not think of drawing attention to things students get right? Why is it important to do so?
5. Should corrective oral feedback to an individual student be given publicly?

Student preferences
6. Do most students want to have their mistakes corrected?
7. Why, probably, do students prefer on the whole to be corrected by the teacher rather than by peers?

8. Do students want teachers to make them rewrite essays that have been corrected?

Oral correction

9. Which is the most common oral correction procedure? Why is it probably not very effective?
10. What can a teacher do to make sure that an oral correction is noticed and learnt?

Written correction

11. List some of the considerations you might take into account when deciding which mistakes, and how many of them, to correct in a piece of written work.
12. List some arguments for and against writing out corrected forms for students when checking written work.

Further reading

Bartram, M. and Walton, R. (1991) *Correction: Mistake Management – A Positive Approach for Language Teachers*, Hove: Language Teaching Publications.
> (A compact, clear, systematic and practical guide to the subject; interesting and relevant reader tasks help to clarify)

Edge, J. (1989) *Mistakes and Correction*, London: Longman.
> (A simple, practical handbook: suggests various techniques for correcting in different situations)

Harmer, J. (1984) How to give your students feedback. *Practical English Teaching*, 5(2), 39–40.
> (Practical guidelines on ways of correcting in the classroom)

Sheen, Y. and Ellis, R. (2011) Corrective feedback in language teaching. In E. Hinkel (ed.), *Handbook of Research in Second Language Teaching and Learning* (pp. 593–610), New York: Routledge.
> (A useful and comprehensive summary of research on corrective feedback, with practical conclusions)

8 Teaching listening

Overview

The sections in this unit are:

8.1. **Goals and problems in teaching listening.** Some reasons why we need to provide systematic instruction and practice in listening comprehension, and associated practical problems.

8.2. **Listening activity design (1): the text.** Characteristics of spontaneous conversation in English that listeners need to be able to cope with.

8.3. **Listening activity design (2): the task.** Guidelines on the design of listening tasks for effective listening comprehension practice.

8.4. **Types of activities.** A list of listening comprehension activities, from those requiring little or no response to those requiring extended interaction.

8.5. **Adapting activities.** Practical ideas for adapting, improving or extending textbook listening comprehension activities.

For assessment and testing of listening skills, see Unit 12: Assessment and testing.

8.1 Goals and problems in teaching listening

After studying French for seven years in school, I went to France and found that I could not understand what French people were saying to me. I needed them to slow down, pause and pronounce things the same way I had been taught they should be pronounced. This was in spite of having had 'listening comprehension' exercises in school. What had gone wrong?

The answer is that my schoolteachers and textbooks had simply not prepared me for real-life listening. The kinds of listening tasks I had been asked to do were similar to those shown on p. 46, and were typically based on the following:

- formal, carefully enunciated language
- written texts read aloud
- audio-recordings
- written comprehension questions to be answered later
- tasks that provided no advance information about the text or listening purpose
- the demand that students understand everything in the text.

This did not simulate real-life listening, most of which takes place in face-to-face interactive situations such as conversation, interviews, lessons, shopping or getting instructions, and which displays the following characteristics:

- The speech is typically in informal, colloquial style. (See below some discussion of the characteristics of this type of discourse.)

- The speech is improvised, not written beforehand to be read aloud. There are a few situations where we might hear prepared written text, e.g. television or radio news, airport announcements or a lecturer reading out his paper, but these are much rarer than improvised speech.
- We can usually see the speaker. The exceptions are when we are on the telephone (without video facilities) or listening to the radio.
- We nearly always respond in real time to what we hear, as it is happening rather than later.
- We have some idea of the kind of topic our speaker will be dealing with, even if we don't know the exact information. And we normally have some purpose in listening (getting information, developing a personal relationship, enjoyment, etc.).
- We rarely need to understand everything. We listen for the gist, or for specific information that we need to know.

Task

Think of a recent situation where you have been listening to someone and needed to understand them: either in your own L1 or in another language. How many of the above features apply to it?

The main goal of teaching listening is to enable our students eventually to cope with the natural listening situations that they are most likely to encounter in real life. And those situations will probably display most of the features above. Students of today have fewer problems with this than I did, for two main reasons. First, as we have seen on pp. 4–6, English as an international language is spoken mainly between people who have learnt English as an additional language. In order to ensure successful communication, such speakers make an effort to speak clearly and use a variety of communication strategies to make sure they understand and are understood (see research summarized by Seidlhofer, 2004, p. 218). Second, today's writers of English-teaching materials are more aware of the points discussed above, and provide more texts and tasks that are modelled on authentic interactional situations as well as samples of speech that are closer to spontaneous talk. Furthermore, at the time of writing, teachers are beginning to use short videos from the Internet as a basis for listening, which at least provide visible speakers and situational contexts. However, the majority of listening materials provided in coursebooks still consists of a relatively long stretch of pre-written discourse, without a visible speaker, accompanied or followed by comprehension questions.

Task

Have a look at an English coursebook used locally. How realistic is the preparation for real-life listening? Use the criteria listed above to help you judge.

At this point, it needs to be said that students listening to each other speak English does not provide useful listening practice, in the same way as giving students each other's written work to read does not provide very useful reading practice. Of course, there is an important place for interaction between students, but this is more for the sake of developing oral fluency than for listening practice. Students can normally understand text that is more difficult than what they can produce themselves (again, there is a parallel in reading and writing). In order to progress in the receptive skill, they need plenty of exposure to text that is slightly, or even substantially, above the level of their own output.

8.2 Listening activity design (1): the text

As we have seen, most of the spoken language we listen to in real life is informal and spontaneous. The speaker is making it up as he or she goes along, rather than reading aloud or reciting from memory. This type of discourse has various interesting features, many of which can be replicated in the texts of listening comprehension activities.

Features of informal spoken discourse

Here is an example of an authentic conversation recorded and transcribed:

A: Are you still playing er

B: Guitar

A: Irish music, yeah

B: No I don't play very much now, not, not at all

A: I thought you were touring the country at one point

B: No, I er ... we go, we listen to it quite a lot, every time we go to Ireland we erm, you know, seek out good musicians and er do quite a lot of listening and of course we still buy a lot of records, bought a lot of records over the last few years, but erm, there's not actually anybody to play with around here, you know there's a there's a session every Sunday night in Cambridge in a pub and that's erm about it ... do you still listen to Scottish music?

A: Ver ... since this pair have arrived very very little, cos you just don't have the time, and with the new house, and with the garden occasionally I take fits of putting stuff on, not as much as before.

(Carter & McCarthy, 1997, pp. 42–3)

Task

Can you identify some of the features of informal spoken language in the conversation above? Can you think of others which are not clearly shown above, but which you know of from your own experience (for example, aspects of pronunciation)? Make a list, and then read on.

Brevity

The discourse is usually broken into short chunks: phrases or short sentences. In a conversation, for example, people typically take turns to speak, often in short 'turns', as at the beginning of the example above. In order to accord with this feature, a listening text can be based on conversation; or, even if it is not, can be broken up by the use of different speakers, pauses and sound effects.

Pronunciation

The pronunciation of words is often slurred and noticeably different from the phonological representation shown in a dictionary and taught to students. There are obvious examples in English, such as *can't* for *cannot*, which have made their way even into the written language. Less obvious examples include the use of the neutral vowel sound 'schwa' in the pronunciation of 'weak' forms (such as /əv/ for 'of') and elision, the disappearance of one or more of the sounds (*orright* for 'all right' or *Sh'we go?* for 'Shall we go?'). However, there is some evidence (Jenkins, 2002) that fully competent English speakers with a different mother tongue tend to pronounce words fairly closely to the way they are written and formally pronounced, which of course makes them more clearly comprehensible. Even so, the pronunciation features described above are still very widespread, and learners need to have opportunities to encounter and understand them.

Vocabulary

The vocabulary is often very informal. You might, for example, use *guy* where in writing you would use *man*, or *kid* for *child*. People also use a lot of vague expressions such as *or something, more or less, stuff* (see the use of *stuff* in the text above), and prefabricated chunks or clichés like *call it a day, that's about it.*

Grammar

Informal speech tends to be somewhat ungrammatical. Utterances do not usually divide neatly into conventional sentences. A grammatical structure may change in mid-utterance, and unfinished sentences or 'fragments' are common. Clauses are joined into long sequences typically joined by *and, but* (see examples in the extract above).

'Noise'

There will be bits of the discourse that the hearer cannot understand and that therefore become, as far as they are concerned, meaningless 'noise'. This is a feature that we cannot distinguish in the extract above, but which is nevertheless a common experience when listening, even in our L1. It may be because the words are not said clearly, or not known to the hearer, or because the hearer is not paying attention. We usually understand less than 100 per cent of what is said to us, making up for the deficit by guessing the missing items or simply ignoring them and gathering what we can from the rest. See the note on *Selective listening* in Section 8.3 below.

Redundancy

The speaker normally says a lot more than is strictly necessary to communicate the message, and much more than in a written text designed to convey the same information. Redundancy includes such things as repetition, paraphrase (see, for example, B's second utterance above), additions that give extra information, self-correction, the use of 'fillers' such as *you know* (see B's longer utterance above). This to some extent compensates for the gaps created by 'noise', as it provides repetition of information the hearer may have missed. It also makes the listening activity more success-orientated by giving listeners extra opportunities to hear the same information and make sure they got it right, or breaks in the discourse when they can 'rest'.

Varied accents

Another feature not shown in the sample above, but which we need to take into account, is the wide variation in the way English words are pronounced by people coming from different speech communities, whether native or non-native. We probably mostly listen to people who speak a similar variety of English to our own, but we need to be able to cope with other accents in various situations outside our home community.

Facial expression and body language

We can usually see the person who is speaking, and their facial expression, gesture and body language in general contribute to understanding. So the speaker in classroom listening exercises should arguably also be visible: either physically present or shown on a video recording.

Summary

Most listening comprehension texts probably need to be based on informal, improvised English, spoken by a visible speaker using colloquial pronunciation, grammar and vocabulary, featuring both 'noise' and 'redundancy' and affording students opportunities to hear a variety of accents, since these represent the kinds of listening they will need to be able to cope with.

Not all such listening discourse has to be authentic recordings of actual conversations. On the contrary: 'authentic' listening texts may well be 'inauthentic' in the classroom: irrelevant to the students, difficult to understand, taken out of context. Effective listening texts can be improvised by actors or teachers based on notes or previous instructions, thus maintaining the spontaneous quality of improvised speech while taking into account the level of the target learners.

It is not my intention to imply that there is no place at all for conventional pre-written recorded texts in formal English. These are the basis for listening texts in many high-stake exams such as Cambridge ESOL and, if only for this reason, many teachers will want to include them in the classroom. Another reason is that they are relatively easy to find on the Internet or to create on your own. However, it remains true that, if you want your students to function easily in real-life listening situations, you need to provide plenty of opportunities for them to hear informal speech.

Practical tips

1. **Don't just use recordings!** The advantage of the use of recordings is that they provide a variety of speakers and accents. However, sound recordings do not allow students to see the speakers, and even videos cannot provide the interactive aspect that characterizes most real listening. Where you can, use real people: see the next two tips.

2. **Teacher talk.** Probably the best listening comprehension texts are those you provide yourself through your own talk. Take time to tell students stories, instruct them to do things, describe, explain and so on.

3. **Bring visitors.** If you can, ask friends or colleagues to come into your classroom and talk to the class (about themselves or their area of expertise, for

example). This gives students opportunities to hear different accents spoken spontaneously by a visible speaker.

4. **Develop your reading-aloud skills.** Most listening texts should, as recommended earlier, be improvised, but there is a place also for occasional reading aloud: for example, stories from picture books with younger learners. When reading aloud, remember to read slowly, maintain occasional eye contact with students, and allow yourself to simplify or occasionally translate bits of the text (see Unit 18: Learner differences (1): age, pp. 259–60).

5. **Make sure you include a varied sample of listening texts.** These should probably be mostly in informal conversational English, as suggested above. However, occasional formal speech types and texts representing a variety of contexts and varieties of English should also be provided. There is a wide range of recorded texts in English on the Internet, both audio and video, some of which are accompanied by listening comprehension tasks.

8.3 Listening activity design (2): the task

There are two main criteria for the design of a listening task.

1. **Does the task provide listening experience that prepares students for real-life listening situations?** Or in other words, does it provide opportunities for students to hear and understand the different kinds of natural English speech that they are likely to need to cope with in the future? This means implementing at least some of the characteristics of natural listening situations discussed earlier in this unit.

2. **How practical is the task to do in the classroom?** Is it easy to present and manage? Can I monitor how well the students are understanding?

Sometimes these two considerations clash. For example, we often want to replay a recorded (audio or video) conversation in order to give students more quantity of listening, to help them understand it by providing extra exposure, and in general to increase the learning value of the exercise as a whole. In real life, in contrast, we almost never have the opportunity to hear exactly the same text twice. Another example has to do with responses: in real life, listener responses to what they hear are normally spoken and ongoing: the listener acknowledges, answers, provides comments or reactions. In class, because we are usually working with large groups of students, spontaneous spoken individual responses are simply not feasible. In both these cases we will probably prioritize the practical over the 'authentic': give our students the possibility of hearing a text more than once, and ask them to respond in writing or action rather than speech (see the next section).

So we need to compromise: maintain as much as we can of the naturalness of a listening task, while making sure that it has maximum teaching/learning value and is practical to administer in the classroom.

Design features which can contribute to a successful listening task
Expectations
Students should have in advance some idea about the kind of text they are going to hear. This both replicates the reality of most listening situations and

facilitates understanding. The instruction *Listen to the passage*, on its own, is fairly useless. It is better to give the students some idea of what they are going to hear. For example: *You are going to hear a husband and wife discussing their plans for the summer* ... This type of instruction activates students' relevant schemata (their own previous knowledge and concepts of facts, scenes, events, etc.) and enables them to use this knowledge to build expectations that will help them understand. We may even discuss the topic with students in advance. It is previous knowledge of the topic which is, apparently, the major factor in facilitating understanding of a listening passage (Chang & Read, 2006).

Purpose

Students should be provided in advance with a task which leads to some kind of clear and visible or audible response. Instead of saying simply: *Listen and understand, then we'll answer questions*, it is better to give an instruction like: *Listen and find out where the family are going for their summer holidays. Mark the places on your map.* Giving them a purpose means that the students can listen selectively for significant information, as we do in real life. This is easier, as well as more natural, than trying to understand everything.

Selective listening

The task should encourage students to listen out for what they need to know. This implies that they also need to learn how to *ignore* irrelevant bits. In the traditional type of listening comprehension task, students are expected to attempt to understand almost everything and are often asked questions about trivial points. Trying to understand every word is an ineffective listening strategy and one that is doomed to failure. A student who adopts this aim and comes across something which they cannot understand early on in the text will immediately have a sense of failure and may give up trying at that point.

Ongoing listener response

Finally, the task should usually involve intermittent responses during the listening. Students should be encouraged to respond to the information they are looking for as they hear it, not to wait to the end. It is not practical, as we have seen above, to ask them to respond orally as the speech is going on. We therefore have to use less 'authentic' but more practical alternatives, such as making brief notes or raising their hands. A visual focus can often provide a basis for such response. For example, the task could involve inserting items in a picture or diagram, or marking or annotating a written text.

Interest

The task should be one that is interesting to do: see the discussion of arousing and maintaining interest in classroom tasks on pp. 51–5.

Exceptions

The above are useful guidelines in the design of most listening tasks: but in some cases we might want to do something different.

No task

We might provide no pre-set task if the listening text is so interesting and easy to understand that we can be sure students will benefit from listening without the need for a focused goal. The classic example of this is a story: anecdote, joke, fairy tale and so on. You do not have to be a brilliant storyteller: any teacher can tell stories they know, and students of all ages react well to them. Reading stories aloud is also a useful thing to do (see *Practical tip 4* in Section 8.2 above). Other examples of such 'taskless tasks' are watching a good movie or an interesting or funny TV show, or listening to a good poem. In such cases pre-set, information-based tasks can actually be counterproductive. If they are used they need to be very carefully planned so as not to spoil the fun, excitement or aesthetic value of the text.

No preparation

We might occasionally want to challenge our students to understand something with no preparation whatsoever, for the sake of the challenge: as when you turn on the television or radio with no idea of what kind of programme you are going to encounter. The task here is to pick up clues to understand what type of text it is, and what it is about.

Practical tips

1. **Don't overload.** A mistake I made myself when I first started designing listening tasks was to ask students to do too much, with the result that they did not have enough time to mark or write their responses during the listening and got frustrated. Even if the listening text is repeated, the initial feeling of failure is something that should be avoided. Use the second listening simply to provide extra listening experience, or to let students check and re-check their responses. See the next tip.

2. **Try it out.** Before presenting a listening task in the classroom, try it out on a colleague to make sure it is doable! You will almost always need to make changes afterwards, but the result in the classroom will be better.

3. **Don't pre-teach too much vocabulary.** Pre-teaching vocabulary is surprisingly unhelpful in getting students to understand a listening text (Chang & Read, 2006). A first presentation of a new word does not ensure that students remember it, as we have seen (Unit 5: Teaching vocabulary, p. 65): students simply cannot recall the new items quickly enough to understand them as they occur in fast-flowing speech. One or two items may help, but more than that will probably not be remembered in time.

8.4 Types of activities

Below is a list of different types of listening activity tasks you might wish to design yourself. They are classified according to the amount and complexity of response required.

1. No overt response: the students do not have to do anything in response to the listening. However, facial expression and body language often show if they are following or not.

2. Short responses: students respond by writing a word or a symbol, or by physical movement.

3. **Longer responses:** students write longer answers, which may be full sentences.

4. **Extended responses:** the listening provides only the first stage in an extended activity involving reading, writing or speaking. In other words these are activities which require a combination of skills.

> **Task**
>
> Can you recall or design yourself at least two kinds of listening activities that would fit each category? If you are working in a group, share and see if you can find three or four for each. Then read on and add to your list any extra ones provided below.

Examples of activities

1. No overt response

Stories. Tell a joke or real-life anecdote, retell a well-known story, read a story from a book. If the story is well chosen, students are likely to be motivated to pay attention and understand in order to enjoy it.

Songs. Sing a song yourself, or play a recording of one. Make sure that you focus students on the words of the song as well as the music. Otherwise, they may just enjoy the tune without listening to the words, when our aim is for them to do both!

Entertainment: films, theatre, video. As with stories, if the content is really entertaining students will be motivated to make the effort to understand without the need for any further task. Use videos from the Internet for texts of manageable length for a lesson. You can find materials you can legally download for educational use at websites such as OER commons at www.oercommons.org/.

2. Short responses

Obeying instructions. Students perform actions or draw something in response to instructions.

Ticking off items. A list, text or picture is provided. The students listen to spoken description, information or narrative and mark the relevant items as they hear them mentioned.

True/false. The listening passage consists of a number of statements, some of which are true and some false (possibly based on material the class has just learnt). Students write ticks or crosses to indicate whether the statements are right or wrong; or they make brief choral responses ('True!' or 'False!' for example); or they may stay silent if the statements are right, and say 'No!' if they are wrong.

Detecting mistakes. The teacher tells a story or describes something the class knows, but with a number of deliberate mistakes or inconsistencies. Listeners raise their hands or call out when they hear something wrong.

Cloze. Like the more conventional written cloze passage, the text has occasional gaps; however, in a listening passage, these gaps are represented by silence or some kind of buzz. Students write down what they think might be the missing word. Note that the gaps have to be much more widely spaced than in a written text, otherwise there is not enough time to listen, understand, think of the answer and write. If you are speaking the text yourself, then you can adapt the pace of your speech to the speed of student responses.

Guessing definitions. The teacher provides brief oral definitions of a person, place, thing, action or whatever; students write down what they think it is.

Skimming and scanning. Students are asked to identify some general topic or information (skimming), or certain limited items of information (scanning) and note the answer(s). Written questions inviting brief answers may be provided in advance; or a grid, with certain entries missing; or a picture or diagram to be altered or completed.

3. Longer responses

Answering questions. Questions which require responses of several words are given in advance. The listening text provides the answer(s). Students write down the answers as they listen.

Note-taking. Students take brief notes from a short lecture or talk.

Paraphrasing and translating. Students rewrite the listening text in different words: either in the same language (paraphrase) or in another (translation).

Summarizing. Students write a brief summary of the content of the listening passage.

Long gapfilling. A long gap is left, at the beginning, middle or end of a listening text. Students guess and write down, or discuss, what they think might be missing.

4. Extended responses

Problem-solving. A problem is described orally. Students discuss how to deal with it and/or write down a suggested solution.

Interpretation. An extract from a piece of dialogue or monologue is provided, with no previous information. The listeners try to guess from the words, kinds of voices, tone and any other evidence what is going on. At a more sophisticated level, a piece of literature that is suitable for reading aloud (some poetry, for example) can be discussed and analysed using both written and spoken versions

Dicto-gloss. Students take notes from a text they hear, and then, in small groups, combine their information and attempt to reconstruct the original text. They may hear the text again during this process. Later, the teacher displays the original text for comparison, and teacher and students discuss together any problems (Wajnryb, 1990).

Task

Choose two of the types of activities listed above, find a suitable text from coursebooks or the Internet, and create your own activity. If you can, try it out with colleagues or a class of students.

If the range of types of listening comprehension activities provided in the students' course materials is very limited, or if you don't like them very much, you may be able to create your own activities, possibly based on the ideas shown above. There are also some good books suggesting a variety of listening activities in *Further reading* at the end of this unit, and of course there are ideas on the Internet. Another possibility is to slightly change or adapt the activities already provided in your coursebook. See the next section for ways of doing this.

8.5 Adapting activities

Most modern course materials include audio recordings of listening texts (though few, unfortunately, are accompanied also by videos), with corresponding tasks in the student's book. Of course, you can simply use these as they stand, but you may find that you wish to adapt or supplement them. The tasks may be too easy or difficult; they may give no useful preparation for real-life listening; they may not be varied enough; or some types of activity that you consider important may be missing.

In the course of a busy teaching schedule, you will probably not have much time to prepare your own supplementary activities. So it is usually most useful and cost-effective to use either the text or the task as your basis and make alterations, involving minimal preparation, to make the activity more effective.

Below are some conventional listening activities, followed by ideas to vary them or make them more effective.

Action task

If you are working with colleagues, try doing the activities below (one of you read out or improvise the text, the others try doing the task). If you are working on your own, simply read through them. What might you do to improve or vary them?

The activities
Activity 1: Instructions

Instructions to learners

1. Listen to the recording of someone giving instructions. What are they talking about?
2. Look at the words below. Use a dictionary to check the meaning of any you are not sure about.
   Nouns: *router, cable, socket, browser, wireless connection, network*
   Verbs: *attach, plug in, register, connect*
3. Listen to the recording again, and use the words to complete the text.

> These instructions will tell you how to install your _____.
> You will need to _____ the router first using an electric _____.
> _____ the _____ to your computer. Then insert the ADSL attachment
> in the ADSL _____ in your wall. Open your internet _____ , and you
> will be able to _____ with us. Later you can _____ your computer to
> our _____ through a _____.

Instructions to teacher
1. Play the recording; then give students time to do the second stage above.
2. Play the recording again, and then check answers.

Listening text

> OK, you've got a new router? Great. Unpack it, and put it in the holder.
>
> Now attach the electric cable and plug it in, but don't turn on the router yet. Next, you need to attach the ADSL cable to the ADSL socket in your wall. OK? Now attach the router to your computer using the yellow cable, and then turn on both the router and your computer.
>
> If you click on your browser, you'll see a screen which will tell you how to register using your username and password. Do you see it? OK, just follow instructions. When you've finished, you'll need to click on the 'wireless connection' icon at the bottom of your screen in order to connect to our network.

Activity 2: Filling in names of animals

Instructions to students
Your worksheet shows a map of a zoo; write the names of the animals in the appropriate cages as your teacher tells you.

Instructions to teacher

1. Explain to the students what they have to do.
2. Using your filled-in map of the zoo, describe to the class where each animal lives; they may ask you to repeat or explain anything they did not catch or understand.
3. At the end, show the class the filled-in map and let them self-check.

Student's map

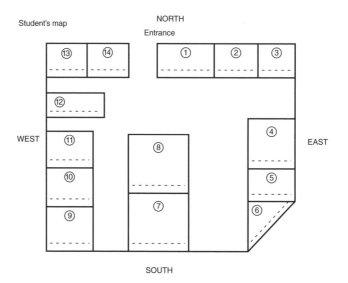

Teacher's map

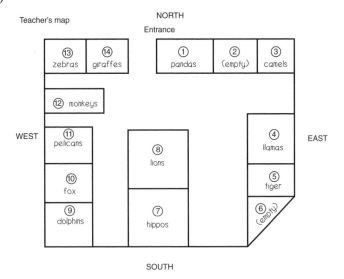

Listening text
> [Improvised by the teacher based on her filled-in map]
> (Adapted from Ur, 1984, 108–12.)

Activity 3: Information

Instructions to students
Listen to the following recorded talk, and then answer the multiple-choice questions below.

Instructions to teacher

1. Play the recording, then give students time to fill in the questions.
2. If there is time, play the recording again to let students check and fill in any questions they didn't manage the first time.
3. Check answers.

Listening text and questions

> One of the most important events in the history of Britain was the Norman invasion headed by their Duke, William. The Normans are normally thought of as French: but their origins, as their name suggests, is from the north: they were originally a Scandinavian tribe who migrated from Denmark and settled in north-western France. They eventually adopted the French language and became one of the most powerful dukedoms of the country.
>
> Harold, king of England at this time, was not in fact related to the previous king, Edward. William, Duke of Normandy, a second cousin of Edward, considered himself the rightful heir, and invaded England in order to

seize the crown by force. He landed at Pevensey in 1066, where he met no opposition, and eventually met Harold's army not far from the town of Hastings. Harold was defeated and killed, and William proclaimed himself king. He was crowned in London on Christmas Day, later the same year.

1. The Norman invasion of England
   a) came from the north, b) had a lot of influence on English history, c) was headed by King Edward, d) took place in the tenth century.

2. The Normans
   a) spoke Danish, b) adopted a Scandinavian tribe, c) came originally from England, d) lived in France.

3. Harold
   a) was the son of Edward, b) was William's cousin, c) was king of Normandy, d) was king of England.

4. The battle between the English and the Normans took place
   a) near Hastings, b) in Hastings, c) at Pevensey, d) in London.

5. William was crowned king of England
   a) at Hastings, b) when he landed in England, c) in 1066, d) in 1067.

Some suggestions for change

Activity 1: Instructions. Although the text is presented as spoken, it is actually adapted from a written instruction. It has hardly been changed and is extremely dense. It has little or no redundancy, and no opportunity later in the text to make up for anything the listener missed earlier. It might be worth saying the text in your own words, taking care to amplify, repeat, paraphrase and generally supply the 'redundancy' that will make it easier to follow.

The task focuses more on vocabulary than listening: most of the time is spent on reading and writing vocabulary. So it scores very low on what I have called 'quantity' (p. 44): there is comparatively little actual listening. It also relies heavily on previous knowledge: a student who was unfamiliar with things like routers, ADSL and wireless connections would find this very difficult, but a student who knew all about them would find it rather boring.

The task needs redesigning. Ideally, a text giving instructions should actually get the students to follow them themselves. So you might improvise the instructions to students as described above, while they actually mime the actions themselves, or label a diagram, asking you questions about vocabulary, or for clarification, as needed.

Activity 2: Filling in names of animals. This activity provides plenty of quantity of listening, and is interesting. It is based on teacher improvisation, so the actual words of the text can be adapted to the level of the class, and the listeners can request clarifications or repetition of information. This type of text involves more work for the teacher than the use of audio or video recordings but is easier for the students and arguably provides a more authentic type of listening text. Resist the temptation to write out the text you are going to say and then just read it out!

However, there is probably too much to do. I would provide the locations of most of the animals in the students' version of the map, and ask them to fill in only a few missing ones. The number of missing items can be varied according to the level of the class. The task may be rather childish for older students: it can be adapted to represent perhaps the location of different people's desks in an office or shops in a mall.

Activity 3: Information. This is a very common and traditional type of listening task which you will still find on a lot of listening comprehension websites. It is used a lot for testing since it is very easy to mark objectively (see Unit 12: Assessment and testing, pp. 178–9). However, it is probably not very effective in giving listening practice. It lacks most of the common characteristics of real-life listening and is based on a dense, obviously written text. Moreover, it gives practice in reading as much as in listening, in the same way that Activity 1 focused more on vocabulary than on listening.

It can be improved if you go through the questions with the class first, checking comprehension. This lightens the reading load when they are answering the questions, gives some previous information and provides for expectation and purpose when students begin the listening. Sometimes I even ask a class to guess what the answers will be before listening. This activates their background knowledge and adds extra challenge and motivation: was I right or wasn't I?

As with Activity 1 above, you may improve the text by using it as an informational basis for your own improvisation, and add 'redundant' extensions such as repetition, paraphrase, extra comment.

To practise selective listening, students can be asked to answer only one or two specific questions each time they hear the text.

Review

Answer as many as you can of the following questions, and then check answers by referring back to the relevant passages in this unit.

If you are working in a group, note down your own answers first alone, and then share with the other members of the group. Finally, check the answers together.

Goals and problems in teaching listening

1. Can you recall at least four characteristics of natural listening situations?
2. Why is it important to take these into account when planning listening comprehension activities?
3. How useful is it to have students listen to each other for listening comprehension practice?

Listening activity design (1): the text

4. Can you define the terms *noise* and *redundancy* in informal speech?
5. What are some characteristics of pronunciation in informal, improvised speech which may produce problems for students?
6. Why might you also want to include formal, pre-written texts as a basis for listening comprehension activities?

Listening activity design (2): the task

7. Suggest some design features you might take into account when creating listening tasks.
8. In what situations might you present a listening text with no accompanying task?

Types of activities

9. Can you give at least two examples of listening activities that elicit very brief responses from students?
10. Can you give an example of an extended activity based on listening that eventually activates students in speaking, reading or writing as well?

Adapting activities

11. Suggest some reasons we may wish to adapt the listening activities provided in coursebooks.
12. Suggest some ways we can improve the more traditional types of listening activities.

Further reading

Chang, A.C. and Read, J. (2006) The effects of listening support on the listening performance of EFL learners. *TESOL Quarterly, 40*(2), 375–97.
> (An interesting study showing the effects of different kinds of support on the results of listening comprehension tasks)

Field, J. (2008) *Listening in the Language Classroom*, Cambridge: Cambridge University Press.
> (Practical guidelines on the design of listening comprehension activities in the classroom, suggesting alternatives to the traditional 'comprehension question' based tasks)

Lynch, T. (2009) *Teaching Second Language Listening*, Oxford: Oxford University Press.
> (Research and theory together with practical suggestions for classroom listening tasks)

Rost, M. (1991) *Listening in Action: Activities for Developing Listening in Language Education*, Hemel Hempstead: Prentice Hall International.
> (A series of suggested activities, classified according to the type of listening, with guiding notes and suggestions)

Ur, P. (1984) *Teaching Listening Comprehension*, Cambridge: Cambridge University Press.
> (Theoretical topics similar to those treated here, with a number of suggestions for listening activities)

Wilson, J. J. (2008) *How to Teach Listening*, Harlow, Essex: Pearson Longman.
> (A practical handbook on teaching listening, providing a range of sample activities as well as principled guidance on task design)

9 Teaching speaking

Overview

The sections in this unit are:

9.1 **Goals and problems in teaching speaking**. The main objectives in teaching oral fluency, and how we might address some typical problems in the classroom.

9.2 **Speaking activity design (1): topic and task**. The respective roles of topic and task in stimulating lively conversational English in the lesson.

9.3 **Speaking activity design (2): sample activities**. Some examples of informal speaking activities, followed by critical discussion.

9.4 **Speaking activity design (3): presentations**. Teaching more formal speaking in the form of classroom presentations at various levels.

9.5 **Pronunciation**. Some aspects of English pronunciation which you may find useful to teach explicitly.

For assessment and testing of speaking skills, see Unit 12: Assessment and testing.

9.1 Goals and problems in teaching speaking

Of all the four skills (listening, speaking, reading and writing), speaking seems intuitively the most important: people who know a language are referred to as 'speakers' of that language, as if speaking included all other kinds of knowing. And many, if not most, language learners are mainly interested in learning to communicate orally.

Classroom activities that develop students' ability to express themselves through speech would therefore seem an important component of a language course. Some courses are explicitly designed to promote oral fluency; others include specific lessons that are labelled 'conversation classes'. Occasionally students may need to develop the ability to produce formal, extended speech in the form of oral presentations. But in most cases, the primary aim is to improve students' fluency in informal conversational interaction.

It is very difficult to design and administer procedures that actually get students to talk: more so, in many ways, than to get them to listen, read or write. So let's start by defining the main goals of such procedures, and the accompanying problems.

The main goals are ...

... that the students should actually talk a lot. As much time as possible during the activity should be used for talk by the students themselves. This may seem obvious, but often a lot of the time is taken up with teacher talk, pauses or classroom management.

... that the language used should be of an acceptable level. Students should express themselves by using language that is relevant, easily understandable and of an acceptable level of accuracy. This does not mean that all the language has to be absolutely correct, only that it is free from pronunciation, lexical and grammatical errors that interfere with the fluent communication of meanings. (For a discussion of the teaching of pronunciation, see Section 9.5 below.)

Task

What, in your experience as either student or teacher are some of the problems in getting students to talk in the classroom? Note down a few ideas, and then read on.

Some problems

Shyness and inhibitions. Unlike reading, writing and listening activities, speaking requires some degree of real-time exposure to an audience. Students are often inhibited about trying to say things in a foreign language in the classroom because they are worried about making mistakes, scared of criticism or losing face, or simply shy of the attention that their speech attracts.

Finding things to say. Even if they are not inhibited, you often hear students complain that they cannot think of anything to say. Just providing an interesting topic, as we shall see in the next section, is not enough. Students need to feel that they have something relevant and original to contribute to the discussion so that it is worth making the effort to speak.

Low participation of individuals. Only one participant can talk at a time if he or she is to be heard; and in a large group this means that each one will have only very little talking time. An added problem here is the tendency of some students to dominate, while others speak very little or not at all.

L1 use. In classes where some or all of the students share the same L1, they may fall back on it when they could, with a bit more effort, use English. They do so because it is easier and feels more natural to talk to each other in their own language. Occasional L1 use is inevitable – and, indeed, can be very helpful in solving specific vocabulary problems, for example – but if students spend most of their time speaking their own language, they will obviously have little opportunity to improve their speaking skills in English.

However, there are a few useful, simple and practical principles that can help achieve the goals while avoiding or reducing the problems.

Task

What would you do in the classroom in order to cope with the problems listed above, and with others you have suggested yourself in the previous task? List a few ideas, and then read on.

Practical principles for the design of speaking activities

Use group or pair work. This increases the amount of learner talk in a limited period of time and also lowers the inhibitions of students who are unwilling to speak in front of the whole class. It is true that group work means the teacher cannot supervise all speech produced by students, and there is a risk, therefore, that errors may go uncorrected and that students may occasionally slip into their L1. Nevertheless, even taking into consideration occasional mistakes and L1 use, the amount of time devoted to talking in English by individual members of the class is still likely to be far more than it would be in a whole-class discussion.

Base the activity on easy language. In general, the level of language needed for participation in the interaction should be **lower** than that used in intensive language-learning activities in the same class. The necessary vocabulary and grammar should be easily recalled and produced so that the participants can speak fluently without too much hesitation. It is a good idea to review essential vocabulary before the activity starts, and maybe even to teach some new items for students to write down and refer to, if necessary, during the activity.

Make a careful choice of topic and task to stimulate interest. On the whole, the more interesting the topic and the clearer the purpose of the interaction, the more motivated participants will be (for the respective roles of topic and task, see Section 9.2 below).

Make students aware of the purpose of the activity and conditions for its success. This is a useful pedagogical principle for any classroom activity, but in oral interaction in groups it becomes essential. Students need to understand how important it is to talk a lot, to make sure that everyone gets a chance to speak, and to try to keep to English all the time so that they will take responsibility for seeing that these conditions are fulfilled. If several groups are working at the same time, you cannot possibly monitor them all: it is the students themselves who should do so.

Practical tips

1. **Discussion leaders.** Appoint one member of the group as discussion leader, whose job it is to make sure that everyone gets a chance to participate and that nobody over-dominates the process, and to keep an eye on the time.

2. **L1 monitors.** With classes who have a strong tendency to overuse L1, invite one student (not the discussion leader) to act as monitor for each group. The monitor's job is to note and tell you later about instances of L1 use. Even if there is no actual penalty attached, the awareness that someone is monitoring their language helps participants to be more careful.

3. **Pair work.** Where feasible, use pair work. That way the amount of talk overall in the class is maximized (at any one time half the members of the class will be speaking). Also, pair work is far easier to organize than group work: it just involves turning to face a partner, rather than actually moving tables and chairs to get into groups.

4. **Correcting errors.** In general, give corrective feedback on errors only rarely during oral fluency work. Stopping students to correct them may distract them, and focusing too much on accuracy will discourage them from trying to express themselves freely. On the other hand, there are places where correction can actually help: if the student is obviously hesitant and needs a confirmation of the correct form, for example. An alternative is for you to note errors and

discuss them with the class later. For more on this topic, see Unit 7: Error correction, p. 96.

5. **Feedback.** If the students have been working in small groups and want to share the results of their discussions at the end, it may get tedious to have to listen to them all. Alternatives are to hear only a selection; and/or to invite the groups to post their results in writing on a class website or on the classroom noticeboard.

9.2 Speaking activity design (1): topic and task

Here are two samples of oral fluency activities, designed to have students engage in informal exchanges of opinion.

Activity 1

Discuss the following conflicting opinions.

Opinion 1. Children should be taught in heterogeneous classes: setting them into ability groupings puts a 'failure' label onto members of the lower groups, whereas putting more and less able students together encourages the slower ones to progress faster, without penalizing the more able.

Opinion 2. Children should be divided into ability groupings for most subjects: this enables the less able ones to be taught at a pace suitable for them, while the better students do not need to wait for the slower ones to catch up.

Activity 2

A good schoolteacher of English should have the following qualities. Can your group agree together in what order of priority you would put them?

sense of humour	enthusiasm for teaching
honesty	pleasant appearance
love of children	knowledge of English
fairness	ability to create interest
flexibility	ability to keep order
intelligence	clear speaking voice

Action task

1. Try out the two oral fluency activities, allowing 5–10 minutes for each. You can do this with colleagues, or with a class of advanced learners. During the activities, try – even if you are participating yourself – to keep an eye on how things are going: how much talk there is, how many people participate, the kind of language they are using, how interested and motivated they seem to be.

> 2. Compare the two: which was more successful in achieving the goals defined at the beginning of this unit? If you felt that one was noticeably more successful than the other, can you identify some reasons why? Was it the topic? The task? The organization?

Topic-based and task-based activities

The main difference between the two activities shown above is that the first is topic-based and the second is task-based. The first simply asks participants to talk about a topic, the main objective being clearly the discussion process itself. The second asks them actually to perform a task, where the objective is the production of some kind of clear result (in this case, a decision about priorities).

Topic

A good topic is one to which students can relate using ideas from their own experience and knowledge. The 'ability-grouping' topic is therefore appropriate for most schoolchildren, schoolteachers or young people whose school memories are fresh. It should also represent a genuine controversy, in which participants are likely to be fairly evenly divided (as my own classes tend to be on this one). Some questions or suggested lines of thought can help to stimulate discussion, but not too many arguments for and against should be 'fed' to the class in advance: leave room for their own initiative and originality.

Task

A task is goal-oriented: it requires the group, or pair, to achieve an objective in the form of an observable result, such as brief notes or lists, a rearrangement of jumbled items, a drawing, a spoken summary (see Unit 4: The task). This result should be achievable only by interaction between participants: so in the instructions for the task, you often find instructions such as 'reach a consensus', or 'find out everyone's opinion'. But make sure that the language needed (mainly vocabulary) is known to students: it might be useful to review some useful words or expressions before beginning the task.

A task is often enhanced if there is some kind of visual focus to base the talking on: a picture, for example, or a text of some kind, as in the example shown in Activity 2 above. You will find more examples of task-based speaking activities in Section 9.3 below.

Which is better?

On the whole I have found that when doing experiments like the one suggested in the *Action task* above, the task-based activity works better: there is more talk, more balanced participation, more motivation and enjoyment. When asked why this might be so, participants say things like: 'I knew what needed to be said'; 'It was a challenge – we were aware that time was running out and we had to get a result'; 'It was more like a game, we enjoyed it'.

The reason why task-based activities generally produce more talking is that they exploit an important component of real-life talking: the purpose. We rarely speak just because a topic interests us. We normally have some goal that we want to achieve with the people we are talking to: to take a decision, to solve a problem, to clarify an issue, to find out the answer to a question and so on. A well-designed classroom task provides students with a purpose of this kind, giving them a reason to speak.

However, it is important to note that there are some students who respond well to topic-based discussions. They say things like: 'I found discussing a topic more interesting: you can go into things more deeply without the pressure of having to reach a decision'; 'I like debating, exploring issues in free discussion'. These students also need to be catered for, so occasional topic-based discussions should be included in a balanced programme.

Most classroom informal speaking activities are based on either topic or task; however, there are some which are neither. With younger beginner learners, for example, we may provide a dialogue to learn by heart (see the beginning of the next section), or a whole play to perform; or at a later stage, we may suggest a role-play situation for improvisation, or a simulation. For examples of both of these, as well as further task-based activities, see Section 9.3 below.

9.3 Speaking activity design (2): sample activities

This unit presents a selection of interactive oral fluency activities, starting with a very simple one for beginners and progressing to more advanced ones, followed by discussion of their strong and weak points.

Task

Discuss with colleagues or think on your own: which of these activities would be likely to produce a lot of talk? What problems might you anticipate when doing them with a class? What might you do to prevent or solve them? Then read on.

The activities
Activity 1: Dialogues
A simple dialogue is learnt by heart. For example:[1]

> A: What's that?
> B: This? It's a frog.
> A: Are you sure?
> B: Yes, of course I'm sure.
> A: Amazing!

Students perform it in pairs, and then again, in various ways, moods, roles, imaginary situations and contexts. For example, they might perform it very fast or very slowly, angrily or sadly; they might play the roles of a teacher and young student, or of two James Bond-type spies where 'frog' is code for a secret weapon. At a later stage they are encouraged to suggest variations or additions to the text.

---

[1] This dialogue is adapted from Hana Raz's *Dramatic Dialogues* (1968), now, sadly, out of print.

Activity 2: Describing pictures

Each group of students has a picture (one of the two shown below) which all its members can see. They have two minutes to say as many sentences as they can that describe it; a 'secretary' marks a tick on a piece of paper representing each

sentence. At the end of the two minutes, groups report how many ticks they have. They then repeat the exercise with the second picture, trying to get more ticks than the first time.

Activity 3: Picture differences

The students are in pairs; each member of the pair has a different picture (either A or B – see p. 124, overleaf). Without showing each other their pictures, they have to find out what the differences are between them (there are 11: see solutions at the bottom of the next page).

Activity 4: Things in common

Students sit in pairs, preferably choosing as their partner someone they do not know very well. They talk to one another in order to find out as many things as they can that they have in common. These must be things that can be discovered only through talking – not obvious or visible characteristics like 'We are in the same class' or 'We both have blue eyes'. At the end they share their findings with the full class.

Activity 5: Role play

Participants are given descriptions of characters and a situation on role cards, and invited to improvise a scene based on these.

ROLE CARD A: Last time your friend borrowed your bike, it came back very dirty and scratched, but you didn't like to complain. Now the same friend has said he/she wants to ask a favour, and you have the feeling he/she wants to borrow the bike again. You really don't want to lend it, but you don't want to lose the friendship …

ROLE CARD B: You don't have a bike of your own, but you need one for a group bike ride tomorrow. So you're going to ask your friend if you can borrow his/her bike (you know your friend isn't planning to go on the bike ride). You are good friends, and you've borrowed this bicycle before, so you don't think there will be any problem …

A

B

1. In picture A the baby is laughing; in B crying.   2. In picture A the mother has a dark sweater; in B she has a white one.   3. In picture A a woman is driving the car; in B a man.   4. In picture A the passenger in the car has dark hair; in B fair.   5. In picture A there is a flag on the building; in B there isn't.   6. In picture A the man in the foreground has a hat; in B he doesn't.   7. In picture A the man directing the car has white trousers; in B he has grey ones.   8. In picture A the woman in the foreground has long hair; in B she has short hair.   9. In picture A the number on the building is 118; in B it is 119.   10. In picture A the man on the ladder has a T-shirt; in B he has a long-sleeved one.   11. In picture A the most distant building has no windows; in B it has lots.

Activity 6: Solving a problem

The students are told that they are an educational advisory committee which has to advise the principal of a school on problems with students. What would they advise with regard to the problem below? They should discuss their recommendation and write it out in the form of a letter to the school principal.

> Benny, the only child of rich parents, is in the 7th Grade (aged 13). He is unpopular with both children and teachers. He likes to attach himself to other members of the class, looking for attention, and doesn't seem to realize they don't want him. He likes to express his opinions, in class and out of it, but his ideas are often silly, and laughed at. He has bad breath.
>
> Last Thursday his classmates got annoyed and told him straight that they didn't want him around; next lesson a teacher scolded him sharply in front of the class. Later he was found crying in the toilet saying he wanted to die. He was taken home and has not been back to school since.

Comment

Activity 1: Dialogues. Learning dialogues by heart is associated with the audio-lingual method (see Unit 1: English teaching today, p. 8), and some people mistakenly assume that it is therefore an outdated and ineffective technique. It is actually extremely useful for the development of oral fluency at elementary levels: it provides the beginner with ready-made meaningful exchanges that they can perform fluently, giving them the confidence early on that they can communicate successfully in spoken English. Some dialogues can also be taught as jazz chants (Graham, 2006): these are very effective, especially with young classes. The expressions that are learnt through memorized dialogues are likely to be easily recalled later when needed in different contexts. Finally, a dialogue can be the starting point for variation, elaboration and continuation into a full scene or even short play whose development will depend on the language level and creative ability of the class.

Activity 2: Describing pictures. This is a simple but surprisingly productive activity for elementary or lower-intermediate classes. The simplicity of the task means that it is very easy to succeed in: this, together with the fact that each English sentence earns a tick, means that participants rarely, if ever, resort to L1. Make sure they understand that it is only necessary for the secretary to put a tick for each contribution; some students tend to assume that every sentence has to be written out – but this cuts down drastically the amount of talk possible. The second time round, with a new picture, the groups almost invariably break their previous record, which adds a sense of achievement and satisfaction.

Activity 3: Picture differences. This is a well-known activity which usually produces plenty of purposeful question-and-answer exchanges. The necessary vocabulary is specific and fairly predictable: so it is a good idea to teach or review and write up these items in advance on the board. The problem here is the temptation to 'peep' at a partner's picture: your function during the activity may be mainly to stop people cheating! You may also need to drop hints to pairs who are 'stuck'. An easier alternative is to allow both students to see both pictures right from the beginning: then all they have to do is help each other to find and describe the differences in English.

Activity 4: Things in common. This is a useful 'ice-breaking' activity for intermediate or advanced students, which creates a feeling of solidarity by focusing on what the participants share. It also produces a lot of interesting talk, and can be lengthened and enriched further if you get students to change partners, perhaps every five minutes or so. There is a problem with the 'feedback' session: if all pairs tell the class everything they found, then it gets quite boring. So it is better to ask a few volunteers to suggest selected 'things in common' that they think are particularly original, amusing or pleasing. (See *Practical tip 5* at the end of Section 9.1 above.)

Activity 5: Role play. Often role play is done in pairs, as in the example shown here; however, it can involve interaction of up to five or six different roles. Normally, the groups or pairs improvise their role play between themselves, simultaneously, with no audience. Sometimes, however, volunteers may perform their role plays later in front of the class. This is virtually the only way we can give our students the opportunity to practise improvising a range of real-life forms of spoken interaction in the classroom, and it is an extremely effective technique if the students are confident and cooperative. However, more inhibited or anxious students find role play difficult and sometimes even embarrassing. Factors that can contribute to a role play's success are: making sure that learners can easily produce the necessary language; your own enthusiasm; careful and clear presentation and instructions. A preliminary demonstration or rehearsal by you together with a student volunteer can also be very helpful. An extension of the role play is the *simulation*, where participants are in an imaginary situation with some task to perform but do not have specific individual roles, as in Activity 6.

Activity 6: Solving a problem. This is particularly suitable for students who are themselves adolescents, or involved with adolescent education, and is intended for fairly advanced students. It usually produces lively discussion, with a high level of participation and motivation. As with many simulation tasks, participants tend to become personally involved. They begin to see the characters as real people, and to relate to the problem as an emotional issue as well as an intellectual and moral one. At the feedback stage, the resulting letters can be read aloud: this often produces further debate.

9.4 Speaking activity design (3): presentations

More advanced classes will need to learn to use spoken English not only for informal interaction, but also for more formal presentations. Training in giving presentations is particularly appropriate for those students studying English for Academic Purposes (EAP) or for a career in business. Presentations involve longer stretches of speech and may be accompanied by written or graphic material displayed on a screen or in the form of handouts. They are often followed by a question-and-answer session or discussion.

Types of presentation
Short
At the early stages, classroom presentations may be very short: one to three minutes long. Even one minute, however, still feels like a long time to have to

speak for a student whose English is limited and who has little experience of presenting even in his or her L1! Here are some kinds of short presentations such students may be asked to do:

- 'Show and tell'. The student shows an object he or she has brought from home and tells the class what it is and why it is significant for them.
- 'Describe'. The student shows a photograph of a person and describes them. Alternatively the photograph may show a scene or an event.
- 'About me'. The student introduces him- or herself to the class: personal details, family, interests, tastes, hobbies.

Medium-length

Later, students may make presentations of five to ten minutes, which may be supported by a picture or text shown on the board. Here are some suggestions:

- Narrative. The student tells a story: a joke, an anecdote, a fable, an urban legend. This can be made easier for the teller and more interesting for the audience if there are illustrations: one or more pictures from a book, or digital pictures projected on a screen or interactive whiteboard.
- Instructions. The student explains to the class how to do something that he or she is an expert in. Again, illustrations or actual objects can be helpful here.
- Recommendations. The student recommends a book, film, television programme or play to an audience. This will involve some narrative but should focus on reasons why the speaker enjoyed the book, film, etc. and thinks the audience will also like it.

Long

The most advanced type is a full-length (15-minute or more) presentation, which simulates presentations the student may later be required to produce in real life. Such presentations need to be based on a clear structure: an introduction telling the audience what the presentation is to be about; the main body, with clearly ordered sections that include explanations and examples; and an ending, summarizing and, where appropriate, drawing conclusions and making recommendations.

- Information. The presentation conveys information about a topic, sometimes in the form of a report, very often based on previous research and presented as a project. It is often accompanied by written materials and/or illustrations on slides.
- Argument. A case is presented, for or against a claim. This may be in the area of politics, linguistics, education or any topic which interests the class. It should include arguments in favour of and against the main thesis, with the speaker's own position made clear.

Advice to students

Your contribution will be mainly in feedback given later to the students, but you can help a lot by giving them tips when they are preparing:

- Prepare! Make notes about what you're going to say; perhaps learn by heart your final sentence, or a few good phrases that can make an impression! But don't learn the whole presentation by heart – see next point.

- **Don't read your text aloud or try to learn all of it by heart!** A text that has been learnt by heart and recited, or read aloud, tends to be boring. It's much more interesting for the audience if you explain things in your own words, even if you occasionally hesitate or repeat yourself. But you can, of course, refer to notes to keep you on track.

- **If using slides (e.g. on *PowerPoint*), don't just read them aloud.** Your audience can probably read English, so you don't need to tell them what's there! Use the text on your slides as cues and reminders, not as your entire text.

- **Keep eye contact with your audience.** It's much more interesting listening to a speaker who is looking at you. And address the entire class, not just the teacher!

- **Speak clearly.** This sounds obvious, but good presentations are often spoilt by the inaudible voice or monotonous tone of the presenter. Speak louder than you normally do, and try to vary the pitch and speed at which you speak.

- **Think about your body language.** Don't walk about too much, and use gesture only when you really need to.

9.5 Pronunciation

The term *pronunciation* as it is understood here includes not only the sounds of the language, but also the rhythm, intonation and stress patterns.

Students do not need necessarily to model their accents on English native speakers – indeed, some native speakers are notoriously difficult to understand! – but their speech does need to be clear. Some learners consistently get particular sounds wrong, and as a result their speech is less 'comfortable' to listen to, and occasionally incomprehensible. In that case, you may wish to spend some lesson time improving your students' pronunciation.

Sounds

Some mispronunciations in international English conversations can actually bring about a breakdown in communication (Jenkins, 2002); for example, the substitution of a long /iː/ sound for the short /ɪ/ in a word like *live* (v.) which then sounds like *leave*. We do therefore need to make sure that our students are differentiating between these two sounds and using them correctly. Other common variants make very little difference: the pronunciation of the 'th' sounds /ð/ and /θ/ as /d/ and /t/, or as /z/ and /s/, does not, apparently, cause problems for most listeners.

It is interesting that in some cases native-speaker pronunciation may actually be less readily comprehensible for the majority of English speakers than that of non-natives. It is a common experience for conference-goers who are non-native speakers of English to find the lectures given by other non-natives far easier to understand than those given by native speakers: largely because of their pronunciation. The shortened pronunciation, or even elimination, of unstressed syllables (the use of the schwa for 'weak' forms such as /əv/ instead of /ov/ for *of*, /tə/ instead of /tu:/ for *to*, or the word *police* pronounced as /pli:s/ instead of /pɒli:s/) may sometimes cause difficulties in comprehension. In general, the nearer the pronunciation is to the actual spelling of a word, the more likely it is to be easily understood by the majority of speakers worldwide.

Rhythm

The speech rhythm of native English speakers is stress-timed. This means that in each phrase or sentence certain words are stressed (usually the lexical words which carry the main content) and the other words are shortened to fit the rhythm. Therefore, how long each phrase or sentence takes to say depends on how many stresses there are in it. For example: *My old GRANDfather used to go SWIMming in the middle of DeCEMber* (three stresses) does not take much longer to say than *My GRANDpa went SWIMming in DeCEMber* (three stresses). Many other languages are syllable-timed: the time it takes to say a sentence depends on how many syllables there are. So the first of the sentences above, if pronounced according to syllable-timing (18 syllables) would take quite a lot longer to say than the second (10 syllables). However, so many people now speak English with syllable- rather than stress-timing – or a mixture – that both are becoming acceptable worldwide, and it may not be worth investing very much effort in training students to produce stress-timed speech themselves. They do, however, need to be able to hear and understand both types: so it is important to give them a varied diet of different accents in listening comprehension.

Intonation

The rules of intonation in English within native-speaker communities are fairly complex and difficult to teach: very few English textbooks, or teachers, attempt to provide rules or practice in these. The issue is complicated further by the fact that, as with rhythm and stress, the increase in the use of English as an international language has resulted in a proliferation of intonation patterns that are used, accepted and understood in spoken English worldwide. So it is probably not worth trying to teach rules of intonation, and what we need to do, again, is provide our students with plenty of exposure to different accents and their accompanying intonations, within comprehensible listening texts.

Stress

English speakers indicate which word they are stressing in a sentence not by increased volume but normally by a rising intonation. Thus, the message conveyed by a sentence like *Eli came by train this morning* will vary according to which word is pronounced at a higher pitch than the others. For example:

1. <u>Eli</u> came by train this morning = It was Eli, not someone else, who came.

2. Eli came by <u>train</u> this morning = It was by train that Eli came, not by car.

3. Eli came by train this <u>morning</u> = It was this morning that Eli came, not this afternoon.

Misuse of intonation for stress can produce misunderstandings. It would seem useful, therefore, to make our students aware of how to convey stress in a sentence and give them practice in it. For example, students might work in pairs on sentences like:

> I don't want to fly to Paris in January.

One student reads out the sentence with a particular stress: for example:

> I don't want to <u>fly</u> to Paris in January.

The other student has to identify what it is, exactly, that the speaker objects to (in this case, the flying).

Task

Make a list of the aspects of pronunciation that you think need to be explicitly taught to learners coming from another language that you know. Then read on.

Selected items that may need explicit teaching

The conclusion is, therefore, that it may not be useful to attempt to teach overall language rhythm or a comprehensive range of intonation patterns, but that there are certain items whose correct pronunciation does need to be insisted on. The most important of these are the following (see Jenkins, 2002):

- **contrast between long and short vowels**, particularly /ɪ/ - /iː/;
- all the consonants, with the exception, as mentioned above, of the /θ/ and /ð/ sounds, which do not seem to be essential for accurate communication;
- in particular, **the contrast between voiced plosives (/p/, /t/, /k/) and unvoiced plosives** (/b/, /d/, /g/);
- **initial consonant clusters** e.g. the /pr/ in a word like *proper*;
- **the use of intonation to signal stress of a particular word in a sentence**.

You may find, however, that you may need to add to, or shorten, this list, in response to the particular needs of students in your own classes.

How do we teach them?

As with grammar, most students can benefit from focused teaching of pronunciation as well as intuitive acquisition through listening. This is because very often they simply do not hear an English sound when listening but perceive it as an approximation to a similar, but not identical, sound in their own language. Many Arabic speakers, for example, have problems perceiving and producing the voiceless /p/, which they hear and pronounce as a sound similar to the Arabic /b/.

It is therefore useful to start by awareness-raising: letting students hear and compare two easily confused sounds either in isolation or within minimal pairs such as *ship/sheep*, and making sure that they can actually recognize the difference. Systematic explanation can help here: you can explain, for example, about the puff of air that accompanies a /h/ or initial plosive consonant, or in what part of the mouth a particular sound is formed.

The next step is to ask students to produce the sounds in single syllables or pairs of contrasted syllables, imitating your pronunciation, or that of a recording.

Learning by heart the correct performance of entire phrases or sentences can help a lot, particularly within the context of dialogues or jazz chants (see Graham, 2006).

Finally, it is important to practise pronunciation within a communicative task: challenging students to convey messages to each other when understanding depends on correct pronunciation or stress (see an example under *Stress* above).

To recap: pronunciation improvement activities may include:

1. **receptive awareness-raising**, perhaps contrasting minimal pairs;

2. **focused explanations** of how particular sounds are produced;

3. **imitation** by the students of pronunciation of single sounds, or sounds within syllables or simple words;

4. **production** by the students of the target pronunciation item within phrases or complete utterances;

5. **meaningful tasks** contextualizing pronunciation items.

Task

Choose a particular item, either from the list *Selected items that may need explicit teaching*, or from the list you yourself made in the previous task, and suggest an activity that might help students to learn it.

Review

Answer as many as you can of the following questions, and then check answers by referring back to the relevant passages in this unit.

If you are working in a group, note down your own answers first alone, and then share with the other members of the group. Finally, check the answers together.

Goals and problems in teaching speaking

1. What are some factors that prevent, or discourage, students from talking in English in the lesson?
2. Why is it a good idea to use group or pair work for oral fluency activities?
3. Can you remember at least two practical tips that can help students participate in a speaking activity?

Speaking activity design (1): topic and task

4. What is a 'task-based activity'?
5. Why do task-based oral fluency activities produce, on the whole, more talking than topic-based ones?

Speaking activity design (2): sample activities

6. Why is it useful to get students to learn dialogues by heart?
7. What are the advantages and disadvantages of using role play as a basis for speaking activities?

Speaking activity design (3): presentations

8. Can you give two examples of short presentations suitable for less proficient classes?
9. Recall at least four useful pieces of advice you might give students when preparing longer presentations.

Pronunciation

10. Why is native-speaker pronunciation sometimes difficult to understand?
11. How important is it to teach intonation, rhythm and stress explicitly?
12. What are some sounds that, if mispronounced, may lead to breakdown in communcation?

Further reading

Bilbrough, N. (2007) *Dialogue Activities*, Cambridge: Cambridge University Press.
(Varied and interesting activities based on the idea of learning and performing dialogues)

Gammidge, M. (2004) *Speaking Extra: A Resource Book of Multi-Skills Activities*, Cambridge: Cambridge University Press.
(Mainly for young adults and adults, but can also be used with adolescents: a variety of speaking activities involving discussion, role play, storytelling)

Hewings, M. (2004) *Pronunciation Practice Activities*, Cambridge: Cambridge University Press.
(A useful set of practical activities providing varied and interesting pronunciation exercises, including communicative tasks)

Klippel, F. (1985). *Keep Talking: Communicative Fluency Activities for Language Teaching*, Cambridge: Cambridge University Press.
(Original and stimulating ideas for getting students to talk, mainly for more advanced students)

Seligson. P. (2007) *Helping Students to Speak*, Slough: Richmond Publishing.
(Basic problems with getting students to speak and how to overcome them; practical ideas for activities)

Ur, P. (1981) *Discussions that Work*, Cambridge: Cambridge University Press.
(A variety of oral fluency activities based on tasks: mainly for intermediate and advanced students)

10 Teaching reading

10.1 What is reading?

In the context of language learning, *reading* means 'reading and understanding'. A student who says, 'I can read the words but I don't know what they mean' is not, therefore, reading, in this sense, but merely *decoding*: translating the written symbols into their corresponding sounds.

In this section I aim to clarify some aspects of the nature of reading by examining critically some generally accepted assumptions expressed in the following statements.

1. We need to decode individual letters in order to read words.
2. We need to read and understand all the words accurately in order to understand a text.
3. If we understand all the words in a text, we will understand the text.
4. The more words there are in a text, the longer it will take to read it.

Task

How far do you agree with the statements above? Try the brief tasks suggested with each text, and then read the following discussion.

Statement 1: We need to decode individual letters in order to read words

Have a look at the words below: can you read them?

You might guess various possibilities, but you cannot be sure you are right. If, however, you look at the whole sentence in which these words appear (see the end of this unit, p. 149), you will probably be able to read the same words without much difficulty.

The conclusion would be that, although we need to learn our letters in order to start reading at the very early stages, we can later recognize words without being able to identify and decode single letters. You can read a word by fitting its general visual 'shape' into a comprehensible context, as in the example shown above.

Statement 2: We need to read all the words accurately in order to understand the meaning of a text

Read the following text as quickly as you can.

> The handsome knight mounted his horse and galloped off to save the beautiful princess. On and on, over mountains and valleys, until his galloping house was exhausted. At last he dismounted … Where was the dragon?

Did you notice that the second time the word *horse* appeared, it was spelt 'house'? If you did not, this does not mean that you are a bad reader, but rather the reverse. You are a good reader, in the sense that you are looking for meanings, and understanding the overall sense of the text. We have an innate tendency to try to make anything we read meaningful to us. If a particular word is irrelevant or meaningless we tend to 'correct' it: to interpret it, as here, in a way which accords with the overall message of the text.

Statement 3: If we understand all the words in a text, we will understand the text

Try reading and understanding the following:

> C++ is an object oriented, general-purpose programming language. It is considered a high-level language but also has low-level features. You can use it with multiple programming styles and without a sophisticated programming environment.

Unless you have a background in computer programming, you will have found this difficult to understand, though you were probably familiar with all the individual words. Knowing the meanings of the words in a text ensures understanding only if you have some knowledge of the subject matter. The use of this knowledge to help us understand what we read is known as 'top-down' reading strategy and is used together with 'bottom-up' (decoding and understanding the words) in order to arrive at overall comprehension. While reading the previous text, for example, you probably had some knowledge of traditional stories with knights on horseback which helped you make sense of it.

It is true (as mentioned in Unit 5: Teaching vocabulary) that a learner needs to know about 95–98% of the words of a text in order to understand it easily. The point is that this is necessary but may not, in some cases, be enough: some background knowledge may also be needed in order to activate top-down strategies. So it may be very helpful as a preparation for reading to activate, share or add to students' previous knowledge of the content of the text.

Statement 4: The more words there are, the longer the text will take to read

Read carefully the two lines of text below. Which takes you more time to read and which less?

> 1. jam hot pin call did tap son tick
>
> 2. How quickly can you read and understand this?

You probably found that the second line was much quicker and easier to read than the first. This indicates that there is not a simple one-to-one relationship between the number of words in a text and the time it takes to read. What appears to be more significant is the number of sense units: words combined into meaningful phrases or sentences. So if you have a text made up of one sense unit (in this case, the full sentence shown in the second line) it will be easier and quicker to read than a text made up of isolated, disconnected words (the first line), even if the total number of words is the same. The difference is one of *coherence*: the words in the first line are difficult and time-consuming to read because there is no connection between them. In contrast, in the second line the same number of words connect with each other coherently to make a meaningful sentence.

Below are some more accurate reformulations of the original statements given above, followed by some implications for teaching.

Statement 1: We usually need to read and decode letters in order to read words, particularly at the early stages of reading. But if the context is clear, even partially illegible writing can be understood.

Statement 2: We do not necessarily need to read every word accurately in order to understand a text. We need to read enough words to understand the main meanings of the text, and can then skip or pay less attention to ones that repeat previous information or are redundant.

Statement 3: If we understand all the words in a text, we are likely to understand the text: but we also need to have some previous knowledge of the subject matter and text-type. When reading a text, we use information given by the words interacting with our own world knowledge in order to access the meaning.

Statement 4: The more clearly the words are linked together to make coherent sense-units (phrases, sentences), and the more clearly sentences are linked together to make coherent paragraphs, the easier the text will be to read.

Implications

The main implication for teaching all of this is the importance of encouraging students to concentrate on understanding the meaning of a text, using their world knowledge and common sense as well as the meanings of the actual words. Decoding single words is, of course, an important first stage in learning to read, particularly for those students whose L1 does not use the Latin alphabet. But we need to be aware that it is only the first stage, and a means to an end. We need to encourage students to read and understand meaningful texts – even very short ones – as soon as we can.

One practical classroom implication of this principle is that it is generally advisable to encourage students to read silently rather than reading aloud. Following a text silently as the teacher reads aloud can be a useful procedure (see Unit 3: The text, p. 32); but when the students themselves read aloud, they are forced to focus on articulating the sounds rather than on the meanings. They have to read all the words at more or less the same speed, paying attention to them all equally. This means that they cannot skip unimportant words or information or choose their own most comfortable speed of reading. Most significantly, reading the text aloud does not allow them enough time or attention to devote to constructing meanings.

Reading aloud is useful at the early stages of learning the letters, as it allows us to monitor how well students are learning the sounds of separate letters. But it does not have much learning value for more advanced reading. Silent reading allows students to study the text at their own pace, with time to focus on meaning, slowing down when they encounter more difficult bits, and skimming, or even skipping, the easy or obvious bits.

10.2 Beginning reading (1): phonemic awareness

Many beginner learners of English need to learn a totally new writing system. For some Asian learners, even the concept of an alphabet is new, as their written symbols may represent syllables or even words. Even if they have already learnt the Latin alphabet for their L1, some letters may be pronounced differently in English. In either case, it is very helpful to do some preliminary work on *phonemic awareness*. This involves making sure the students can hear and differentiate between the different sounds, or phonemes, of English which they will need to match with the letters or letter combinations that represent them. They need, for example, to be able to identify the difference between /p/ and /b/, or between /ɪ/ and /iː/. Various kinds of oral exercises can be used, usually based on getting students to listen to sounds and do various identification tasks.

Below are some types of phonemic awareness activities. Each has one example, but can be expanded into a series of similar items. They are listed roughly in order of difficulty.

1. Tell students to put their hands up when they hear a particular phoneme. Say a series of phonemes including the target one and others that may be confused with it.

> Put your hands up when you hear /θ/. Now listen: /d/, /θ/, /p/, /t/, /d/, /t/, /ʧ/, /ð/, /θ/.

2. Ask students which is the odd one out of a series of phonemes. Let them hear the series twice.

> Listen for the odd one out. /t/ /t/ /t/ /d/ /t/. Now, put your hands up when you hear it: /t/ /t/ /t/ /d/ /t/.

3. Ask students to identify which words rhyme. Give two options.

> Which word rhymes with 'patch'? Say 'one' or 'two'. One: cash; Two: catch.

4. Challenge students to identify whether a sound is at the beginning, middle or end of a word.

> Tell me if the /iː/ sound is at the beginning, middle or end of the word. 1. even 2. three 3. steep.

5. Add an extra sound to a word, and ask students if they can say what sound was added.

> Here's a word: *sand*. Now I'm going to say the word with another sound added – can you tell me what the new sound is? The word I said before was *sand*. The new word is *stand*.

6. Ask students to count the sounds in a simple word, where these correspond with letters in the written form.

> How many sounds can you hear in the word *man*? What are they?

7. Provide students with the component sounds of a word, and challenge them to put them together to make a word they know.

> Here are some sounds. If you put them together, what word do they make? /m/, /æ/, /n/.

Task

Choose one of the tasks above that you feel would be particularly useful in developing students' phonemic awareness. Create a complete exercise of about seven or eight items based on it.

Action task

If you are teaching an appropriate group of beginner students, try out this exercise in the classroom.

10.3 Beginning reading (2): practical principles

When beginning reading, there are some important preliminary decisions that we need to take. Some of these are more relevant to situations where the students are having to learn a totally new writing system. But even if they are only learning different pronunciation for some of the letters, you need to think about how to teach them. Here are some questions that we need to consider.

1. Should I teach my students only orally for a while, so that they have basic spoken proficiency in English before starting reading? Or start reading and writing from the beginning?
2. Should I teach them single letters, and gradually build these up into words (the 'phonic' method)? Or should I teach the written form of meaningful words first and analyse the different component letters later ('global reading method')? If letters, should I teach them in the same order that they appear in the alphabet?
3. If I decide to teach single letters, should I teach their names first, or their (usual) sound?
4. Should I teach upper- and lower-case letters together, or first the lower case of all the letters, because they are more common?
5. At what stage should I teach the conventional order of the alphabet?

Task

How would you answer the questions above?

Beginning reading: some guidelines

1. Both for students learning a new alphabet, and for those who already know it, it is generally preferable to begin reading only after acquiring some basic knowledge of the spoken language. Then reading can quickly become a matter of recognizing meanings, rather than just decoding symbols. This also means we can give much more interesting tasks for reading practice. For those learning a new alphabet, teaching letters before they know much spoken English would mean that we would have to provide exercises based on meaningless combinations of letters, which would be boring and demotivating.

2. With students learning a new alphabet, it is probably most practical to begin with single letters (the conventional 'phonic' method), starting with the most common and useful. As soon as they have a few of the most common

letters (for example, *a, e, i, o, s, n, t, r*), students can read and write an enormous number of common words. The most common digraphs (two-letter combinations that make a single sound, like *th, sh, ee*) are worth teaching even before you teach the least common letters like *q, z*.

Having said this, I would add the reservation that it is worth teaching very early on a few very common words whose spelling and pronunciation are not 'transparent' (for example: *the, he, she, what, are*) and practising recognition through tasks that involve searching for and identifying them within an authentic, unsimplified text.

Students who already know the Latin alphabet, on the other hand, are likely to pick up the different sound–symbol correspondences as they encounter them in context: from your reading aloud of texts or single items, or from reading texts in their course materials. (This, of course, will work only if they already know the spoken forms, as recommended at (1) above.) However, there may also be a place for taking time early on to clarify explicitly the sounds of single letters if these are obviously different from those in the L1: for example, for French speakers, how English *u* is usually pronounced (/ʌ/), or for German speakers, how the *w* is pronounced (/w/).

3. It is more useful for reading if the student knows the most common sound of the letter. The name of the letter is used only for explaining spelling. It is possible, of course, to teach both – 'This letter is called "aitch" and is pronounced /h/' – if the class can cope. This would be appropriate for older beginners; but with younger ones, it is arguably more helpful to teach them first how to pronounce the letter as it is read in a word, and leave the names until later. Note that even students who already know the Latin alphabet are going to have to learn new letter names as well as some sounds.

4. (This question relates only to students learning the Latin alphabet for the first time.) My own preference is to teach the two forms of the letters together. This slows down the process a little but means that the letters the students do know can immediately be recognized in authentic texts outside the classroom (even in countries where the local writing system is different, English names regularly appear on signs in public spaces). Another reason is that proper nouns, which regularly begin with upper-case letters, are very useful for reading practice with classes of beginners who do not yet have a very wide vocabulary. Names of people, commercial products or places provide a lot of extra words that the students can read and recognize.

5. (Again, students who already know the Latin alphabet will probably also know the conventional alphabetical order, so this question would not be relevant.) Conventionally, the order of the alphabet is taught very early, particularly in younger classes who learn to sing the 'alphabet song'. However, there is not much justification for this. The order of the alphabet is only needed when students start looking up words in paper dictionaries or other reference books, which for most classes happens quite a lot later. Moreover, many students today look up words using electronic dictionaries, apps on their mobile phones or dictionary websites, for which the alphabet is not needed. But sooner or later, even today, they will find it useful to know the order of the alphabet. So

I am not suggesting that we don't teach it at all, only that it is not essential at the early stages of learning to read.

The teaching of new letters is only a preliminary stage: the ability to read and understand English is acquired mainly through later reading activity in which the students have the opportunity to engage repeatedly with written texts.

10.4 Beginning reading (3): reading tasks

In order for students to start developing reading fluency, they need a lot of practice at the early stages in reading and understanding very short simple texts, at word and sentence level. Your course materials will supply a number of these, but there may not be enough or they may not be very varied or interesting. You may want to supplement them with your own tasks, using worksheets or work cards (see Unit 14: Materials, p. 211). Here is a variety of tasks for beginning reading, ordered from the easiest to the most difficult. I have given only sample items for each, which can be expanded into longer exercises. Note that at this level, instructions would normally be provided in L1.

Letters in words

These exercises focus on single letters, but students have to identify the letters in words which they already know in their spoken form. These exercises are particularly useful for classes which are learning a new writing system. They can easily be designed to use only a limited set of letters, and so can be used even before the class has learnt the entire alphabet.

Task 1

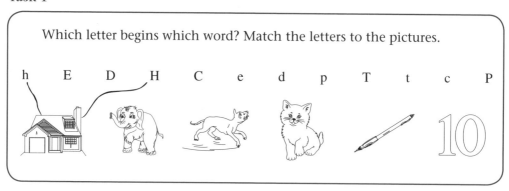

Task 2

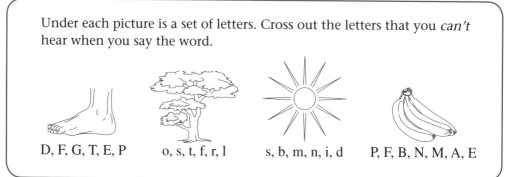

Single words 1: cognates

Here, students are asked to identify words that are likely to be the same, or roughly similar, in their own language. The purpose is simply to provide a wider range of vocabulary for them to practise reading.

Task 3

> Can you translate these words into your own language?
>
> pasta   television   dragon   video

Task 4

> Write out the names of the countries in your own language. (And perhaps find them on a map.)
>
> England   Brazil   Canada   Japan   India   Poland

Task 5

> Are these names for boys or girls?
>
> Maria   Peter   David   Sarah   Anna

Single words 2: English words

Students identify the words and do something with them to demonstrate comprehension.

Task 6

> Copy these words in the order of size of the object, the biggest first.
>
> a   bag   a tree   a mouse

Task 7

> Which words go together? Draw a line between words that are connected.
>
> table   hand   woman   down   up
>   man   foot   chair

Task 8

> Circle the words that are the names of animals.
>
> head   dog   table   pencil   cow   horse

Task 9

> Which is the odd one out?
>
> run   walk   sit   jump

Phrases and short sentences

Here, students need to understand whole sense-units and demonstrate understanding: the last stage before beginning full texts.

Task 10

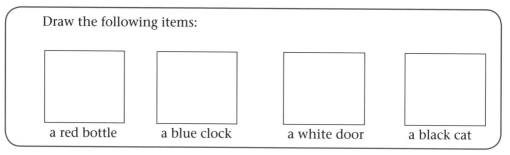

> Draw the following items:
>
> a red bottle   a blue clock   a white door   a black cat

Task 11

> Copy out only the sentences that are relevant to the picture.
>
>
>
> 1. There is a table here.   4. They are not eating.
> 2. They are under the tree.   5. They are drinking.
> 3. They are not happy.

Task 12

> Write what this is (in your language if you don't know the word in English):
>
> It is in Australia. It is big. It can jump.

Task

Can you suggest a new elementary reading exercise? Where would it fit in this list?

Fluent reading

Once our students have mastered basic reading comprehension, we need to help them deal with more sophisticated texts and tasks quickly, appropriately and skilfully. Note that the focus here is not on reading texts intensively for the sake of the language learning (which was dealt with in Unit 3: The text), but on activities which foster the ability to read better. The aim is for our students to become *fluent readers* in the same way that we want them to be fluent listeners and speakers: to access the meaning of a text successfully and rapidly, with minimum hesitations. A large 'sight' vocabulary (lexical items the student identifies and understands at a glance) is the first requirement for this (see Unit 5: Teaching vocabulary). But in order to foster fluent reading, we also need to make sure that students have plenty of successful reading experience through encounter with a wide range of texts read for a variety of purposes.

One useful way of defining how best to provide for such experience is to look at the features which facilitate fluent reading.

> ### Task
>
> Look at the following list, and think for yourself what the teacher could do, through text selection, task design and classroom interaction, to promote the necessary abilities and strategies. Then read on.

Characteristics of fluent reading

1. **Language level:** The text is easy enough to be comprehensible to learners.
2. **Content:** The topic is accessible to learners. They know enough about it to be able to apply their own background knowledge.
3. **Speed:** Learners read fairly fast, meaningful unit by meaningful unit, rather than word by word.
4. **Selective attention:** Learners concentrate on the significant bits and skim the rest. They may even skip parts they know to be less significant.
5. **Unknown vocabulary:** Learners are not worried by unknown vocabulary. They guess its meaning from the surrounding text, or ignore it. They use a dictionary only when these strategies are insufficient.
6. **Prediction:** Learners think ahead, hypothesize and predict.
7. **Motivation:** Learners are motivated to read: by interesting content or a challenging task.
8. **Purpose:** Learners are aware of a clear purpose in reading, beyond just understanding: for example, to find out something, or to enjoy reading.
9. **Different strategies:** Learners use different strategies for different kinds of reading.

Implications for teaching

1. **Language level.** The texts chosen for reading practice should be of a level that is easily comprehensible to the students. As noted earlier (pp. 63–4), a knowledge of between 95% and 98% of the words is necessary for fluent reading and understanding of a text. If students cannot understand vital information without looking up words, then work on the text may improve

their vocabulary (as discussed in Unit 3: The text), but it will be less useful for improving their reading skills as such.

2. **Content.** The texts should be based on information or world knowledge that the students are familiar with. If a particular text you use does not deal with something the students know about, then you can use various pre-reading strategies to supply the missing information. You can elicit what students already know, and then add any further necessary input yourself; you can provide an easy introductory text which provides the information; or you can send students to the Internet to find it out themselves.

3. **Speed.** There is some controversy over whether you can in fact improve reading speed, or get students to read for sense-units rather than single words, through training. The crucial factor here is, again, the provision of a large amount of experience of successful reading. Beyond this, we can, perhaps, best help our students to read faster by giving them tips as to reading strategy: see *Advice to students* later in this section.

4. **Selective attention.** Again, paying more attention to key information and less to redundancies or repetition is a reading strategy which fluent readers apply intuitively. We can help students by providing 'scanning' tasks: ask them to find out a specific item of information in the text and to raise their hands when they have done so. In order to do this, they will need to search for content which is relevant to their task, and identify and ignore those parts of the text which are not. It is also helpful to do some explicit strategy instruction here, by making students aware that it is not only legitimate but actually desirable to ignore redundant or repetitive items or chunks of text while reading. Another useful preliminary instruction is to tell students first to glance through the text ('skim') and summarize the main points they have understood.

5. **Unknown vocabulary.** Pausing reading in order to look up the meaning of a new word is a useful strategy for vocabulary expansion, but it can be counterproductive if the aim is reading fluency. Of course, students should know how to use the dictionary, but they should also be aware when it is necessary and when an intelligent guess based on context ('inferencing') is preferable. The dictionary is often overused, resulting in slower, less fluent reading, as well as frequent misunderstanding when students choose the wrong dictionary definition.

Inferencing the meaning of a word from a text is a useful reading strategy, provided the text as a whole is easy enough to provide a clear context (for the impossibility of guessing meanings in a difficult text, see Unit 5: Teaching vocabulary, pp. 63–4). It is something that students should be encouraged to do, even if their guess results in only a rough approximation to the actual meaning.

Finally, the fluent reader will occasionally simply ignore a new word completely, if the general meaning is clear and the unknown word not necessary for comprehension. Skipping 'redundant' words in this way means missing an opportunity to learn a new item, but if our main priority is fluent reading, then it is an important strategy.

6. **Prediction.** This is, again, something which fluent readers do naturally. At the conscious level, just to tell students 'remember to predict as you read' is not very helpful. But there are tasks which specifically encourage prediction, such as 'Read up to the end of the first paragraph of the story: what do you think will happen next?' or 'Read to the end of the page. What do you think the next few words are likely to be, more or less?'

7. **Motivation.** Texts should be selected with reader interest in mind: topics that are likely to be at least partially familiar to students, but with enough extra information to invite curiosity and increase knowledge. The task is even more important: a boring text can be made interesting through a stimulating task, but a boring task can 'kill' a potentially interesting text.

8. **Purpose.** When reading a story or a very interesting or entertaining text (see Section 10.6 below), no actual task may be necessary: students will be motivated to read anyway, and a task may actually spoil their enjoyment. But in most cases we will need to provide a task, given in advance, so that the student has a purpose in reading. Some examples of this are: to find out a specific piece of information; to summarize the main points; to respond to the writer's point of view.

> **Task**
>
> Look at the reading texts and tasks supplied in a foreign-language textbook you know. How far do they accord with the recommendations above? And what might you do to compensate for any weaknesses you discover?

Advice to students

Your students will benefit from some tips on useful strategies for improving their reading fluency.

- If you aren't familiar with the content, find something out about it before you read the text.
- Read whole 'chunks' of meaningful text: word combinations rather than single words.
- Try not to 'vocalize' (pronounce the words in your head) as you read.
- Focus on information that is vital for understanding.
- Feel free to skip parts of the text that you find are not necessary for understanding.
- Where possible, try to guess unknown words from context ('inference').
- Use the dictionary only when absolutely necessary.
- Be aware of your purpose in reading.

There is some controversy over how far such strategies can be explicitly taught. My own experience is that we can teach them only up to a point. It is definitely helpful to raise students' awareness of them with explicit recommendations and classroom discussion, eliciting individual students' experience of how they have used particular strategies when reading. The formulation of tasks on the specific text you are teaching that focuses on a particular strategy (see some examples in the previous discussion) may also be helpful. Then students can, later, use or reject the various strategies according to how well they work for them. It is worth emphasizing, however, that long sessions on focused practice of particular strategies, such as prediction or inferencing, may not be worth the investment of time, which would be better spent increasing students' vocabulary or general reading fluency.

Some procedures have been designed that combine a series of strategies to use when approaching a reading text. Two of them are described below: more can be found in Grabe (2009, pp. 231–2).

1. KWL stands for 'Know – Want to know – Learnt'. The reader looks at the title or topic of an informative text, notes what he or she already knows and what he or she wants or expects to learn further from reading the text. After reading, he or she notes what new information has been learnt. This is a short and simple procedure that is very easy to implement in the classroom.

2. SQ3R stands for 'Survey, Question, Read, Recall, Review'. Survey means skimming through the title, main headings, illustrations, and maybe taking a quick glance at the main points of the text. The Survey is followed by, or accompanied by Question: what questions occur to the reader about the text or its topic or writer? Then there is Reading: the reader goes through the text more thoroughly, while bearing in mind the questions asked previously. Recall means checking that the reader can remember the main points made. Finally, at the Review stage, the reader rereads and reviews the content of the text.

10.6 Extensive reading

Extensive reading is the silent reading by individual students of long, interesting texts (such as stories or books). It is sometimes known as 'reading for pleasure' or 'sustained silent reading' (SSR). It necessitates a class or school library from which students can borrow books to read at their own speed and exchange as needed. Like the teacher-initiated reading of texts in Section 10.4 above, its main aim is to increase reading fluency and confidence. It therefore shares many of the principles already mentioned: the texts should be relatively easy, reading should be fast, passages that are not necessary to understanding can be skipped, and so on. However, it goes further in developing the ability of the student to read independently in English, and implements the following principles:

1. Students have access to a large variety of reading material to choose from.
2. Each student chooses his or her own reading material. The teacher may advise but does not choose for them.
3. Students can stop reading material that they find boring or too difficult and swap it for something else.
4. The purpose of reading is enjoyment and interest, not a task from the teacher or textbook. In principle, the reading is its own reward, just as when we read a novel in our L1.
5. The role of the teacher is to encourage students to read and swap books, to help them choose, and to be a role model as a reader.

Problems

Extensive reading programmes are implemented far less than you might expect: mainly because of the practical problems involved.

Time

Teachers are worried about getting through the coursebook or preparing for an exam and are unwilling to devote parts of classroom sessions to extensive reading. They see it as a possible waste of valuable class time which could be spent on more intensive language learning.

Money

Some institutions do not have the necessary financial resources to set up and – just as important – to maintain and keep adding to a library. Ironically, many schools seem to be able to find more money to buy advanced technological equipment than they do to buy books, which cost far less! One solution is for students to read stories onscreen, assuming that there is one computer or other reading device available for each student. Books are still, however, most people's preferred medium for their own reading for pleasure.

Monitoring

It is sometimes difficult to know whether students are actually reading their books, and you may need to check. Many teachers insist on a 'book report' for each book. This, of course, spoils the pleasure and motivation associated with extensive reading and takes time away from the reading itself. There are other, easier options such as oral presentations recommending the book, drawings to illustrate it, or posters to advertise it. But again, this leaves less time for reading. It's a tricky dilemma: personally, I prefer not to have follow-up assignments and to rely on my own perceptions of students' body language in the classroom to check that they are in fact reading and understanding; but many of my colleagues do not agree!

Practical tips

1. **Class time.** Set aside a regular scheduled time for extensive reading: at the beginning of lessons, or half a lesson a week. Don't leave it just for homework: devoting lesson time to extensive reading conveys a message about its importance and provides opportunities for exchanging books.

2. **Read yourself.** If you can, use the extensive reading lesson to get on with whatever book you are reading; example is a powerful instructor.

3. **Bring books to the class.** If your library is not in the classroom, bring a box of books at the appropriate level to the classroom for students to exchange. Sending them to the library in class time is time-wasting and does not allow you to help them choose.

4. **Have reserve reading materials ready.** Students sometimes forget to bring their books. Have some short stories or booklets at an appropriate level ready to give these students. Alternatively, if computers are available, prepare website addresses where they can read interesting material at an appropriate level.

Review

Answer as many as you can of the following questions, and then check answers by referring back to the relevant passages in this unit.

If you are working in a group, note down your own answers first alone, and then share with the other members of the group. Finally, check the answers together.

What is reading?
1. What is the difference between *decoding* and *reading*?
2. Why do we not necessarily have to pay attention to all the words in a text?

Beginning reading (1): phonemic awareness
3. What is *phonemic awareness*?
4. Can you remember at least two activities that help phonemic awareness?

Beginning reading (2): practical principles
5. What are the 'phonic' and 'global reading' methods of teaching reading?
6. Which is more important to teach: the names of the letters or their sounds? Why?

Beginning reading (3): reading tasks
7. Why is it useful to use cognates in early reading tasks?
8. Can you suggest at least three ideas for simple reading activities based on the comprehension of single words or phrases?

Fluent reading
9. Can you recall at least six features which are likely to facilitate fluent reading?
10. How might a fluent reader cope with unknown vocabulary?

Extensive reading
11. Can you list at least three of the main principles to bear in mind when setting up 'extensive reading'?
12. What are the advantages and disadvantages of requiring a book report after reading?

Further reading

Day, R. and Bamford, J. (1998) *Extensive Reading in the Second Language Classroom*, Cambridge: Cambridge University Press.

> (A guide to the theory and practice of extensive reading)

Day, R. and Bamford, J. (2004) *Extensive Reading Activities for Teaching Language*, Cambridge: Cambridge University Press.

> (A collection of practical procedures and classroom activities for the support of extensive reading)

Grabe, W. (2009) *Reading in a Second Language*, Cambridge: Cambridge University Press.

> (A comprehensive discussion of the research and thinking on reading and reading instruction in a second language)

Janzen, J. (2002) Teaching strategic reading. In J. C. Richards and W. A. Renandya (eds.), *Methodology in Language Teaching* (pp. 287–94), Cambridge: Cambridge University Press.

   (An interesting discussion of the use of reading strategies to enhance comprehension)

Nuttall, C. (1996) *Teaching Reading Skills in a Foreign Language* (new edn), Portsmouth: Heinemann.

   (A thorough and sensible introduction to the subject; plenty of practical teaching suggestions, with underlying rationale)

Full context of handwritten words shown on p. 134.

She's a "natural" teacher! (And it was a pleasure to have her with us)

11 Teaching writing

11.1 What is writing?

The teaching of writing, as noted in Unit 1: English teaching today, p. 3, has assumed much greater importance in recent years with the arrival of new forms of rapid written communication. This means that we need to pay more attention to helping students learn how to write well than previous generations of teachers did.

Some characteristics of writing

Writing is fundamentally different from the other four skills, not only because it is visual as contrasted with oral/aural, or productive as contrasted with receptive, but also because of how it is produced and the way it communicates.

It is permanent. A text once written is there on paper or on the screen, to be easily reread or rewritten, either very soon after it was written or later. Speech, on the other hand, is normally fleeting, with no possibility of changing and editing.

It is dense. The content of a written passage is, unlike speech, presented relatively densely, with little or no 'redundancy'. Writing takes more time and effort than speaking: the writer simply does not want to waste time writing any more words than are necessary to convey the message, and the reader can always go back and reread if they feel repetition is necessary.

It is asynchronous, or time-independent. We usually read text some time after it has been written. Even with 'synchronous chat', there is a time-lapse between production and reception. Spoken discourse, in contrast, is in most cases produced and received simultaneously.

The person or people being addressed are not physically present. The target audience for a written text – whether a single addressee, closed group or the public at large – is rarely physically present. Spoken interaction is mostly face to face.

It is produced slowly. Writing is much slower than speaking, reading or listening. This is one reason why it is used least of the four skills in real-life communicative activity.

It is a learnt and high-prestige form. Most people acquire the spoken language (at least of their own mother tongue) intuitively, whereas the written form is normally taught and learned in school. Literate people are more respected, in general, than the illiterate.

It uses more standard forms. English speech typically varies widely, in accent, lexis and grammar, according to the cultural or linguistic background of the speaker; writing, in contrast, is more uniform and tends to observe conventional usages (formal or informal).

Some implications for teaching

We have seen that writing cannot normally be 'picked up' but has to be systematically taught. This means that we actually need to devote a lot of attention to teaching it, even though it is actually used by most people far less than the other skills.

In speech, students express their ideas in linear fashion, as they occur to them; in writing, they have time to rewrite and edit. So we need to help them ensure, through such rewriting and editing, that their writing uses acceptable language and that the text is organized and coherent (see Section 11.5 below).

11.2 Formal and informal writing

Most writing is formal. Stories, reports, most webpages (wiki entries, for example), newspaper articles, fiction, the book you are reading at this moment … all these are formal texts. Informal writing was in the past only used for quick notes or reminders; but these days it is used much more: in online 'chat' and texting (SMS), for example.

Here is an example of informal writing: in this case a 'chat' between friends about an upcoming wedding (between Jane and Joe):

> Emma says:
>> taxi? to register office? yes? no?
>
> Emma says:
>> unless you'd rather walk
>
> Jane says:
>> if raining, then yeah, a taxi

Emma says:
  excellent

Emma says:
  anything you need for the day that we could bring?

Joe says:
  me

Jane says:
  nooo

(Crystal, 2006, p. 251)

Task

List the differences you can find between formal writing, using the example of the text of this book, and informal writing, using the example above. Then read on.

Some differences between formal and informal writing are listed in the table below.

	Formal writing	Informal writing
Grammar and lexis	The text follows standard grammatical rules and uses conventional, formal vocabulary.	The text may not use full sentences or formally 'correct' grammar and spelling; uses colloquial vocabulary (e.g. *yeah* for 'yes') and contracted or abbreviated forms like *you'd*.
Punctuation	Punctuation follows standard rules.	On the whole, punctuation is used less. Some 'special effects' punctuation may sometimes be inserted, for example rows of exclamation marks for emphasis.
Detachment	The writer is detached from the reader personally, in time and in space. The text is therefore not normally designed to be immediately responded to.	The text is usually targeted at a specific audience, personally known to the writer, often read immediately, or a very short time, after it is written, and responded to quickly.
Editing and redrafting	The text is written first as a draft, and then edited and redrafted to polish the language, style and organization.	The text is not normally edited but sent to the recipient as a 'first draft': it may therefore often include slips or 'ungrammatical' usages and will not have a systematic structure.

	Formal writing	Informal writing
Length	Most texts are more than a paragraph in length: reports, letters, articles, stories, even complete books.	Most texts are short: a few words, a sentence, occasionally more.
Explicitness	The text is explicit: little shared knowledge is taken for granted and all necessary information is provided.	The text may be largely implicit, assuming a large measure of shared knowledge; there will therefore be ellipses (missing words assumed to be easily guessed by the reader), and pronoun or other references to real-world subjects may not be explained.

Formal and informal writing are presented in the table above as two distinct types or styles: but of course, there are gradations: some emails and blogs, for example, are written semi-informally, with characteristics from both columns.

In teaching, however, it is important to make students aware of the difference in principle, and in what contexts and circumstances each may be appropriate. They should know, for example, that they should not use informal vocabulary or contracted forms like *can't* or *u* (for 'you') in formal academic writing.

Most writing is formal, and students need to learn the necessary skills and knowledge to enable them to compose formal texts of different kinds. If they are able to do so, we will not have much difficulty teaching them the specific 'shortcuts' and stylistic peculiarities of informal writing – but the converse is not true. So it is probably best in teaching writing to focus mainly on the formal mode.

11.3 Beginning writing: the letters

Note. This section is appropriate for monolingual classes whose L1 uses a non-Latin alphabet or another writing system. Such classes are very often composed of young learners (aged between 7 and 11).

Task

Think back to when you yourself were taught to write Latin script – whether in your L1 or when you learnt English or another Latin-alphabet-based language. How were you taught? Can you remember what was useful (or not) in helping you to learn letter formation?

Some basic aspects of the teaching of writing to beginners apply equally to the teaching of reading, and have already been dealt with in Unit 10: Teaching reading, pp. 136–42. As with reading, it is important to know some simple conversational English before beginning to learn the letters; and we are likely to teach single letters before we teach letter combinations in words. We will probably teach the most common and useful letters before the less common and useful ones, and cover the lower- and upper-case forms at the same time. But there are other skills students need to master that are specific to handwriting and, later, typing. Here are some of them, with practical teaching implications that you may have already thought of if you did the task above.

Direction

Other writing systems often go in a different direction from English: from right to left instead of from left to right (Arabic, Hebrew) or vertically (Chinese). This involves not only getting used to moving one's hand in a different direction along the line, but also often learning to form the letters in a different direction. For example, speakers of Arabic or Hebrew are used to drawing circular letters in a clockwise direction and will now have to learn to form them anti-clockwise. If they are not deliberately taught otherwise, they will continue to write these letters clockwise, which will slow down the flow of handwriting and make it difficult to join up letters should they wish to do so later (see *Cursive writing* below).

Practical implications
We need to provide students with models of correct-direction writing: by modelling the letter writing on the board, and perhaps also by providing the alphabet written out with little arrows showing in what direction it should be written.

It can help as a preliminary exercise to get the students to write rows of waves or loops, running from left to right, as follows:

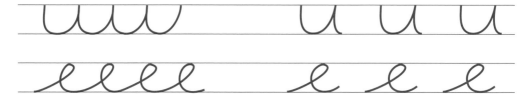

Then they need to practise writing out rows of similar letters, and later combinations of different ones in words, while the teacher makes sure they are forming them correctly.

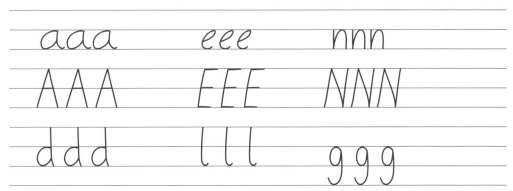

Height, depth and level

One thing students learning the Latin alphabet often find tricky is getting the height and depth of letters right: making sure that letters like *d, l, b* in fact have 'arms' that are of a similar height to capital letters, and that letters like *p, y, g* have 'tails' that are sufficiently long beneath the line. Some students also have problems with maintaining level horizontal writing. In both cases, they need the guidance of ruled lines at the early stages of writing.

Practical implications

Early writing should be done within parallel lines, which limit the height of letters and make sure they are level. These have two parallel lines in the middle which limit the height of the smaller letters such as *c, m, o,* and two added lines above and below to show how far the taller and deeper letters should reach.

Cursive writing

There is some debate over whether or not to teach students to write *cursive (joined-up) script*. If their L1 uses the Latin alphabet, then this will depend how they have already been taught to write it. If, however, the Latin alphabet is a new writing system for them, you will need to decide whether or not to teach cursive. Sometimes the decision will be taken for you: there is a clear general policy in your school, and perhaps in the country in general. Elsewhere, it is more a question of clarity (non-cursive) versus more attractive appearance (cursive).

Practical implications

The overriding criterion here has to be comprehensibility; and letters written separately are more likely to be legible than joined-up letters. A possible compromise I used in my own primary classes was to insist that everyone used non-cursive for the first year. In the second year I taught them cursive, and anyone who wished was told that they could continue to use it provided it was clearly legible. Most of my students in fact reverted to the non-cursive and later, as adults, used a combination, joining up some letters and not others.

Typing

For the foreseeable future it will still be necessary for our students to know how to handwrite in English: for personal greetings, form-filling, quick notes, shopping lists, etc. But it is becoming more and more necessary for them to learn to type in English as well, as most writing today is done on a computer. In my opinion, they should be taught to touch-type in their own language in elementary school: but for some reason, even where computers are available, this is rarely done.

Practical implications

Normally there is no time in an English course to provide the hours of practice needed to acquire touch-typing skills, though we might suggest that they teach themselves using a computer or internet-based program (you can find free programs online by searching for 'touch type'). In any case, we should give our students plenty of opportunities to use the keyboard, as well as a pencil or pen, to do writing exercises, in order to increase their typing speed. If they have already learnt this elsewhere, it is also useful to teach them how to use word processing tools to format their compositions: different fonts, sizes and spacings, different colours and positions. Basic copying or simple composition exercises can be made more motivating by allowing students to use these tools to improve the presentation of a text.

Speed and legibility

When teaching writing, the two main aims are to enable students to write reasonably fast, and to write legibly. However, emphasis on the one may be at the expense of the other. If you write very fast, your writing may be difficult to understand (true of typing as well as handwriting!). If you write very carefully, so as to be legible, you may sacrifice speed.

Practical implications

Having taught the letters, we need to give students plenty of practice in using them to write words and sentences so that they get to do so faster, but not at the cost of legibility. See *Beginner writing tasks* below for some ideas.

Later, any grammar or vocabulary written exercises will obviously give practice in speed and accuracy of handwriting or typing as a useful side benefit.

Beginner writing tasks

Apart from the first two ideas, which clearly relate to handwriting, all the following task-types can be done either on paper or on the computer.

- Copying. Copying is a useful way for students to practise letter formation with the 'scaffolding' of a model. It can be done by tracing (using tracing paper or following dotted lines) or copying lines of letters or words.

- Colour copying. Since early letter-writing practice can be boring, invite students to use different-coloured pens, or decorate their exercises with coloured frames or underlining.

- Thoughtful copying. Another way of making early writing practice interesting is to ask students to copy according to particular criteria: to copy, for example, only words that are names of animals (or any other lexical set you choose); or in a different order; or into different categories; or in order to label pictures.

- **Transliteration.** Students transliterate single letters or words (cognates or names of people or places are particularly useful) from their L1.

- **Dictation.** Students write down single letters or simple words from dictation.

- **Completion.** Students fill in the missing letter(s) from a known word, perhaps illustrated by a picture.

- **Labelling.** Students label pictures with simple phonetically spelt words.

11.4 Tasks that promote fluent writing

Most of students' writing in an English course is not done primarily in order to develop writing skills, but because writing is a convenient means of engaging with aspects of language. For example, students write down new vocabulary; copy out grammar rules; write out answers to reading or listening comprehension questions; do written tests. In these examples, writing is used as a means of getting the students to attend to and/or practise a particular language point, to make a note of new language for later reference, or as a convenient method of testing it.

Fluent writing tasks, in contrast, aim to improve students' ability to compose written text for communicative purposes. Aspects of accuracy (grammar, vocabulary, spelling) are, of course, important in formal writing, as discussed earlier in this unit; but the main focus is on meaningful writing following the conventions of a particular genre. (Tasks that focus on the forms rather than the communicative purposes of writing will be discussed in Section 11.6 below.)

Some criteria for the planning or selection of writing tasks are:

- **Interest.** The task should be motivating and stimulating.

- **Level.** The language required should be appropriate to the level of the class.

- **Relevance.** At least some of the tasks should be similar to the kinds of things students may need to write themselves, now or in the future.

- **Simplicity.** The task should be easy to explain. Often the provision of a model text can help to clarify.

- **Personal appropriateness.** The task should be one that you, the teacher, feel comfortable with and that fits your own teaching style, goals and preferences.

Task

Choose four or five specific writing tasks from the seven categories below, and think about how they might work with an intermediate-level class (if possible, one you are familiar with yourself). Suggest criticisms and any improvements or additions you can think of. Then read on.

Writing tasks

1. Creative writing
   a) A **story** based on some kind of given stimulus: a title, a picture or series of pictures, or a first or last sentence.
   b) A **personal anecdote** describing an occasion when you were disappointed (or afraid, surprised, relieved, etc.).
   c) A **poem** based on a given stimulus: topic, a particular structure, first or last lines.
2. Instructions
   a) An **instruction sheet** for something you know how to do (for example, prepare some kind of food).
   b) **Directions** how to get somewhere.
3. Interpersonal communication
   a) A **letter or email applying for a job**.
   b) A **letter of complaint**.
   c) A **reply** to a letter.
   d) A **comment on a blog**: either one that already exists, or one set up for the class.
   e) An **email** telling a friend what you've been doing recently and suggesting a meeting.
4. Description
   a) A **description of a view, a place** or **a person**.
   b) A **description of a process**, such as a scientific experiment, the life-cycle of an animal, a sequence of events represented by a flowchart.
5. Responses to literature
   a) A **synopsis** of a book, play or film.
   b) A **review** evaluating a piece of literature the class has read.
6. Persuasion
   a) A **recommendation** for some kind of change in your home community or place of work/study, addressed to the appropriate authority.
   b) An **advertisement** for a product.
   c) A **leaflet** promoting an institution, a tourist attraction, a course.
7. Information
   a) A **newspaper report** on an item of news, genuine or imaginary.
   b) A **short paper** providing information on a particular person, event or invention, previously researched on the Internet.

Comment

1. Creative writing. Some students respond well to tasks that demand imagination and creativity: others really don't like them! For the less creative students, you will need to provide much more structure and support.

Poems are surprisingly easy and pleasurable to write if based on an appropriate stimulus: see some excellent practical ideas in *Writing Simple Poems* (Holmes & Moulton, 2001).

The results of such tasks are often enjoyable for other students to read: post them on the class website, or on a noticeboard in the classroom, or read them out to the class (with the author's permission, of course).

2. Instructions. These tasks may be interesting for students if they relate to processes or places they know a lot about. They may require some preliminary vocabulary review or teaching; and you may wish to give some advice on the layout of instructions: numbered steps, for example, or illustrations where necessary.

    They are particularly useful for classes in English for Specific Purposes, such as engineering or nursing.

3. Interpersonal communication. Assignments like a letter or email applying for a job or a letter of complaint are probably most suitable for adults or older teenagers. Students also need to be aware that such texts would demand far more formal English than the blog comment or email. If they are written as paper letters rather than email, then you will need to teach some conventions of letter writing: address, date, addressee, formal beginnings and endings.

    The blog task is often highly motivating, and can continue later, with other students adding further comments.

4. Description. This can be done at a fairly basic level of proficiency. To make it even easier, you might ask for phrases or single words, rather than full sentences in a coherent paragraph.

    For the personal description, it is helpful to provide in advance some topics that the writer might relate to: appearance; occupation; personality; interests; life story.

    Apart from the flowchart, descriptions of processes can often be laid out in other ways, such as tables or graphs.

5. Responses to literature. Just providing a synopsis can be rather boring. The review is more difficult, but more interesting to do, with the challenge to analyse and criticise, and the purpose of encouraging (or discouraging) potential readers or viewers.

6. Persuasion. The recommendation task is suitable for rather more advanced classes as it demands fairly careful planning of content and organization.

    The advertisement may be easier and can be decorated with coloured fonts and designs, and illustrated by pictures.

    The leaflet may be done collaboratively, each student in a group writing a different section: and again there is the possibility of illustration and decoration.

7. Information. The newspaper report can be based on a model: an authentic news report which has been read in class.

    The short paper is a first step on the way to academic writing, though it may be done at intermediate level. It can be highly motivating if the student is researching something that interests him or her personally. Note that you may need to do some preliminary instruction not only on the need for formal language, but also on the need for structure: introduction, headed sections, conclusion.

An alternative is to require such assignments to be formatted as presentations with slides. In this case, there is less actual writing, but the student will need to be careful with the choice of headings and notes to be shown on the slides, and with the formatting: size of font, line spacing, use of punctuation and so on.

Writing in class

After having explained the task, you are likely to send the students to do most of the writing on their own at home. However, it is useful to be able to vary this routine by occasionally doing shorter writing assignments in class. For example:

- **Collaborative planning.** Students plan their texts in pairs or small groups in class, before going off to do the actual writing alone. They later come together to compare results.

- **Five-minute writing.** Students have exactly five minutes – no more, no less – to write something in class. The time limitation usually increases concentration and is a useful quick way of providing extra writing experience.

- **Multiple contributions.** Students are given a topic and are asked to write a phrase, a word or a sentence on it at the top of a sheet of paper. They then pass the paper to their neighbour, who adds another line, continuing the idea which the first student has expressed (not just adding another sentence about the topic). The process continues until there are 5 to 15 contributions. Note that the paper remains open, not folded, so that every new writer can see all the previous contributions. The results are then read out to the class. The same can be done with a story: the first line is given, and students continue adding further events to the narrative.

Practical tips

1. **Length.** Give students a clear idea of how long you intend the composition to be. If they are writing on computers, then they can easily check the number of words; if not, an A4 page of double-spaced lines is about 300 words. As a rough guide, beginner classes can be asked to write about 50 words, intermediate classes between 100 and 200, and advanced classes 300 or more.

2. **Rewriting.** Get students to rewrite their compositions at least once: see Section 11.5 below.

3. **Collaborative writing.** Most writing is best done by students working on their own; it can be planned collaboratively, but if you ask students to do the actual writing together, the result will usually be that one of them does all the work and the other(s) is (are) passive! For collaborative editing using wikis, see Section 11.5 below.

11.5 Process writing

When they have mastered the basics, students need to progress and improve their writing. This can be helped to some extent by focused instruction on spelling and punctuation (see Section 11.6 below); however, the best way to promote students' writing ability is through the *process-writing* cycle: the experience of writing a first draft, getting feedback and rewriting. The main problems for teachers are how to help students write their first draft(s); and how to give effective feedback on these that will help them produce as good a final draft as possible.

First draft

No assessment

Students need to be aware that the first draft is not graded and nor are any other preliminary drafts (if the process-writing cycle is repeated more than once). The assessment is given only on the final draft.

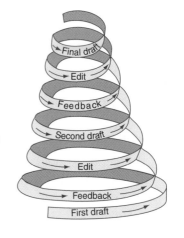

Not giving a grade for preliminary drafts has two important results. First, it lowers stress: students feel freer to experiment and to use language they are not quite sure of but want to try out: they know that they will not be penalized if they get it wrong and will be shown how to get it right. Second, they are highly motivated to implement feedback and improve in order to achieve a better final draft. (For some detailed guidance on later assessment of the finished assignment, see Unit 12: Assessment and testing, pp. 181–2.)

Support

Having given the assignment, we need to provide support in order to ensure that students write their first draft as well as possible. This support can include:

- providing key vocabulary that you think students might need or that they ask for;
- providing a 'model' text similar to the one required by the task;
- some discussion of possible content;
- guidance on the organization of texts of the relevant genre, and occasionally conventional formats (e.g. the placing of the address or date on a paper letter);
- allowing the beginning of the writing in class so that students have the opportunity to consult you as they write. They can then continue at home.

Feedback FAQs

Below are some Frequently Asked Questions (FAQs) that relate to feedback on process writing, an analysis of the basic problem in each case, and some advice.

1. **What should feedback be mainly on: language? content? organization?**
   The problem. When a student submits a piece of original writing, the most important thing about it is, arguably, its message: does it succeed in conveying the content required in the task? Then there is the organization and presentation: are the ideas arranged in a way that is easy to follow and interesting to read? Finally, there is the question of language forms: is the grammar, vocabulary, spelling and punctuation of an acceptable standard of accuracy?

   Many teachers are aware that content and organization are important but find themselves focusing mainly on language forms in their feedback, conveying the implicit message that these are what matter, sometimes to the exclusion of the other aspects. There are various reasons for this:

1. Mistakes in spelling or grammar catch the eye and seem to demand to be corrected; they are very difficult to ignore.
2. Students also usually want their language mistakes to be corrected (see Unit 7: Error correction, p. 93).
3. Language mistakes are far more easily and quickly diagnosed and corrected than problems of content and organization.

Advice. We should correct language mistakes. Our problem is how to do so without suggesting that this is our only (or main) basis for evaluation, and the only aspect which needs to be improved in a second draft. So corrections to language or style should be noted, but we should also take care to include comments on content and organization.

2. **Should all mistakes be corrected?**
The problem. If we accept that language (including punctuation) should be corrected, another problem arises: should *all* language mistakes be noted, even if there are so many that the page will be covered with corrections? If not, how do we judge which to relate to and which not?

Advice. The problem is one of potential conflict between two of our functions as teachers: language instruction versus support and encouragement of learning. Correcting mistakes is part of the language instruction, but too much of it can be discouraging and demoralizing. Also, over-emphasis on language mistakes can distract both students' and teachers' attention from the equally important aspects of content and organization, as noted above.

The answer is obviously some kind of compromise, which will vary according to the course objectives, class and student. We might correct only mistakes that actually affect meaning (i.e. might lead to misunderstanding or confusion), and/or those which are very basic. Or, of course, we can vary our response according to individual need. In any case, it is important to ask the students themselves (even younger ones!) how, and how much, they want to be corrected.

3. **Should we let students correct or give feedback on each other's written work?**
The problem. Correcting written work is very time-consuming, particularly with large classes. It helps to let students correct and edit each other's writing. They may not be able to identify all its good or bad qualities, but they will detect at least some of them. The problem is: will students feel uncomfortable correcting, or being corrected by, their classmates? Will they accept criticism (positive or negative) from each other?

Advice. Students on the whole, it appears, prefer to be corrected by the teacher rather than by their peers (see Unit 7: Error correction, p. 94). On the other hand, peer correction can be a time-saving and useful technique. Also, from the point of view of the 'peer-corrector', critical reading for style, content and language accuracy is a valuable exercise in itself. See *Practical tip 4* below for the use of wikis.

Practical tips

1. **Give feedback quickly.** Students get much greater benefit from your corrective feedback if it is given immediately, or very soon, after they have submitted their work. They should also be required to rewrite and re-submit within a fairly short time limit.

2. **Use 'track changes'.** Word processing on a computer means you can make changes or corrections and add comments to a document, while the original text can still be clearly seen. This is a very useful and time-saving way of correcting. Similar editing tools are available on PDF document readers as well.

3. **Use 'share documents'.** If you want your students to do multiple rewrites, then instead of sending documents by email attachment, try using a file hosting service that allows you to share documents online (for example, Windows Live Skydrive, Dropbox or Google Docs). Your student uploads a document and names you as a 'sharer': you can then annotate or correct it, and the student can immediately see what you have done and implement the corrections in a second version, which again you can see immediately. LMS programs also allow you to do this (see Unit 16: Classroom interaction, p. 241).

4. **Use wikis for collaborative editing.** The use of the wiki for editing makes the whole process much easier, more collaborative and more learner-friendly. A text is uploaded onto a class wiki, and then any student, including the author, can insert changes or suggestions, which can then be immediately checked by the teacher. Previous drafts are preserved in a 'history' file within the wiki, so you can always go back and check an earlier version.

11.6 Spelling and punctuation

Spelling

Contrary to general belief, the large majority of words in English (about 84%, according to Pinker, 1995) are actually spelt either phonetically or according to regular rules which are fairly straightforward to teach and practise.

This means that teaching students to spell correctly is not as difficult as you might have thought. And most of the words that have irregular spellings are very common ones which students learn anyway very early on: *the, to, what, one*. Other irregular spellings can be taught as the individual words come up.

Some basic spelling rules that are worth teaching are:
* the digraphs *th, ch (tch), sh, wh* and the less common *ph*;
* the final *e* which causes a previous vowel to be pronounced like its name, as in *late, these, time, hope, tune*;
* the letter *c*, usually representing the sound /k/, regularly pronounced /s/ before *i, e, y*;
* the suffixes *-tion, -sion, -ssion*;
* the prefix *al-* spelt with one *l* in words like *always*;
* the suffixes *al, ful* spelt with one *l*;
* the letter *g*, usually representing the sound /g/, but sometimes (not always) pronounced /dʒ/ before *e, i*;
* the *u* following *q*;

- *ck* instead of *c* at the end of one-syllable words;
- the combination *-all* in short words, pronounced /ɔ:l/;
- the combinations *-ight, -ought*.

Advice to students
As well as teaching these rules, it is quite useful to give students advice on some generalizations that apply to a variety of words.

- The letter *z* is rare: usually when you hear the sound /z/ it will be spelt with an *s*.
- The letter *j* is rare: usually when you hear the sound /dʒ/ it will be spelt *g* or *dg/dge*.
- The letter *k* is relatively rare: usually the sound /k/ is represented by *c* (except at the end of short words, where it is likely to be *ck*, see rule above).
- A double consonant usually causes the previous vowel to be pronounced short, not like its name, in words like **app**le, **fill**ing (compare **pap**er, **fil**ing). Hence the rule about doubling the consonant when adding the *-ed, -ing* suffix to short verbs, or making the comparative of short adjectives.

Practice tasks for spelling
Dictations. Dictate a set of words that you have taught which follow a rule the students have learnt. Other variations are as follows:
- Dictate a set of words that the students don't know yet, but whose spelling follows a rule they know, and challenge them to spell them right.
- Provide the students with the target words, but with some key letters missing. You read out the full words, and they fill in the missing letters.
- Dictate only the definition of a word, students write down the word.
- Provide the L1 translation, students write down the English word (only, obviously, if this is a monolingual class whose L1 you know).

For more variations on dictation, see *Dictation: New Methods, New Possibilities* (Davis & Rinvolucri, 1988).

Recall and share. Write the target items on the board, give students a minute to look at them, and then delete them. The students try to remember all of them, first individually and then sharing. Finally, you display all the items again. This is particularly useful for words spelt irregularly. (It is also an appropriate exercise for vocabulary consolidation: see Unit 5: Teaching vocabulary, p. 48.)

> ### Task
> Add three or more spelling activities to those given above. They can be ones you experienced as a student yourself, or from a book, or of your own creation.

Punctuation and capital letters
The most common punctuation signs are likely to be used in the students' L1 in a very similar way; for example, the full stop or period (.), the comma (,), the question mark (?) and the exclamation mark (!). There may, however, be marked differences in the way quotation marks (single or double, ' ' or " ") are used. There are also specific punctuation usages in some other languages which are different from English. Spanish adds an upside-down question mark at the beginning of

questions, for example, and German inserts a comma before the equivalent of 'that' in relative or noun clauses. If you are teaching a monolingual class whose language you know, you will probably be aware of such differences and will teach them as they occur in reading texts, or as errors in students' compositions.

Students whose L1 does not use the Latin script may have problems mastering the use of capital letters to mark the beginning of sentences and proper nouns: these will need some focused teaching at the early stages. See the *Practice tasks* below for some ideas.

Task

Think of another language you know. What similarities and differences in punctuation have you noticed between English and that language? What difficulties might a native speaker of this language have in learning English punctuation?

Practice tasks for pronunciation and capital letters

Inserting punctuation. Give students a text with no punctuation or capital letters and invite them to correct it. It is, perhaps, best with most classes to provide texts from which only specific items have been excluded. For example, there are no capital letters, or no commas; or no quotation marks in a conversation. Students are told which type of item is missing and to insert them where appropriate.

Capitals. Dictate a mixed list of common and proper nouns. Students write them down, inserting the initial capital where appropriate.

Dictation. Dictate a short and fairly simple text, where the spelling is not a problem but which needs quite a lot of punctuation and capital letters.

Recall and share. As in the 'recall and share' activity suggested for spelling, give the students two minutes to look at a text similar to the one described in the preceding dictation task (3). Then they try to reproduce it without looking back at it, with the punctuation and capitals accurately inserted. They can share their results before checking with the original.

Review

Answer as many as you can of the following questions, and then check answers by referring back to the relevant passages in this unit.

If you are working in a group, note down your own answers first alone, and then share with the other memebers of the group. Finally, check the answers together.

What is writing?

1. Can you recall at least four aspects of writing that distinguish it from the other four skills (other than the fact that it is written!)?
2. What are the implications of these differences for teaching?

Formal and informal writing

3. For what purposes might formal or informal writing be used?
4. Can you specify at least three important differences between formal and informal writing?

Beginning writing: the letters

5. What are some problems in learning to write English for students whose L1 uses a different writing system?
6. Why is it important for students to be able to type as well as handwrite?

Tasks that promote fluent writing

7. What kinds of tasks can be used to promote creative writing? And to give information?
8. Can you suggest two writing tasks that might be appropriate for elementary or intermediate classes, and two that are appropriate for more advanced ones?

Process writing

9. What is 'process writing'?
10. Suggest two problems associated with the giving of feedback on a preliminary draft, and then some solutions.

Spelling and punctuation

11. How irregular is English spelling?
12. Can you suggest two activities that might help students practise punctuation?

Further reading

Ferris, D. and Hedgcock, J. (2005) *Teaching ESL Composition: Purpose, Process, and Practice* (2nd edn), Mahwah, NJ: Lawrence Erlbaum Associates.
> (A useful practical guide to the teaching of mainly academic students, providing guidance on stimulating, supporting and providing feedback on student writing)

Hyland, K. (2003) *Second Language Writing*, New York: Cambridge University Press.
> (A particularly clearly written and accessible guide to the teaching of second-language writing)

Kroll, B. (2003) *Exploring the Dynamics of Second Language Writing*, Cambridge: Cambridge University Press.
> (An interesting collection of articles covering both research-based theory and practical topics such as providing feedback)

Shemesh, R. and Waller, S. (2000) *Teaching English Spelling*, Cambridge: Cambridge University Press.
> (Presents the basic rules of English spelling, with plenty of practical classroom activities to help learn them)

Truss, L. (2003) *Eats, Shoots and Leaves*, London: Profile Books Ltd.
> (A 'must read' for the English teacher: the basic rules of punctuation entertainingly presented)

12 Assessment and testing

12.1 Functions and types of assessment

Functions of assessment

The main reasons for trying to assess English proficiency are as follows:

1. **In order to evaluate students' overall level**: for example, we may want to specify their level according to the Common European Framework of Reference for Languages (CEFR), or let them or their parents know how good their English is, or register them for an appropriate course.

2. **In order to evaluate students' progress**: for example, we may need to give them a grade showing how much they have improved since the last assessment.

3. **In order to evaluate how well students have learnt specific material during a course**: for example, we may wish to assess how well they know a set of vocabulary items, a text or a grammatical feature.

4. **In order to evaluate students' strengths and weaknesses ('diagnostic' assessment)**: so that the students themselves can be aware of what they need to learn, and so that we can plan our teaching appropriately.

We may get added benefits from assessment procedures. For example, we might learn some useful information about successes or failures in our own teaching, and they may help us to predict how students will progress in the future ('prognostic' assessment).

Summative and formative assessment

The most formal and prestigious types of assessment, such as state school-leaving exams, or international exams such as IELTS, Cambridge English: First or TOEFL, are *summative* in nature: they provide only a grade, often expressed as a percentage, offer no specific feedback on aspects of performance, and are designed to summarize or conclude a period of learning. Summative assessment may be used as a basis for selection, as final school grades, or for acceptance into further education or employment. It may contribute little or nothing to ongoing teaching and learning; however, it is a part of the teacher's job and we need to know how to do it effectively. Items 1 and 2 of the list above are used mainly for summative purposes.

In contrast, most of the assessment that we carry out during a course (tests at the end of units in a coursebook, for example) is *formative* in nature: it may, like summative assessment, provide a grade in the form of a number, but it happens in the middle of a period of learning rather than at the end, provides clear feedback in the form of error correction and suggestions for improvement, and has the primary aim of enhancing future learning. For example, we might respond to a dictation with a grade like $\frac{6}{10}$ and the comment 'You need to work on the spelling of the words I have underlined' (corrective feedback). So the types of assessment described in items 3 and 4 above are essentially formative.

Summative assessment is normally carried out either by the class teacher or by an external authority: a ministry of education, for example, or an internationally recognized body such as the British Council or Cambridge Assessment (ESOL). In contrast, formative assessment is almost always done by the class teacher as part of the teaching process, though it may be supplemented occasionally by the student's own self-assessment (see below).

Assessment tools

Various tools are used to assess students' language ability.

Tests

Testing is by far the most common basis for assessment. The criterion for success is a fixed level which the student is expected to reach ('pass'); and the result is usually expressed as a percentage. Tests are relatively easy to design and check, take place at pre-set times and places, give clear-cut results, and are in general (rightly or wrongly) accepted as reliable bases for course grades.

Tests also have useful functions in the course other than the assessment outcome.

- They act as 'stations' in the course programme, marking off the ends of units.

- They encourage students to review material in preparation.

- They are motivating, in the sense that students will work hard to do them well.

- They can give a sense of achievement and progress.

- Their content often provides some useful learning or review.

- In classes with discipline problems, they often provide a welcome oasis of quiet, concentrated work during the lesson.

However, there are problems with tests as a basis for evaluation:

- They are not always valid (actually testing what they say they are). For example, a listening test based on long multiple-choice written questions may actually test reading rather than listening comprehension.

- They may not be reliable. For example, similar classes may get quite different results on the same tests because their teachers mark them differently.

- They are a one-off event which might not give a fair representation of the student's overall ability.

- They discriminate against students with test anxiety who perform badly under test conditions.

- If they are the basis for crucial summative assessment in the student's career, they can be extremely stressful for all students.

Alternative assessment

Other tools are available, sometimes termed 'Alternative assessment'. These may solve some of the problems associated with testing, but they raise others.

Teacher assessment. The teacher gives a subjective estimate of the student's level. This is based on the performance of the student over time in a wide range of tasks, and it takes into account aspects such as the student's effort and progress, or particular learning disabilities. On the other hand, it is inevitably subjective to some extent and may be seen by students, parents or school principals as unreliable.

Continuous assessment. The final grade is some kind of combination of the grades the student received for various assignments during the course. Again there may be a problem of subjectivity, as the grades are given by the teacher. Also, the assignments and criteria for the different grades may vary from class to class, which makes it difficult to achieve standardization between classes.

Self-assessment. The students evaluate their own performance, using clear criteria and grading systems. This is not very popular, even with students themselves, for summative assessment. And again there is the problem of subjectivity. However, for formative purposes, self-assessment can be very valuable, since it encourages students to reflect on and take responsibility for the evaluation of their own learning. It is particularly helpful when it is combined with teacher assessment and discussed in a tutorial.

Portfolio. The student collects examples of his or her own work over a long period to create a portfolio, which provides the basis for evaluation. This is a more student-oriented method of assessment, as although the teacher decides on the overall composition of the portfolio (for example, one essay, one test, one text comprehension assignment, etc.), the exact assignments that will go into it are chosen by the student. Portfolio assessment avoids the stress and 'one-off' problems of testing. It also provides a much broader basis for evaluation, though there is likely to be a disproportionate focus on writing. Portfolio assessment is widely used in secondary schools in Europe today. Its main disadvantage in practice is the amount of work for the teacher, who has to keep track of students' work on the portfolios during the year to ensure they collect all the required components, as well as read and assess the portfolios of entire classes.

> ### Task
>
> What experience do you yourself have of any of these assessment tools, as teacher or student? What comments would you add to the definitions and criticisms shown above?

12.2 Giving a grade

The most common practical problem relating to assessment that we face as teachers is how to decide the final grade of a student, whether it is at the end of a course, at the end of a term or at the end of a year.

Criteria

The first decision to be made is what standard you will use to judge your students' level: whether you are going to use criterion-, norm- or individual-referenced assessment.

Criterion-referenced assessment means that you judge the student according to some fixed criterion. This can be based on an estimation of what it is reasonable or desirable to demand from students according to their age, career, level, stage of a course, etc. The criteria might also be based on the levels of the CEFR, for example.

Norm-referenced assessment means that you evaluate the student's performance relative to what you would expect from the particular group.
In this case, a group of less advanced, or learning-disabled, students would be assessed according to different standards from those applied to an advanced student within the same school.

Individual-referenced assessment means that you relate the assessment of an individual student to his or her own previous performance, or to an estimate of his or her individual ability. You would give a student a high grade if he or she has worked hard and made impressive progress, even if by norm- or criterion-referenced standards the student might have received a fairly low one.

Components of the grade

Having decided what your criterion (or combination of criteria) will be, you then need to decide what *information* you will use as a basis for the grade. You may not have much choice: some schools have rules for their teachers about what the final grade must be based on. But if you have a choice, then it is probably best to take into account ongoing work as well as tests: whether a student has made an effort and progressed, whether he or she has consistently submitted homework assignments, has assembled all the components of a portfolio satisfactorily and so on. In some classes, particularly the younger ones, you may also want to include behaviour as a component: whether or not the student has been punctual, attentive and cooperative.

The use of such components in a grade is fairer than assessing students only on the basis of a one-off test, which may not, for reasons given earlier, provide a fair sample of what they can do. It also helps student motivation. This may not be very 'educational', but it is a fact of life: if we know that something is going to affect how we are assessed, then we are more likely to make an effort than if we know it is not. For example, if students know that completing homework assignments throughout the term accounts for 10% of their grade, they are more likely to do them.

We need to decide what weighting (percentage of the final grade) we will give to the different components: which means, of course, rather more work for us than just copying out the results of a test. For example:

> Final test or portfolio – 50%
> Class tests – 10%
> Ongoing class work and attentiveness – 10%
> Homework assignments – 10%
> Personal effort – 10%
> Overall progress since last assessment – 10%

In different situations, it might be appropriate to remove or change some of these criteria, or add others, or change the weighting. Your own pedagogical approach and student expectations will also make a difference.

Task

Think of a class you have taught or observed (or, perhaps, one you have been a student in). Do you think the components and weighting shown above would be suitable? If not, how would you change them?

How the grade can be expressed

How do you express the grade you give the student at the end of the course? There are various possibilities:

Percentages are probably the most common, though in different places the actual value placed on the different percentages may vary. For example, in some places 40% is a pass, in others it is 60%; some student populations consider 75% a high grade, others would think anything below 85% unsatisfactory. So you would need to find out how the different percentages are regarded at your school.

Letters, words or phrases, such as 'A' or 'B'; 'Good', 'Very good' 'Excellent' look a little less impersonal, less definitive than percentages; however, the students and other stakeholders (e.g. parents, employers) often 'read' them as definitive number-type grades, exactly as they read percentages.

Profiles are a totally different kind of expression of assessment, comprising a number of separate grades on different skills or sections of knowledge, so that there is a possibility of describing the performance of an individual student in more detail, showing his or her various strengths and weaknesses. So you might, for example, provide a rubric with categories such as reading, writing, speaking, listening, grammar, vocabulary, and give a grade, or remark, for each. This provides a more rounded view of the student's level, but obviously involves a lot more work for the teacher.

Evaluative comments, such as 'Well done! You have worked hard', without any expression of level of achievement, avoids the difficult and sometimes unpleasant job of actually having to give a grade; however, the institution will normally demand a grade, as will other stakeholders, such as parents. Students also, in my experience, want to see a grade: they need some kind of clear-cut evaluation of how well they are doing. So it is probably best in most contexts to give an indication of achievement through a grade, but accompany it with encouraging and constructive comments.

Task

Consider the way grades are awarded and expressed in a teaching context you are familiar with, either as a student or as a teacher. What would be your criticisms (positive or negative)? What improvements can you suggest?

Practical tips

1. **Tell students early on what your criteria are.** Right at the beginning of the term or course, make sure you explain to the students on what basis the grades are given: whether you are taking into account aspects of ongoing work, or only results of a final test. Don't leave it to the last minute: students should know from the start how they are going to be assessed.
2. **Discuss the grade with individual students.** If your class is not too big, and if time allows, try to set up individual meetings with students. Give them general feedback on their performance, tell them what grade you intend to give them, ask them what grade they consider they deserve; clarify and discuss any differences. You may sometimes change the grade after this consultation. This will remove the stress of not knowing what the final grade is until they get it in writing; and in some cases it may help you decide on a fair grade. If you are short of time, the meetings can be done in class time while the rest of the class is doing individual work.
3. **Keep grades private.** Don't make the grades public (unless your institution insists on it). Students usually prefer to be told privately what their grade is, and then choose themselves whether, and with whom, to share it.

12.3 Test design (1): testing accuracy

There are various types of test items for checking accurate usage of vocabulary, grammar, spelling and punctuation. You may already have come across some of them if you have read Unit 5: Teaching vocabulary or Unit 6: Teaching grammar. In this section you will find a list of the most common types of test items, with some notes on their advantages and disadvantages. For testing techniques for the assessment of listening or reading comprehension, or of spoken or written ability in general, see Section 12.4 below.

The test items below are normally used in conventional class tests given at the end of a teaching unit, term or year. They usually appear within a written test which includes several sections using different types of items.

Occasionally some of these test items may be used in an oral test, such as an interview. This provides the tester with information about how well the student can understand and produce the spoken forms. Interviews are, however, rather time-consuming as well as expensive, since testers need to be paid for their time. So schools with tight budgets tend to use written tests.

Some test items can be administered, answered and graded using the computer: but these are normally only ones that have a limited set of clear, predetermined right answers, such as multiple-choice, matching or gapfilling. See *Computer testing* on p. 178 below.

We need to take into account various considerations when selecting items to use for a particular test.

- **What will it tell me about the student's knowledge?** For example, will it reveal the student's ability to produce the item, or just show that they understand it? Will it provide evidence that the student can use the item in appropriate contexts or not?

- **How easy is it to compose?** Will it take me a long time to think up and write out the item? Is there a source (the coursebook, a website) which will provide me with ready-made items I can use?

- **How easy is it to check?** Does it require only a quick, objective check based on a single possible right answer, or will I need to use my own judgement in assessing the answer?

- **Can it be used in the design of a computer test?** Are the answers clear and objective enough to enable it to be administered and checked through a computer?

The test items that are listed below are divided into two groups: those which are conventionally used quite a lot and which you are likely to be familiar with; and those which are used less but have various useful functions that are worth considering.

Task

Choose five test items from the list below, and comment on them based on the questions above. Then read on.

Frequently used test items

1. **True/false.** This may either be in the form of a statement ('true' or 'false'), or as a question ('yes' or 'no').

> *Underline 'True' or 'False'.*
> a) London is the capital of France. True / False
>
> *Write 'Yes' or 'No'.*
> b) Is London the capital of France? _____

2. **Multiple-choice.** There is one correct option out of (usually) four.

> *Circle the right answer.*
>
> A person who writes books is called
> a) an engineer.   b) an accountant.   c) an author.   d) a baker.

3. **Gapfill.** The 'base form' of the word that is to fill the gap may or may not be provided; the placing of the gap may or may not be shown.

> *Complete the sentences.*
> a) They _____ (go) to Australia in 2007.
> Or
> b) The money was _____ from the bank. (steal)
> Or
> c) _____ you like action movies?
> Or
> d) I've seen that film. (never)

4. **Matching.** Each item is to be matched with one other.

> *Match words that mean the same.*
>
> a)   large   small
> b)   unhappy   many
> c)   a lot   big
> d)   little   sad

5. **Dictation.** The tester dictates a passage or set of words; the student writes them down.
6. **Focused cloze.** The target lexical or grammatical items are omitted from a passage.

> *Insert words in the past tense.*
>
> Beowulf 1.____**was**____ (be) a great warrior 1000 years ago. He 2.
> _____(win) many battles against monsters and dragons. Grendel
> _____ (be) a terrible monster from Denmark. He 3. _____
> (have) big teeth and he was very strong. Grendel 4. _____(not
> sleep) and 5. _____(not eat). He 6. _____(drink) blood. ...[1]

7. Transformation. This usually involves alterations such as changing the
   tense or voice (active/passive), or number (singular/plural).

> *Put into the past tense*:
> I go to school by bus.

8. Rewrite. A sentence is to be written that paraphrases the one provided.

> *Complete the second sentence so that it means the same as the first.*
>
> He came to the meeting in spite of his illness.
> Although ...
>
> _____

Less frequently used test items

9. Sentence completion. The student may complete the sentence any way
   he or she likes provided the language is acceptable.

> *Complete the sentence.*
>
> She will come to the party if ...

10. Translation. This may be either from the L1 into English, or from English
    into the L1.
11. Mistake correction

> *Correct the mistake.*
>
> *We talked to the man which is in charge of the project.

12. Wordsearch. The target items are hidden within a criss-cross of words
    within a grid, to be identified by the student.
13. Unscramble sentences. The sentences have words in jumbled order: the
    student has to write out the words in the correct order.

---

[1] Davis, F. and Rimmer, W. (2010) *Active Grammar 1* (p. 27). Cambridge: Cambridge University Press.

Comment

A characteristic of all the more **frequently used test items** is that they are easy to check. Most are also fairly easy to compose, with one notable exception (multiple-choice, see below).

1. **True/false** items check only receptive knowledge: the fact that students got the answer right does not indicate that they would be able to produce the target item themselves correctly or appropriately. And note that they have a fifty-fifty chance of getting it right even if they are guessing.

2. **Multiple-choice** may be used for the same testing purposes as true/false items and checks knowledge more reliably since it offers more options (there is only a 25% chance of getting it right by chance). Good multiple-choice questions, however, are surprisingly difficult to design. They often come out with more than one possible right answer, or no clear right answer at all, or one over-obvious right answer. Also, the punctuation and aligning of the 'stem' and 'options' can be tricky. Finally, less experienced test-writers tend to make the right answers the longest ones, which may give them away to students who are aware of this tendency.

3. **Gapfills**, again, test mainly receptive knowledge. You need to be careful to design a gapfill item so that there is only one right answer, or a very limited number of right answers, otherwise it becomes difficult to check. For this reason it is generally advisable to limit choice by including a root word in parenthesis or in a 'word bank'.

4. **Matching** can be used not only to elicit knowledge of synonyms, as shown in the example, but also for opposites, collocations and grammatical cohesion (appropriate sequence of tenses, for example). Design is not too difficult, but as with multiple-choice questions, you do need to take care that there is only one right 'match' for each item.

5. **Dictation** mainly tests spelling, sometimes punctuation and, perhaps surprisingly, listening comprehension (people can usually write things down accurately from dictation only if they understand them). It may supply some information on students' receptive knowledge of pronunciation, grammar and vocabulary. Note that when checking, you may have a problem deciding how much weight to attribute to different mistakes. If you are teaching a monolingual class whose language you know, you might use 'translation dictation': dictate a word or short text in the L1, the students write down the translation. But here again, there may be different possible right answers which you will need to take into account when checking.

6. **Focused cloze** can be used to test grammar, vocabulary, spelling or punctuation, depending on which items you choose to delete. Marking can be slightly less straightforward than for previous items: you may find it difficult sometimes to decide if a specific item is acceptable or not. If you insert multiple-choice options at each gap, composition is more time-consuming, but the marking becomes easier.

7. **Transformation** items are still in use, though less popular than they used to be. Their validity may be suspect: they check the ability of the student to

produce correct forms as transformations (to write, for example, *went* as the past of *go*), which is not the same as testing productive knowledge of grammar. A student may perform well on transformation items without knowing the meaning of the target structure or how to use it in context.

8. **Rewrite** tests the same sort of thing as transformation. However, it is likely to reflect more thorough knowledge of the target items since it involves paraphrasing the entire meaning of a sentence rather than just transforming a particular item. As with the focused cloze, you may occasionally find it difficult to decide if a specific answer is acceptable or not.

The **less frequently used test items** are not so popular for a variety of reasons.

9. **Sentence completion** is difficult to check, since there is often a very large number of possible right answers. Its big advantage is that it tests production: shows whether the student can produce correct sentences and use the target items in appropriate (though limited) contexts.

10. **Translation** is still frowned on by some teachers and methodologists, though far less than it was a generation ago. It is actually a useful technique in a monolingual class whose teacher also speaks the students' L1. The translation of a language item to or from English can give very quick and reliable information about what the student does or does not know, particularly when it involves entire units of meaning (phrases, sentences) within a known context. Items are fairly easy to design and may be more, or less, easy to check depending on how close and obvious the translations are.

11. **Mistake correction** is, again, something which many teachers feel uncomfortable with. There is always the worry that exposing students to a mistake in print might reinforce that mistake rather than correcting it. If used, it has to be very clear what the mistake is. One possibility is to cross out the wrong words (for example, '*We talked to the man ~~which~~ is in charge of the project') so the students only have to decide what words should replace them. Another is to write an 'insert' symbol ˄ where something is missing. But both design and checking are fairly straightforward.

12. **Wordsearch.** This is a fairly motivating test item for teenage or younger learners, though not so good for adults. It is a useful item to put at the end of a test to keep the faster workers busy while the others are finishing. But of course it does not provide information on the students' ability to produce the item or use it in context, and may not even tell us if they know the meaning; and it is extremely difficult for students with some forms of dyslexia. It can be produced and checked through computer programs (e.g. Word Search Maker: http://puzzles.about.com/od/wordsearches/tp/word-search-makers.htm). It is relatively easy to check.

13. **Unscramble sentences.** Most of the same positive and negative criticisms that apply to Wordsearch apply here too; though it is less attractive to learners and rather more difficult. It is particularly useful when testing aspects of grammar where word order is crucial – in questions, for example, or other structures that demand inversion.

Computer testing

The computer is very good at testing receptive knowledge and mechanical knowledge of forms (e.g. irregular past tenses) through dual- or multiple-choice, gapfills and matching items. There is online software for creating your own tests with those exercise types: see, for example, the Hot Potatoes website (http://hotpot.uvic.ca/). There is also a large number of 'test yourself' sites online, where students can test their own knowledge and get instant feedback: for example, Easy English (www.easyenglish.com/), or Learning English – Quizzes (www.bbc.co.uk/worldservice/learningenglish/quizzes/).

Computer software, however, is not yet able to assess students' ability to use the target language items to express themselves in longer, more open responses, such as sentence completion. For this kind of assessment, there is at the moment no alternative to tests composed (or adapted) and assessed by the teacher.

Practical tips

1. **Clarity.** Make sure the instructions for each item are clear. They should usually include an example with its solution. For low-level, monolingual classes, it may be appropriate to have the instructions in the students' L1, as well as in English.

2. **'Doability'.** The test should be quite doable: not too difficult, with no trick questions. It's sometimes difficult to judge the doability of your own tests, so it's worth asking a colleague to read through and check they can answer the questions before you give the test to students.

3. **Marking.** Decide exactly how you will assess each section of the test, and how many points you will give each out of the total. Make the marking system as simple as you can, and inform the students what it is: write in the number of points assigned to each section on the test sheet itself.

4. **Interest.** Try to choose interesting content and tasks in order to make the test more motivating for the students.

5. **Varied level.** Lower-level students should feel that they are able to do a substantial part of the test, while the higher-level ones should have a chance to show what they know. So make the earlier items fairly easy, and define one or more of the more difficult ones as optional. (For more discussion of tests and worksheets for mixed-level classes, see Unit 19: Learner differences (2): teaching heterogenous (mixed) classes.)

6. Occasionally, let students compose their own tests. Students can be told exactly what you intend to test, and then write their own test items, individually or in groups. You then collect these items, correct them if necessary, and use some or all of them as a basis for the test. This is in itself an excellent review of the test material and also reduces test anxiety.

12.4 Test design (2): testing comprehension and fluency

Tests that assess comprehension through listening and reading, and fluency and accuracy in speaking and writing, rather than knowledge of specific language items, need a different set of testing techniques.

Listening comprehension

This is usually tested as a skill on its own, although in real life it normally occurs in conjunction with speaking (for discussion of the teaching, rather than testing, of listening skills, see Unit 8: Teaching listening). A test which involves both speaking and listening is the interview, described under *Speaking* later in this section.

Dictation and repetition. As mentioned previously, a student can only normally write down more than a word or two accurately from dictation if he or she has understood it. The same applies to oral repetition. So one way of assessing listening comprehension at the most basic level is to ask students to repeat what they have heard, either in writing or orally. They should, of course, hear the source text more than once.

Text + comprehension questions is probably the most common form of listening comprehension test. The student hears a text, usually two or three times, and is asked to answer questions on it. The questions may relate to gist or details of content. For convenience of checking, they are very often multiple-choice. See, for example, the listening task shown on p. 54, which is a fairly typical test format. This kind of test can easily be computerized using audio texts followed by questions with a limited possible set of right answers.

Taking notes is a useful test of listening comprehension, but one that demands, of course, the ability to write quickly and clearly as well as understand what is heard. It is a component of some international examinations, such as the Cambridge English: Key and Cambridge English: Preliminary.

Reading comprehension

Ideas for teaching students to cope with reading texts have been discussed in Unit 3: The text, and the promotion of reading fluency in general in Unit 10: Teaching reading. This section deals only with tools for **assessment** of reading comprehension.

Reading aloud of single words can, obviously, show only that the student can decode the letters accurately; however, reading aloud of a text with appropriate prosody (pause, intonation, stress) can be done well only if the text is understood. So reading a text aloud is a very easily designed and administered test of reading comprehension, in very much the same way as dictation and repetition are tests of listening comprehension. It is, on the other hand, time-consuming because it has to be done through one-to-one interaction with the teacher. The student should usually have time to read, reread and prepare before such a test: only at very advanced levels can we expect students to sight-read competently.

Text + comprehension questions, as with listening, is the most common format of the reading comprehension test. The students study a text and answer questions, which are commonly gapfills and multiple-choice but may also be open, inviting the students to respond in their own words.

Cloze is another way of checking general reading comprehension. Unlike 'focused cloze', where specific target items are deleted, the reading comprehension cloze test normally has words deleted at regular intervals (commonly every seventh word), so it is unpredictable whether these will be grammatical or lexical items. However, it is possible to be flexible with this point.

Jumbled paragraphs. Students are given a text with the paragraphs in the wrong order, and they have to sort them out. Their success depends not only on their comprehension of the content, but also on their awareness of the typical discourse structure of the genre and of cohesive devices (use of pronouns, connectors such as *however, moreover*, discourse markers such as *first, on the one hand, finally*).

Speaking

The assessment of a student's ability to speak fluently, accurately and appropriately is particularly problematic for two reasons. One is practical: unlike the other three skills, speaking can only normally be tested in individual (or, occasionally, pair- or small-group) interaction. This means that it takes a long time to test an entire class, and it is expensive to pay the testers. The other problem is reliable assessment: there cannot possibly be 'one right answer', so there is no possibility of objective or computer-based grading. Moreover speech is fleeting; it cannot usually be 'reread' and reconsidered for assessment. It is also difficult to retain speech in the memory long enough to assess its level. It can help to record the student's speech and then listen to it again later, but this increases the time and expense even more.

The use of scales of standards, or rubrics can help to solve the problem of reliability by making sure that there are clear criteria for the different possible grades. Here is an example, assuming that the test is based on an interview (see below).

The following are some common formats used in oral testing:

1	Does not speak at all
2	Single-word responses to interviewer cues; difficult to understand.
3	Communicates in brief, hesitant phrases; often difficult to understand; only speaks in response to cues from interviewer.
4	Uses short sentences, and communicates limited messages; can give slightly longer responses to interviewer cues.
5	Can use longer sentences and convey clear messages; occasional hesitations; able occasionally to show initiative and prolong an exchange with interviewer.
6	Speaks fluently and clearly; engages in a cooperative dialogue with interviewer; takes initiative.

Interview consists of a conversation between two people. It is the most common context for speech in daily life and therefore should provide useful and reliable evidence of the ability of the student to converse in English. It should be noted that it does in fact test listening comprehension as well as speaking. Its main disadvantage is the problem of attention for the interviewer who has to initiate and maintain a conversation as well as assessing. With an unwilling or shy interviewee, this can be very difficult. The problem can be avoided by having one person interview and another assess, but the expense of two testers is not acceptable in most places.

Picture description is particularly suitable for younger learners or beginners. The student describes a picture or a series of pictures. It is easier for the tester, who does not have to initiate conversation and can devote his or her attention to assessing the student's performance.

Presentation is a longer, more advanced procedure. The student is asked to present an extended description, explanation or other oral account, while the tester simply listens and assesses. The problem here is that students may memorize their presentations in advance, which gives no idea of their ability to compose and deliver spontaneous speech. An alternative is to give the student a topic, two minutes to prepare, and then ask them to speak about it for a minute or two.

Group or pair discussions can be used in order to assess the speaking ability of two or more students at the same time, while the tester simply sits at the side and listens. This possibly saves time, but there is always the chance that the less assertive students, however good their spoken English, may not get sufficient opportunities to speak. Discussion needs to be skilfully led to ensure that everyone gets a reasonable chance to participate.

Writing

A written assignment used for assessment purposes can of course be done on a computer, in which case students can use computer tools to check their spelling and grammar. Some teachers prefer not to let students use computers when doing writing tests for this reason. However, in my opinion, the use of such tools cannot disguise poor writing ability; and in any case since much, if not most, English writing is now done with these tools available, it does not make sense to exclude them from tests.

A trickier problem with using computers is the possibility that students will copy-paste passages – or, indeed, full essays – from the Internet. However, it should be possible to make sure that your students do not have internet access. You can usually tell if the writing is not at the same level as writing assignments you have received from the same students previously; and they should also be aware that whole texts copied from the Internet can usually be fairly easily identified through search engines.

Assessing free writing is very difficult. We do not have the problem of the fleeting nature of the input, as in speaking, but we do need to assess various aspects: accuracy, coherent organization, content and so on. How much weight should be given to each? The suggested rubrics shown on the next page are adapted from a variety of assessment scales from different sources (e.g. Weir & Roberts, 1994) and are appropriate for writing at an intermediate or advanced level.

Compositions are probably the most common form of tests of writing skills at intermediate or advanced level. The student is given a topic, or sometimes a genre, communicative purpose and target audience (see, for example, the set of writing tasks listed in Unit 11: Teaching writing, p. 158), and asked to write a composition of a set length.

Brief descriptions and dialogues can be used to test writing at elementary level. The student is given a picture to describe, or the beginning of a dialogue to continue with a set number of exchanges. Care has to be taken when selecting the picture or writing the beginning of the dialogue to limit the lexical and grammatical knowledge required to do the test.

Level	Content	Organization and coherence	Vocabulary and spelling	Grammar and punctuation
5	Clear and appropriate content	Content well organized and coherent	Wide range of vocabulary, very few errors	Wide range of structures, very few minor errors
4	Appropriate content, but could be more fully extended	Logical organization, occasional misuse of cohesive devices	Adequate vocabulary, occasional spelling errors	A variety of structures, occasional errors
3	May be some missing or irrelevant content	Somewhat disorganized, repetitive, sometimes incoherent	Minimally adequate vocabulary, errors in spelling, etc. that may impede communication	A limited range of structures, may make errors that impede communication
2	Limited range of ideas, largely irrelevant	Does not organize ideas logically	Limited range of vocabulary; lexical errors may lead to incomprehensibility	Errors in grammar and punctuation predominate, leading to incomprehensibility
1	Content is completely unrelated to the topic	Disorganized and incoherent	Can only use a few isolated, simple words	Most of the grammar is erroneous
0	Writes text copied from elsewhere or memorized, or nothing.			

Action task

Download two sample tests of listening, reading, speaking or writing at different levels from the Internet: either internationally accredited ones like the ESOL, TOEFL or IELTS tests; or national school-leaving English exams. Which of the above test types are used and which not? Are there further testing techniques not mentioned here which you found in the exams you looked at?

12.5 Administering tests in class

In practice most tests are actually run by the teacher in his or her own class, and it is important to know how to administer them. The test experience can be a frightening one for students; even those not badly affected by test anxiety may perform less well under test conditions, thus not providing a fair sample of their knowledge and abilities. It is important for students to feel that, although we have to assess their performance and will be as fair as we can in doing so, we are 'on their side' and want them to do as well as possible. These are practical pedagogical issues: this brief section is therefore based mainly on a series of tips.

Practical tips

1. **Inform your students about the test well in advance.** Don't suddenly announce the test a day or two before it, and don't do 'surprise tests'. Tell them exactly when it will be and how long it will take. Let them have enough time to prepare themselves, and review any material they need to.

2. **Allot some class time to preparation.** If the test is based on particular material, don't leave all the review for homework. Lead some focused review in lessons, and give some class time for individual preparation.

3. **Provide, or review, essential information about the test as you present it.** You may need to remind students about the test content, format and marking system before giving out the papers, and sometimes run through the instructions with them after doing so in order to make sure that everything is clear – as well as wishing them good luck!

4. **Help students with instructions.** You may find that you need to provide individual weaker students with some quiet help with understanding instructions.

5. **Check and return tests as soon as you can.** This is so that you can discuss specific points while the test is still fresh in the students' minds.

Review

Answer as many as you can of the following questions, and then check answers by referring back to the relevant passages in this unit.

If you are working in a group, note down your own answers first alone, and then share with the other members of the group. Finally, check the answers together.

Functions and types of assessment
1. What is the difference between 'formative' and 'summative' assessment?
2. What are some disadvantages of the test as an assessment tool?
3. What other assessment tools might be used in English courses?

Giving a grade
4. What is the difference between criterion-, norm- and individual-referenced assessment?
5. Suggest some ways of expressing the assessment of a student's achievements at the end of a course, other than as a percentage.

Test design (1): testing accuracy

6. What are some important criteria for the selection of test items?
7. What are the advantages and disadvantages of multiple-choice test items?
8. What other kinds of test items can you recall? Try to remember at least six.

Test design (2): testing comprehension and fluency

9. In what different ways might we test reading comprehension?
10. Suggest two problems with testing speaking? What can help?
11. When assessing a written composition, what are some of the main aspects, other than correct grammar and vocabulary, that we should evaluate?

Administering tests in class

12. Suggest some ways in which we can mitigate test anxiety.

Further reading

Bachman, L. (1990) *Fundamental Considerations in Language Testing*, Oxford: Oxford University Press.

(A good summary of the basic theoretical concepts and terminology associated with testing and their practical implications)

Chapelle, C. A. and Douglas, D. (2006) *Assessing Language through Computer Technology*, Cambridge: Cambridge University Press.

(Discusses practical issues associated with computer testing, and provides guidance for teachers wishing to use it)

Cohen, A. D. (1994) *Assessing Language Ability in the Classroom* (2nd edn), Boston: Heinle & Heinle.

(Discusses the various methods of assessing language, with particular attention paid to alternative methods such as self-assessment and portfolio assessment)

Hughes, A. (2003) *Testing for Language Teachers* (2nd edn), Cambridge: Cambridge University Press.

(Criteria for good test design, an overview of test items and guidance on the testing of younger learners)

McKay, P. (2006) *Assessing Young Language Learners*, Cambridge: Cambridge University Press.

(This deals with mainly practical issues associated with assessment of young learners)

Websites

Hot Potatoes accessible from: http://hotpot.uvic.ca/

Word Search Maker accessible from: http://puzzles.about.com/od/wordsearches/tp/word-search-makers.htm

Easy English accessible from: www.easyenglish.com/

Learning English – Quizzes accessible from: www.bbc.co.uk/worldservice/learningenglish/quizzes/

13 The syllabus

13.1 What is a syllabus?

A syllabus is a document which presents information on what topics or content are to be covered in a course of study. For example, it may present information on what is to be taught

- in order to reach levels specified internationally (e.g. the CEFR);

- in a national school system;

- in order to pass a particular examination, for example Cambridge English: First;

- in a specific course (no matter what materials are used);

- in a specific coursebook.

Syllabuses may be *synthetic* or *analytic*. Synthetic syllabuses provide a set of isolated language items (grammatical structures or lexical items, for example). The learner is asked to learn these separately and then combine them to create or understand meaningful phrases or sentences in order to deal with language in context. Analytic syllabuses work the other way round. They describe communicative abilities, tasks or functions (conveying simple information, for example, or understanding the main points of a text). These can then be analysed, and the required words or structures are taught as an outcome rather than as a starting point. See the description of the situational or topic-based syllabus, described in Section 13.2 below, as an example of an analytic syllabus.

Basic features of a syllabus

A syllabus is essentially a list that specifies all the things that are to be taught in a course. It is therefore comprehensive. The actual components of the list may be content items (words, grammatical features, topics), or process ones (tasks) or communicative 'can-dos' (standards). The items are ordered, usually with components that are considered easier or more essential earlier, and more difficult and less important ones later.

The syllabus has clear objectives, usually explained in an introduction. These objectives are then used as the basis for selecting and ordering the components.

Another characteristic of the syllabus is that it is a public document. It can be read not only by teachers who are expected to implement it, but also by the consumers (learners, their parents or employers), by the relevant authorities (inspectors, school principals), by other interested members of the public (researchers, people involved in teacher-training courses). So a syllabus observes the principle of accountability: the writers of the syllabus are answerable to their target audiences for the quality of their document.

There are further components that are displayed by some syllabuses and not others. Some syllabuses define the time frame, for example requiring that certain items should be dealt with in the first year, others in the second, etc. A particular approach or methodology may also be specified. Some may list recommended materials (coursebooks, visual materials or supplementary materials) for all or some of the course.

To summarize, a syllabus

1. consists of a comprehensive **list** of content items (e.g. words, structures, topics), or process items (e.g. tasks);

2. is **ordered** (easier, more essential items first);

3. has **explicit objectives** (usually expressed in the introduction);

4. is a **public document**, and therefore **accountable**;

5. may indicate a **time schedule**;

6. may indicate a **preferred methodology** or approach;

7. may recommend **materials**.

Action task

Look at an English-language syllabus used in a local teaching context. Check how the different basic elements (1, 2, 3, 4 in the list above) are implemented in it. Which, if any, of the optional elements (5, 6,7) are included?

13.2 Types of language syllabus

A number of different kinds of syllabuses are used in English language teaching: the main types are listed below. The last two (standards-based and multi-strand) are most commonly used today. The others have been influential in the development of theory about syllabus design, and you may occasionally come across them. Most of them are included in multi-strand syllabuses.

The structural, or grammatical, syllabus

This is based on a list of grammatical structures and items, such as the present tense, definite and indefinite articles, comparison of adjectives. It is the most traditional syllabus type but is still in use in many places. It is particularly convenient for coursebook design: each unit has a grammatical feature as its primary jumping-off point, and texts and tasks are selected or composed that relate to it, either directly (as in grammar explanations and exercises) or indirectly (as in communicative activities or texts where the grammar comes up incidentally).

Some grammatical syllabuses also include a core list of vocabulary (see *The lexical syllabus* below) and may add other components as well: it is often the primary basis for a multi-strand curriculum as described later in this section.

The structural syllabus has been criticized by some on the assumption that it is likely to lead to an over-emphasis on accuracy at the expense of meaningful communication. In fact it is perfectly compatible with an overall communicative approach (see Unit 6: Teaching grammar, and Ellis, 1993).

For an example, see the extract below from a structural syllabus proposed for the Cambridge ESOL KET exam:
(www.cambridge.org/servlet/file/EIM_L1_PED_KETStructuralSyllabus. pdf?ITEM_ENT_ID=621530&ITEM_VERSION=1&COLLSPEC_ENT_ID=7)

MODALS
can (ability; requests; permission)
could (ability; polite; requests)
would (polite requests)
will (future)
shall (suggestion; offer)
should (advice)
may (possibility)
have (got) to (obligation)
must (obligation)
mustn't (prohibition)
need (necessity)
don't have to (lack of necessity)

TENSES
Present simple: states, habits, systems, processes and with future meaning
Present continuous: present actions and future meaning
Present perfect simple: recent past with *just*, indefinite past with *yet*, *already*, *never*, *ever*; unfinished past with *for* and *since*
Past simple: past events
Future with *going to*
Future with *will* and *shall*: offers, promises, predictions, etc.

The lexical syllabus

This comprises a list of lexical items (for example, *girl, happily, go away*), sometimes including multi-word expressions (for example, *in any case, call it a day*) and collocational links (for example, *take + a decision, hard + work*). It relates to grammar also, and so includes items such as *that* or the suffix *-ing*, but treats them in very much the same way as a lexical item. An extract from the lexical syllabus designed as part of the CEFR follows: (http://tvo.wikispaces.com/file/view/20386024-Common-English-Lexical-Framework.pdf.)

BNL	HeadWord	A1	A2	B1	B2	C1	C2
1	blue	blue			blues		bluish
1	board	board, boards			boarding	boarded	boarder, boarders
1	boat	boat, boats	boating		boatmen		
1	body	body	bodies			bodily	
1	book	book, booklet, books		booklets			
1	both	both					
1	bottom	bottom					bottoms
1	break	break, broke, broken	breaking, breaks	unbroken		breakers	
1	bridge	bridge	bridges				

The situational and topic-based syllabuses

The situational syllabus takes real-life contexts of language use as its basis: sections are headed by names of situations or locations such as 'Eating a meal' or 'In school'. A variation of this, the topic-based syllabus, lists particular topics such as 'Animals' or 'The family'. In either case, a fairly clear set of vocabulary items, and sometimes grammatical features, is indicated, which may be specified.

Both situational and topic-based syllabuses are particularly suitable for courses in English for Specific Purposes: tourism, business, etc. Such syllabuses have obvious advantages as the basis for coursebook design, and this is, indeed, their main use in practice. Here is an extract from a topic-based syllabus for a business coursebook, *English for Business Studies* (Mackenzie, 2009).

> **Management**
> • Management
> • Work and motivation
> • Company structure
> • Managing across cultures
> • Recruitment
> • Women in business
> **Production**
> • The different sectors of the economy
> • Production
> • Logistics
> • Quality
> **Marketing**
> • Products
> • Marketing
> • Advertising

The functional-notional syllabus

Notions are concepts that language can describe. General notions may include things like *number, time, place* and *colour*. Specific notions look more like vocabulary items: *man, woman, afternoon. Functions*, in contrast, are things you can do with language: purposes or outcomes of a specific language use; examples include *identifying, denying, promising*.

The functional-notional syllabus was an early attempt to create an appropriate syllabus for the communicative approach. The idea was to get away from a focus on correct forms and move towards the use of language to express meanings. An example is shown below. Today it is mainly used as part of a standards-based syllabus (see *The standards-based syllabus* below).

Below are some functions listed in *Threshold 1990* (Van Ek & Trim, 1990), a precursor of the modern CEFR curriculum.

> 1 Imparting and seeking factual information
>   1.1 reporting (describing and narrating)
>   1.2 correcting
>   1.3 asking
>   1.4 answering questions

And some notions, from the same publication:

1. personal identification
2. house and home, environment
3. daily life
4. free time, entertainment
5. travel

The standards-based syllabus

A standards-based syllabus describes what learners should be able to do at specific levels, often through 'can-do' statements. The standards can be divided into functional areas of language use: usually the four skills of listening, speaking, reading and writing, but also possibly wider, more communicative categories such as 'social interaction' or 'access to information'. Within these categories, the standards are often defined as functions such as 'greeting' or 'expressing agreement or disagreement'.

The CEFR is probably the best-known standards-based syllabus, but this type is also often used in the United States. Here are some extracts from the Michigan English Language Proficiency Standards for K-12 Schools.

> (www.michigan.gov/documents/Draft_ELP_Standards_Benchmarks_att_A_10-03_76961_7.pdf)

Michigan English Language Proficiency Standards	
Domain	English Language Proficiency Standards
Listening	Follow simple and complex directions Understand spoken English to participate in social contexts Identify main ideas and supporting details from spoken English Identify the meaning of vocabulary in the content areas Identify speaker attitude and point of view Make inferences and predictions
Speaking	Use spoken language for daily activities within and beyond the school setting Engage in conversations for personal expression and enjoyment Use spoken English and non verbal communication in socially and culturally appropriate ways Use English to interact in the classroom Provide and obtain information; express and exchange opinions Demonstrate comprehensible pronunciation and into nation for clarity in oral communication Present information, concepts, and ideas to an audience of listeners on a variety of topics Use strategies to extend communicative competence
Reading	Recognize concepts of print literacy Demonstrate phonological awareness and the relationship of listening/speaking to decoding Build vocabulary to develop concepts Understand and use grammatical rules of English to improve comprehension Read and demonstrate comprehension of main ideas and supporting details Apply reading skills in social and academic contexts Read for research purposes Make inferences, predictions, and conclusions from reading Analyze style and form of various genre Identify author's voice, attitude, and point of view
Writing	Use conventions and formats of written English Use grammatical conventions of English Write using appropriate vocabulary choice and variation Construct sentences and develop paragraphs to organize writing supporting a central idea Use the writing process to produce written products Use various types of writing for specific purposes Use multiple sources to extend writing Use tone and voice to engage specific audiences

The standards-based curriculum is commonly used at national or international level and can be used to assess the level of individual students. However, it has been found rather difficult to use as a basis for course or coursebook design because it is analytic (see Section 13.1 above for a definition of analytic and synthetic syllabuses) and does not specify which particular language items (pronunciation, grammar, vocabulary) should be taught.

The mixed or multi-strand syllabus

Increasingly, modern syllabuses are combining different aspects in order to be as comprehensive and helpful as possible to teachers and learners. Many people have come to feel that one kind of syllabus is unlikely to answer the needs of all those involved in using it: the researchers, the education authorities or heads of institutions, the teachers, the materials writers, the assessors and, of course, the students themselves.

Multi-strand design may come about through two main routes:

1. Structural syllabuses did not answer the needs of teachers and test-writers looking for more communicative and meaning-based components. So syllabus writers first added a lexical syllabus, and then components such as topics, situations and communicative functions, notions and communicative 'can-dos' in the four skills.

2. Some modern standards-based syllabuses were criticized by teachers and materials writers who felt they needed to know the actual language items to be taught. These were then added as separate 'strands'.

In the following example, you can clearly see the different strands: functions, notions and standards in the first column; grammar and vocabulary in the second; situations and topics in the third; and an added component in the fourth column providing opportunities for reflection, further learning and cultural aspects taken from the coursebook *English Unlimited* (Rea, Clementson, Tilbury & Hendra, 2010).

Goals	Language	Skills	Explore
Media around the world	**Vocabulary** Habits and preferences p6 Talking about facts and information p8 Evaluating and recommending p9 Describing books and TV shows p10	**Listening** TV and radio habits p6 What's on TV? p7 Four people describe books and TV shows p10	**Across cultures** Intercultural experiences
talk about entertainment media talk about habits express preferences talk about information media evaluate ideas make recommendations describe a book or TV show		**Reading** Can you believe what you read? p8	**Writing** write a book review for a website
	Grammar Talking about the present p7	**Writing and speaking** Media habits p7	
Target activity Describe a book or a TV show	**Pronunciation** Common pairs of words 1 p7	**Speaking** Is it true? p9 Make recommendations p9	**Look again** Spelling and sounds: /f/
Good communication	**Vocabulary** Expressing opinions p15 It's + adjectives p15 Using the Internet p16 Expressing probability p17 Speculating about consequences p18	**Listening** Keeping in touch p14 Eric and Graham discuss a management decision p18	**Keywords** so, such
talk about methods of communication express opinions talk about using the Internet speculate about the present and future speculate about consequences		**Reading** Online friendships p16 *Email Survival Guide* p18	**Speaking** ask for clarification clarify what you're saying
	Grammar will, could, may, might p17	**Speaking** Express opinions p15 Socialising online p17 Is it likely? p17	
Target activity Discuss an issue	**Pronunciation** Sentence stress p15		**Look again** Spelling and sounds: /t/

Look at an English-language syllabus used in a teaching context with which you are familiar. Can you classify it, according to the types listed above? If it is multi-strand, what are the main components?

13.3 Using an approved syllabus

By 'approved syllabus', I mean a published document which is approved by an authority (rather than the specific syllabus that may appear in a coursebook).

How might you use an approved syllabus? Would you keep to it carefully, consulting it regularly? Or would you refer to it only rarely, to check yourself? Or would you ignore it?

Here are statements by five teachers describing how they use an approved syllabus.

Task

Look at the five statements below. If you are teaching at the moment, which one do you most identify with? If you are not teaching yet, which one do you imagine will be closest to your future teaching situation? Do you have any comments on or criticisms of the others?

Anna: The syllabus of my language school is very comprehensive. It includes grammar, vocabulary, functions, notions, situations, and it refers to material I can use. I use it all the time and could not do without it. When preparing a class or series of classes, I go first to the syllabus, decide what to teach next according to its programme, plan how to combine and schedule the components I have selected, and take the relevant books or materials from the library as I need them.

Joseph: I teach English for Academic Purposes, in a university. There is a syllabus approved by the institution, rather like Anna's, but we don't have to use it. I simply ignore it, because I prefer to do my own thing, based on the needs of my students. I use materials and activities from different sources (books for teachers, textbooks, supplementary materials, literature) to create a rich and varied programme that is flexible enough to be adapted to student needs during the course.

Maria: I teach in a state school, and was trained in a state institution. They made us read the national syllabus in my teacher-training course, but I haven't looked at it since. What for? I use an approved coursebook which lays out all the language I have to teach as well as giving me texts, exercises and ideas for activities. I assume the Ministry would not have authorized the book if it didn't follow the syllabus, so there's no reason for me to double-check if I'm teaching the right things.

Lilly: I have the syllabus, and look at it occasionally, but mostly I work from the coursebook that my school chose for the class. It's just that sometimes I get a bit fed up with the coursebook and want to do something different. So I do my own thing for a bit, and then use the syllabus as a retrospective checklist, to make sure I'm still reasonably on target with the content. After all, I am being employed to teach a certain syllabus, so I can't stray too far.

David: I'm a new teacher, just qualified, and not very confident of my knowledge of English. The school can't afford books for all the children, so I'm supposed to base my lessons on the syllabus, and create my own lessons and materials. But the syllabus isn't very helpful to me: it's all about general standards ('the pupils at this level will be able to hold simple conversations'), and I really need to know what language to teach! Luckily I have very helpful colleagues.

How teachers use the syllabus varies very widely between different countries and institutions, and depends on financial resources as well as on teaching approach.

In situations where there are enough resources to invest in creating very detailed syllabuses and buying a wide variety of teaching materials, teachers may find it most effective to work mainly from the syllabus, using specific materials as they need them, as Anna does.

In other relatively affluent settings, there may be a policy of allowing teachers complete freedom in designing their teaching programme. In these cases the syllabus may be non-existent or ignored, and teachers like Joseph may develop new, independent programmes, based mainly on their preferences and students' needs. A competent and creative teacher working with mature students can turn this into a unique, exciting and satisfying teaching/learning experience. However, in most contexts the disadvantages outweigh the advantages. Apart from an enormous amount of work for the teacher, the abandonment of a carefully pre-planned syllabus may result in significant gaps in the language content. This may not matter so much in a situation where the students are already very advanced, or if the students are studying in an English-speaking country and have plenty of exposure to the language outside the classroom. In other situations, however, it may make it very difficult to plan a systematic and effective teaching programme. Also, the lack of clear structure may make it difficult for teacher or learners to feel a sense of progress or evaluate learning outcomes.

When only one coursebook per student can be afforded, the book tends to take over the function of a syllabus, particularly if (as in the case of Maria) the book has been recommended for use by the same authority that drew up the syllabus. Here the use or non-use of the syllabus to supplement the book depends on the personality of the teacher, and his or her willingness to put in extra effort – as exemplified by Lilly.

There are some situations, like David's, where even one book per student is an unknown luxury. In such cases the teacher needs to rely heavily on the syllabus. If, as in David's case, the syllabus does not provide very helpful guidance, then the teacher has to resort to the help of colleagues or his or her own creativity. Note that sometimes the syllabus has an extra role to play: as a source of information and reassurance for teachers who are not confident of their own knowledge of English. In such cases a multi-strand syllabus is far more helpful than a standards-based one.

13.4 Evaluating the syllabus

A fairly frequent situation these days is that new English-language syllabuses, often quite different from previous ones, are introduced by a ministry of education or by some other authority in an institution or group of institutions. If you are teaching in the same country you were educated in, you may well find you are teaching from a syllabus that is quite different from the one in use when you were a student.

The vital question is: has this new syllabus improved English language teaching and learning? After it has been given a fair chance to 'prove itself' (perhaps five years or more), the new syllabus needs to be evaluated, both by the authority which approved it in the first place, and by the teachers themselves.

Syllabuses are sometimes evaluated by checking whether overall proficiency among students has risen since its introduction, as measured by exam results. There is a problem with this, of course, as there may be all sorts of reasons for rises or falls in exam results: changes in the difficulty of the exams, the publication of more/less effective course materials, or a demographic change in the student population caused by an influx of immigrants, for example.

Perhaps a better way is to ask the people who are involved in the implementation of the syllabus in the field: the teachers, teacher trainers, exam designers, coursebook writers and the students themselves.

Even if a full evaluation is not initiated by the relevant authority, it is important for the teachers themselves to reflect on how the syllabus is working in their own situation. This may be done through the use of evaluation sheets such as the one below. The respondent gives each criterion a rating from 0 to 5, 0 being 'strongly disagree' and 5 'strongly agree'.

Task

Would you add any further items to the evaluation sheet below? Would you delete or change any?

Criterion	Rating
1. The syllabus is in accordance with the latest thinking on language acquisition and language-teaching methodology.	
2. The syllabus clearly states the basic principles (linguistic and/or educational) on which its design was based.	
3. The syllabus shows clearly what language performance will be appropriate to the different levels, and how this progresses from beginner to advanced.	
4. The syllabus is comprehensive: it covers all the language or language abilities that the students should learn.	
5. The syllabus provides a rational breakdown of the target knowledge (the language) into clearly defined divisions.	
6. The syllabus is 'transparent', i.e. easily understood by teachers and coursebook writers.	
7. It is clear how the syllabus can be implemented in classroom practice.	
8. It is clear how the syllabus can be used to design materials.	
9. It is clear how the syllabus will be used as a basis for learner assessment or testing.	
10. It is my impression that the syllabus has led to a rise in learner achievement.	
11. It is my impression that the syllabus has led to an improvement in course materials.	
12. It is my impression that the syllabus has led to the composition of more effective examination papers.	
Other specific positive criticisms:	
Other specific negative criticisms:	
Suggestions for change:	

Action task

Having made your changes, complete the evaluation sheet yourself, relating to a syllabus that was approved for a course you have taught or observed.

Review

Answer as many as you can of the following questions, and then check answers by referring back to the relevant passages in this unit.

If you are working in a group, note down your own answers first alone, and then share with the other members of the group. Finally, check the answers together.

What is a syllabus?
1. What are the basic features of all syllabuses?
2. Can you recall one or two optional features of a syllabus?

Types of language syllabus
3. What is a 'structural' syllabus?
4. For what kinds of courses are situational and topic-based syllabuses most used?
5. What is a 'standards-based' syllabus?
6. What may a 'multi-strand' syllabus include?

Using the approved syllabus
7. In what kinds of situations may teachers prefer to work directly from the syllabus when planning their courses?
8. In what situations might the syllabus not be very helpful?
9. What other function(s) besides helping to plan a course can the syllabus perform?

Evaluating the syllabus
10. What are the problems with evaluating a syllabus by checking if student performance has improved?
11. When eliciting opinions about the functioning of a new syllabus, who should be asked?
12. What 'agree/disagree' questions could be asked to elicit feedback on a new syllabus? Write down all you can recall (there are 12 listed in the unit).

Further reading

Language syllabuses in general

Brumfit, C.J. (ed.) (1984) *General English Syllabus Design (ELT Documents 118)*, Oxford: Pergamon Press.

> (An old but still very relevant collection of articles on different kinds of English-language syllabuses: useful summaries by Brumfit and Stern)

Richards, J.C. (2001) *Curriculum Development in Language Teaching*, Cambridge: Cambridge University Press.

> (A comprehensive summary of the issues involved in curriculum development and course planning)

Specific types of syllabus

Common European Framework of Reference for Languages (2006), Cambridge: Cambridge University Press.

(The multi-strand syllabus of the Common European Framework, including standards-based 'can-do' specifications)

Ellis, R. (1993) The structural syllabus and second language acquisition. *TESOL Quarterly, 27*(1), 91–113.

(A rationale for the inclusion of a structural syllabus as a basis for the teaching of grammar in English courses)

Willis, D. (1990) *The Lexical Syllabus: A New Approach to Language Teaching*, London: Collins.

(Gives the rationale for a lexical syllabus, how it would be organized and how to use it in teaching)

Wilkins, D.A. (1976) *Notional Syllabuses*, Oxford: Oxford University Press.

(A slim volume providing the original rationale underlying functional-notional syllabuses)

Websites

Syllabus Design Links: www.udel.edu/cubillos/622links.htm

(A useful list of websites that gives information about the design and implementation of various different kinds of syllabuses)

14 Materials

Overview

The sections in this unit are:

14.1 **How necessary is a coursebook?** Alternatives to the coursebook, advantages and disadvantages.

14.2 **Coursebook evaluation and selection.** Discussion of criteria for evaluating and choosing a coursebook for your class.

14.3 **Adapting course materials.** Some ideas on how to add to, shorten or change course materials to make them more appropriate for a particular class.

14.4 **Supplementary materials (1): paper.** A summary of various types of paper materials available to supplement the main coursebook.

14.5 **Supplementary materials (2): digital.** Some computer-based software and hardware that can be used to facilitate teaching and learning.

14.1 How necessary is a coursebook?

The word *coursebook* here refers to the material which is used as the basis for a course, whether it is an actual book or an online course.

Task

Before reading this unit: what would your own answer be to the question in the heading of this section?

In some places it is taken for granted that coursebooks are used as the basis for courses. In others they may not be used at all, and the teacher bases his or her teaching on a syllabus, or his or her own programme, using personally selected teaching materials when necessary. A third situation is a compromise, where a coursebook is used selectively, not necessarily in sequence, and is extensively supplemented by other materials.

In most situations today, the coursebook is in fact a conventional paper book but online or digital course materials are on the increase. The following list of advantages and disadvantages apply to either paper or digital coursebooks.

Task

Read through the arguments below, ticking those you agree with, adding a cross to ones you don't. Write any criticisms or comments in the margin. Add any other arguments that you think of, based on your own experience as a student or teacher.

Advantages of a coursebook

- **Framework.** A coursebook provides a clear framework. Teachers and students know where they are going and what is coming next, so there is a sense of structure and progress.

- **Syllabus.** In many places the coursebook is used as a syllabus. If it is followed systematically, a planned selection of language will be covered.

- **Ready-made texts and tasks.** The coursebook provides texts and learning tasks which are likely to be of an appropriate level for most of the class. This saves time for the teacher who would otherwise have to prepare his or her own.

- **Guidance.** For teachers who are inexperienced or unsure of their knowledge of the language or teaching skills, the coursebook can provide useful guidance and support.

- **Autonomy.** The student can use the coursebook to learn new material, and review and monitor his or her own progress autonomously. A student without a coursebook is more teacher-dependent.

Disadvantages of a coursebook

- **Inadequacy.** Every individual class has their own learning needs. No single coursebook can possibly meet these satisfactorily.

- **Irrelevance, lack of interest.** The topics in the coursebook may not be relevant or interesting for your class. And they may 'date' rapidly, whereas materials you choose yourself can be more up to date.

- **Cultural inappropriateness.** The content of a coursebook may be culturally inappropriate, which not only may make it irrelevant or uninteresting, but can also cause discomfort or even offence.

- **Limited range of level.** Coursebooks target a particular student population and rarely cater for the variety of levels of ability or proficiency that exist in most classes.

- **Possible negative effect on teaching.** Teachers may follow the coursebook uncritically and are discouraged from using their own initiative: they may find themselves functioning merely as mediators of its content instead of as teachers in their own right.

Task

Were any of the arguments new to you? If they were, and you agree with them, would you now change your answer to the question at the beginning of this unit? Or is your previous opinion unchanged?

The final decision as to whether or not to use a coursebook has to depend on your own teaching style, the resources available and the accepted policy in your school.

In my own situation – teaching English in a state school in a non-English-speaking country – I preferred to use a coursebook. I found that a set framework helped me to regulate and time my programme. Perhaps surprisingly, it also provided a firm basis for my own supplementary teaching ideas. I could do my own thing occasionally, knowing that I had a structured programme to return to.

It is my experience that students also prefer to have one. The classes which I have tried to teach using a selection of materials from different sources have complained of a sense of lack of purpose. And, interestingly, that they feel that their studies – and, by implication, they – are not taken seriously. It seems that having a coursebook may carry a certain prestige.

14.2 Coursebook evaluation and selection

Whether or not you choose to base your course on a coursebook, it is worth thinking about how you recognize a good one, and why you might reject or criticize it: in other words, what are your main criteria for evaluation. These criteria may be general (suitable for any language-teaching materials) or specific (looking at the appropriateness of a set of materials for a certain course or group of learners). An example of a general criterion might be: 'clear layout and font', or 'provides regular review or test sections'. A specific criterion for a class of younger learners might be: 'attractive and colourful illustrations', or for a class of medical students: 'vocabulary and texts relevant to medicine'.

The general criteria suggested below are my own, but they rely on ideas suggested in a number of books and articles on the subject (see some useful sources in *Further reading* at the end of this unit).

Task

Read the list of criteria for evaluating language-learning coursebooks below. In the left-hand column, use the following symbols to note how important you think each criterion is:

✓✓ for 'essential' (without this I wouldn't use the coursebook)
✓ for 'quite important'
? for 'not sure'
✗ for 'not important'
✗✗ for 'totally unimportant' (it wouldn't make any difference to me if it was there or not)

Then, optionally, add further criteria you feel are significant in the spaces left at the end, and mark in their importance. Ignore the Applied column for the moment.

If you are working in a group, compare your ideas with those of colleagues. Then read on.

Checklist for coursebook evaluation

Importance	Criterion	Applied
	1. The objectives are clearly explained in the introduction, and implemented in the material.	
	2. The approach is educationally and culturally acceptable to the target students.	
	3. The layout is clear (both the book as a whole and single pages) and the print is easy to read. If digital, then it is easy to 'navigate' from page to page.	
	4. The material is attractive.	
	5. The texts and tasks are interesting.	
	6. The texts and tasks are varied, appropriate for different learner levels, learning styles, interests, etc.	
	7. Instructions are clear.	
	8. There is an explicit syllabus, which is covered systematically.	
	9. Content is clearly organized and graded.	
	10. There are regular review and test sections.	
	11. There are pronunciation explanations and practice.	
	12. There are vocabulary explanations and practice.	
	13. There are grammar explanations and practice.	
	14. There are tasks that activate the students in listening, speaking, reading and writing.	
	15. The material encourages learners to develop their own learning strategies and to become independent in their learning.	
	16. There is adequate guidance for the teacher (teacher's guide, or teacher's notes).	
	17. There are audio recordings available.	
	18. There are visual materials available: posters, video, flash cards, etc.	
	19. There is a coursebook website, with guidance and supplementary materials available.	
	20. The material is easily available and not too expensive.	
	21.	
	22.	

1. **Objectives.** This is important, but check that the objectives expressed in the introduction to the coursebook are in fact implemented. Often they are not!

2. **Approach.** How important this is depends on your approach and the student population. Some communities are more sensitive than others.

3. **Layout.** This is vitally important. The material has to be clear and 'navigable': both you and your students need to be able to find your way around it easily and smoothly. You need to be able to read the texts easily (so it is not a good idea to have artistic fonts, or pictures behind text which make reading difficult). You also need to be able to move around it easily if it is a digital course composed of a lot of webpages and links.

4. **Appearance.** This is particularly important for younger classes, but may be less so for older ones. Children and adolescents are used to colourful and eye-catching books, television and websites and may be demotivated by black and white or uninteresting design.

5. **Interest.** I would rank this as quite important. On the one hand, skilful and imaginative teaching can make even the most boring texts and tasks interesting (and bad teaching can 'kill' the most interesting ones!). On the other hand, it helps a lot if the book provides interesting material that you can use, adapting as necessary for your classes.

6. **Variation.** This quality is one that is often missing in coursebooks. There should be some texts which are easier or more difficult. Tasks should be designed to allow for performance at different levels. Texts and tasks should vary also in the topic, the kind of language style, the type of participation or learning strategies they require, etc. The lack of variation is not a reason to reject the book, but if it exists it is a positive feature. So I would rank it as quite important (see Unit 19: Learner differences (2): teaching heterogeneous (mixed) classes).

7. **Instructions.** Essential. For a monolingual class of beginners, this may mean providing instructions and explanations in the L1.

8. **Syllabus.** Essential. Check what kind of a syllabus the coursebook has. This should be clear from the table of contents at the beginning (see Unit 13: The syllabus). Does it provide coverage of all the items you think are essential? And are these items in fact covered in the material itself? You may need to check that the coursebook follows syllabuses which are relevant to your teaching situation, such as the CEFR, a national syllabus, or the syllabus of an exam such as ESOL.

9. **Organization.** Systematic progress in difficulty is very important for courses in primary and secondary schools. However, it may not be as important for courses in academic English or other more advanced programmes.

10. **Review and test.** The inclusion of these features may or may not be important to you. Review exercises and tests are sometimes provided on the course website, rather than in the main materials themselves. Often, however, you will prefer to create your own. What you actually teach is never exactly

what the coursebook provides: you may skip some bits and add others, in which case the coursebook reviews and tests might not be suitable. So this component is probably less essential than some of the others.

11. **Pronunciation.** How much emphasis is put on pronunciation teaching depends on the approach in your teaching situation, so the evaluation here would also vary. Pronunciation problems can often be dealt with as they come up, so you do not necessarily need a systematic programme in the coursebook.

12. **Vocabulary.** This is an essential component. The materials should provide plenty of vocabulary expansion and review activities.

13. **Grammar.** Like pronunciation, how much emphasis is put on grammar depends on the local teaching situation. In many contexts substantial grammar coverage is required, but in others it is not. So the evaluation is likely to range from 'essential' to 'not sure'.

14. **Listening, speaking, reading and writing.** Tasks activating the four skills are the main basis for communicative practice. And they are essential. The coursebook should provide texts and tasks that promote fluency and accuracy in the four skills in communicative situations, as well as activities that provide opportunities for students to do 'mixed-skills' activities.

15. **Learner independence.** Whether the materials encourage learner independence and autonomy is quite important, but it is a very difficult aspect to evaluate. Some things to look for are computer-based tasks which enable self-checking, and research tasks that students do on their own, such as 'webquests'.

16. **Teacher's guides.** Teacher's guides are quite important, particularly – but not only – for novice teachers. The teacher's materials provide not only answers to exercises, saving time and effort, but also useful tips on ways of dealing with texts and tasks.

17. **Audio recordings.** This is an essential component for listening comprehension. Without them, you would have to look for material on the Internet or on CDs. It is very difficult to find suitable material for your class from either source, so you really need ready-made ones that accompany the course. If the recordings are on video, so much the better.

18. **Visual materials.** Visual materials such as posters and flash cards, whether on paper or displayed digitally, are essential for classes of younger learners. They provide an enjoyable break from the coursebook, focus attention and are likely to improve learning. However, they may be unnecessary for older and more academic classes.

19. **Website.** The course website is a fairly standard component these days. Often the audio recordings and teacher's guide can be found there, as well as supplementary exercises, tests and texts, and links to other useful websites. It is not absolutely necessary, but it may be quite an important added resource.

20. Availability. This is perhaps obvious, but essential. The most desirable coursebook in the world is no good if it is too expensive for your institution or students to afford, or if it is not easily available in your country.

Action task

Now take a coursebook and examine it, applying the criteria you have in your list. Write your ratings in the Applied column of the table. You could use a similar code to the one used above in the first task in this section (✓✓ or ✓ indicates a high or very high score, ✗ or ✗✗ a low or very low score, and **?** indicates that you are not sure, or that the criterion applies partially).

Again, you can compare notes with colleagues who have looked at the same materials, and see how far you can agree on the different items.

14.3 Adapting course materials

This section applies both to standard coursebooks, as discussed in Sections 14.1 and 14.2 above, and to materials such as published grammar exercises, reading comprehension texts, worksheets – all of which may, of course, be presented either on paper or on a computer.

All teaching materials should be related to critically by the teacher. We need to be aware of their strengths and weaknesses in order to make the most of the former and compensate for or neutralize the latter. If there are gaps in the material (for example, if the coursebook does not provide enough reading texts or grammar practice), the problem can be solved by a quick 'surf' through the Internet, or by adding supplementary grammar or reading books. But problems with specific components within teaching units can only be solved by the teacher in the classroom. You may find it necessary to make substantial changes, deletions and additions.

Here is a sample of problems that teachers in particular situations might encounter, where the solutions might involve such changes to the text or task. Note that no criticism is intended of the extracts in themselves: they are all interesting and well written. It's just that they may not, for various reasons, address the needs of a particular group of students.

Task

Look at the teachers' criticisms, and think about how you might go about solving the problems. Then read on to the *What we can do* section below, and annotate with any further ideas you had yourself that I had not thought of.

Paolo (teaching in a primary school in Italy): It's important to do lots of grammar practice with my students, but exercises like this one are rather boring, the students get fed up doing them. And they're too short: don't give enough opportunities for practice.

Complete the sentences:

1. Venice is .... (beautiful) than London.
2. This school is .... (big) than that one.
3. This was .... (bad) day of my life!
4. Which is .... (heavy): a pound or a kilo?
5. Which supermarket has the .... (cheap) vegetables?
6. She was .... (popular) singer in the festival.
7. For me, mathematics is .... (difficult) than English.

Suad (teaching in a girls' school in Egypt): The reading passage is culturally inappropriate for my adolescent female students. In our culture it is not acceptable for young people to have girlfriends and boyfriends or 'go out'. So I have a problem with the following reading passage, though the rest of the book is excellent.

Where did New Yorkers ever get the reputation for being unfriendly? It's so completely the opposite that it is unbelievable that anyone could subscribe to the idea for more than five minutes. The only reason the idea survives is that New Yorkers themselves love to affirm it and that many people who visit the city stay in a few midtown blocks of the business area and fear to walk the neighborhoods, west and east. The truth is that New Yorkers are almost embarrassingly friendly and helpful, so much so that it is bewildering to the uninitiated, who think they are up to something.

Nearly all New Yorkers talk to one another all the time, and they love to give advice. A woman at a bus stop dropped some books and muttered that everything was terrible today. Another asked her what was wrong (while everyone else listened carefully), and she said her boyfriend had broken up with her. Nearly every person had consolation to offer, and then a very elegantly dressed lady at the back of the group said, 'You should meet my brother Jimmy; he's a great guy and he's not attached. Look, here's his phone number; I'll tell him to expect your call. You can have coffee – what could it hurt?'

If you are a stranger, all the stops are pulled out. Recently, on a full subway car a man asked where to get off for Wall Street. Everyone jumped to instruct him, but that was just the beginning. The passengers on the subway wanted to know why he wanted to go to Wall Street, explained that Saturday was no good since the Stock Exchange wasn't open, demanded to know what he'd already seen in New York, and arrived finally at an agreement about where he should go that day – and three of them made sure he got off at the right stop for it.

Why is such a huge city so sociable? My own theory is that it's an island mentality. They want to know everything about everybody on their little island, or at least in their own neighborhood, and everyone who sets foot on it.

(Slightly abridged from http://wps.prenhall.com/hss_wassman_effective_3/55/14087/3606342.cw/content/index.html)

Emilia (teaching in a private school in Brazil): This reading passage is interesting, and my students relate well to the topic, but it's a bit too short and easy for my class of 12-year-old students. They need more challenge.

Who was Robin Hood?
Nobody knows. In the film, *Robin Hood: Prince of Thieves*, Robin was rich, but this probably wasn't true. We know that he was a popular hero in the 13th century. It's possible the real man was born before then.

Who were the Merry Men?
Little John and Will Scarlet were famous Merry Men. Robin Hood was the leader of this group of men (and women).

Why were Robin Hood and his Merry Men famous?

They were famous for robbing rich people. But Robin Hood and his Merry Men weren't robbers – the money was for poor people.

(Adapted from *Active Grammar 1*, F. Davis and W. Rimmer, Cambridge University Press.)

Takumi (teaching in a boys' school in Japan): This reading passage is too long and difficult for my class: teaching it would mean translating a lot of the words, and they would find it hard and perhaps boring.

A young emperor penguin took a wrong turn from the Antarctic and ended up stranded on a New Zealand beach – the first time in 44 years the aquatic bird has been sighted in the south Pacific country.

Local resident Christine Wilton was taking her miniature schnauzer dog Millie for a walk on Peka Peka beach on the North Island's western coast when she discovered the bird.

'It was out of this world to see it … like someone just dropped it from the sky,' Wilton said.

Conservation experts say the penguin is about 10 months old and stands about 80cm (32 inches) high.

Emperor penguins are the tallest and largest species of penguin and can grow up to 122cm high and weigh more than 34kg (75lbs).

Colin Miskelly, a curator at Te Papa, the Museum of New Zealand, said the bird was likely to have been born during the last Antarctic winter. He said emperor penguins can spend months at a time in the ocean, but did not know what might have caused this particular one to become disoriented. Miskelly said the penguin appeared healthy and well fed, with plenty of body fat, and probably came ashore for a rest.

However, Miskelly said the penguin would need to find its way back south soon if it were to survive. Despite the onset of the New Zealand winter, the bird was probably hot and thirsty, he said.

Peter Simpson, a programme manager for New Zealand's department of conservation, said officials are asking people to stand back about 10m from the creature and to avoid letting dogs near it.

The last confirmed sighting of a wild emperor in New Zealand was in 1967 at the southern Oreti beach, he said.

(Slightly abridged version of an article that appeared in *The Guardian*, on 21 June 2011. www.guardian.co.uk/world/2011/jun/21/emperor-penguins-detour-new-zealand)

What we can do

Paolo: boring and too-short grammar exercises. Here are some ideas for adaptation to add interest and length.

Having led the students through the exercise once conventionally, tell them to:

1. close their books and try to recall all seven of the completed sentences. They can work in pairs. Then, in full class, check answers.
2. ignore the sentence endings, and invent their own: so sentence 5 might be 'Which supermarket has the freshest fruit'?
3. ignore the adjective in brackets, and suggest any other comparative or superlative adjectives that make sense with the rest of the sentence. For example, the first sentence could be 'Venice is warmer than London' or 'Venice is smaller than London'.
4. change selected statements (it doesn't work for questions) in whatever way they like in order to make them true for them. So for sentence 7, for example, they might say 'For me, mathematics is more difficult than Italian'.
5. use only the comparative or superlative adjective in each case, ignoring all the rest of the sentence given, and make true sentences of their own.

Note that in ideas 2, 3, 4 and 5, the students do not have to go through every item in the exercise, and are certainly not confined to the order in which they appear in the original. On the other hand, they may produce a number of different answers to any single item.

Suad: cultural inappropriateness. There are various options here, and which you choose depends on various factors: the opinions and personalities of the students, their parents' attitudes, your own cultural background and beliefs, and school policy.

1. You can simply skip this reading passage, which may mean omitting an entire unit. Or you could replace it with one you find yourself.
2. If you have a digital copy of the text, you could either delete the inappropriate paragraph, or change the text so that the woman's problem is something more acceptable to your students' culture.
3. You might use the text as it is, and simply acknowledge that this relates to a foreign culture and would not be acceptable at home.
4. You might go further: take the opportunity to draw students' attention to the differences in cultural norms between the USA and the home culture and discuss the issue of cultural differences in general.

Emilia: short, easy reading passage. This is indeed quite an easy text, though you might need to teach your students words like *leader*, *merry*. Some things you might do to make it more challenging are:

1. Give students five minutes to work on their own, inserting as many adjectives and adverbs as they can in the passage. Then share the results.
2. Tell students to take pairs of simple sentences from the text, and combine them into one sentence. They can change the wording as necessary. For example 'In the film *Robin Hood: Prince of Thieves*, Robin was rich, but this probably wasn't true.' Might be changed to 'Although in the film *Robin Hood: Prince of Thieves*, Robin was rich, this probably wasn't true.'
3. Send students to the Internet to find out as much as they can about Robin Hood, write notes, and share the information they have found in the following lesson, either orally or in writing.
4. a) If you have an interactive whiteboard (IWB), show the text on the board and invite students to add whole phrases or sentences of at least three words, wherever they like and make sense. If they have done the internet research, as suggested at 3. above, then the insertions should relate to what they have found out.
   b) If you don't have an IWB, then ask students to say what their additions would be, and where they would put them. Write up on the board only the additions. Students copy them down, and then for homework try to remember or work out where to insert them and write out the entire text.
5. Select specific words from the text (for example, *hero*, *real*, *rich*, *popular*, *merry*, etc.), and tell students for homework to find out from dictionaries, thesauri or by searching online as many other words of similar meaning as they can for each.

Takumi: long, difficult passage. The problem with difficulty is essentially the level of vocabulary. The aspect of length is dealt with later.

1. *Vocabulary*. There are two useful strategies here:
   a) Pre-teach the key words necessary for understanding the main topic of the passage. These might be *emperor penguin*, *sight (v.)*, *stranded*. Don't try to pre-teach all previously unknown vocabulary before reading. That would just overwhelm and discourage the students. They need to discover the rest of the new items gradually, preferably in context. The main key words can also provide the basis for a pre-reading discussion of the topic.

b) Before presenting the passage, delete the difficult bits wherever you can without altering the basic message, and present the text the first time without them. For example:

> A young emperor penguin took a wrong turn from the Antarctic and ended up ~~stranded~~ on a New Zealand beach – the first time in 44 years the ~~aquatic~~ bird has been sighted in the south Pacific country.
>
> ~~Local resident~~ Christine Wilton was taking her dog Millie for a walk ~~on Peka Peka beach on the North Island's western coast~~ when she discovered the bird.
>
> "It was ~~out of this world to see it~~ … like someone just dropped it from the sky," Wilton said.
>
> ~~Conservation~~ experts say the penguin is about 10 months old and stands about 80cm (32 inches) high.

Tell students to cross out these items lightly, in pencil on their copy (or use 'delete' or 'strikethrough' if they have a digital version). Or, if you are able to retype the passage, it can be presented to the students as:

> A young emperor penguin took a wrong turn from the Antarctic and ended up on a New Zealand beach – the first time in 44 years the bird has been sighted in the south Pacific country. Christine Wilton was taking her dog Millie for a walk when she discovered the bird. "It was … like someone just dropped it from the sky," Wilton said. Experts say the penguin is about 10 months old and stands about 80cm (32 inches) high.

2. *Length*. The answer here is to do the text bit by bit, so that the students are not faced with the entire text at one session.
   a) In the first lesson, work only on the first few sentences, simplified as suggested above, teaching new vocabulary as necessary.
   b) Challenge students to predict what more information will be provided later in this report; then continue reading, working on each paragraph on its own before progressing to the next.
   c) When you have finished working through the entire passage, read it aloud to the students again, to familiarize further.
   d) Only after the students know the basic content and sequence of argument of the simplified passage, let them read the original with the deleted items reinstated, and work on these as necessary.

Summary

The coursebook provides you with useful texts and tasks which you can use as the basis for your teaching programme. But that is essentially what it is: a good basis. The coursebook authors do not know your class: you do. You are the best person to decide how much of the material to use, and how. Be selective and critical, using your own professional judgement to decide where it needs to be changed and where it does not. As the examples above show, coursebook materials can be adapted (sometimes quite drastically) in order to create appropriate, learning-rich and interesting activities for your class.

14.4 Supplementary materials (1): paper

Most language-teaching coursebooks probably need some supplementing in order to adapt them to the needs of a particular class or to offer extra texts, exercises or visual materials. Below is a list of paper supplementary materials that you should try to have access to, either in your staff room or at home.

Reference books

The main type of reference book is, of course, the dictionary. It is useful to have a monolingual English dictionary available in the staff room (the *Concise Oxford English Dictionary*, for example), as well as a good learner's dictionary (like the *Cambridge Advanced Learner's Dictionary*). If you are teaching students who all (or mostly) share a single L1, then you will need also a good bilingual dictionary. Other useful reference books are the thesaurus (*Roget's Thesaurus of English Words and Phrases*) and a good teacher's grammar (for example, Michael Swan's *Practical English Usage*).

Your students should also have paper or electronic dictionaries with them – usually bilingual– unless they are always carrying mobile electronic hardware with easily accessed dictionary sites.

Textbooks

You will find it useful to have a variety of English-teaching textbooks on your shelves. These would include various coursebooks, but also books focusing on particular aspects of language such as grammar, vocabulary, pronunciation, style and so on. You might want to use extracts to supplement your own coursebook where you feel something is missing or inadequately covered.

Teacher handbooks

There is an enormous range of handbooks available to the English teacher, covering almost any aspect of teaching you can think of. Some of them are too theoretical, or focus on a specific student population which may not have much in common with yours, or suggest activities that are not practicable in your classes. Others are excellent and can enrich your teaching as well as make it more enjoyable. Take every opportunity to browse through the teacher handbooks at teachers' conferences and bookshops; and ask experienced colleagues which handbooks they have found useful.

Books for extensive reading

The importance of extensive reading has already been discussed in Unit 10: Teaching reading, pp. 145–6. A library of suitable books is therefore a 'must' for any school or insitution where English is taught. This should include plenty of simplified readers at different levels as well as unsimplified books.

Getting a group of students to read such books regularly is easier said than done, as many experienced teachers will testify. It requires ongoing monitoring of book borrowing and returning, and constant investment in new books. However, it is certainly worthwhile: the expense, compared to computer hardware, for example, is relatively small, and the benefits for language learning are substantial.

Worksheets, test papers, work cards

Teachers very often prepare worksheets for their students with extra reading or language practice as well as tests. There is also an enormous number of worksheets and tests available on the Internet, although finding what you want can take hours – and even then you might not find exactly what you need.

Teacher-made worksheets or test papers are copied onto A4 paper and have room to write in answers. As compared to work cards (described below), they have the advantages that they can be written on, are less time-consuming to make, and are in fact often provided in workbooks that come with course materials.

Having created and used the worksheets or tests, there are two important things you need to do with them later. One is to share them with colleagues, some of whom may be using similar materials with similar students and may find the extra material useful. The second is to file them: see the last paragraph of this section.

Work cards are small pieces of coloured card (perhaps about one-quarter the size of an A4 sheet of paper), which can be laminated. Each card displays one short task, designed to be done in five minutes or less. Students do one, and then exchange it for another, as described below. If you are focusing on reading, then each card would show the same type of reading task, but obviously using different actual content each time. If you are focusing on grammar, each might show one item of a ten-item exercise, with instructions. The same can be done for writing, vocabulary and various other topics.

Here is an example of a simple reading card for an elementary class of young learners:

Draw in your notebooks

This is a big bus. It is red. There are people in the bus.

The other cards would consist of similar easy descriptions for students to draw.

Usually there are ten or so different cards in a set, but each would need to be copied three or four times, depending on the size of your class. For a class of 20, you would need about 30 cards to make sure you have a constant 'reserve'. You begin by giving each student a card. Leave the 'reserve' in a central location in the classroom. As they finish, students come to exchange their card for a new one.

The main advantage of the use of work cards is that all students are engaging with the task all the time, each working at his or her own speed. I have also found them very motivating. This is is partly because the items are done quickly so there is a sense of achievement: the student does not have to wait to the end of the whole exercise to feel he or she has finished something. And it is partly because of the actual movement – getting up to exchange cards and returning with a new card – which provides a change from the generally static classroom.

Pictures: posters, flash cards

Materials with pictures are invaluable, particularly for younger learners, and teachers of children find that they constantly use them. The time is gone when teachers used to spend hours leafing through glossy magazines and colour supplements of newspapers to find suitable pictures: today you can find and download all the pictures you need at the click of a mouse. These can then be glued onto card, or laminated if you think you will use them repeatedly, and filed (see below). It is, of course, possible to display visual material on IWBs, but paper materials have the advantage that they can be easily handled, moved and exchanged rather than stuck at the front of the class.

All supplementary materials based on separate sheets of paper or card need to be carefully filed. It is very frustrating to invest a lot of time creating them and then find that you cannot lay your hands on them when you want to use them again! Label and classify files clearly, either in a folder on a computer or in a box file. It is often a good idea to preserve paper versions even of material you have on your computer in digital form, as a useful ready-to-copy back-up.

14.5 Supplementary materials (2): digital

A large amount of teaching and learning these days is done with the help of technology. The term CALL (Computer Assisted Language Learning) is, however, used less and less, as people become aware that the use of technology is not a supplement (as implied in the word 'assisted'), but a staple component in the materials and facilities used for learning and teaching worldwide. Computers, in their various forms, with a wide range of software and access to the Internet, are, in many teaching contexts, taken for granted, in much the same way as the black- or whiteboard is.

Below is a list of the digital tools that can be useful in teaching. For more information on how to use them, see Unit 16: Classroom interaction, pp. 238–41.

The interactive whiteboard (IWBs) and data projectors

You can use both data projectors and IWBs to display texts, pictures, pages from the textbook, presentations and video. IWBs can be controlled by the touch of a finger or special 'pen', which means that a teacher can write and erase in the same way as with a conventional board. But it is useful to take advantage of an IWB's other tools: hide and display text and pictures; play audio and video directly from the textbook page; type in answers; insert your own files. The material can be saved, to be displayed later, filed on the class website or emailed to students later.

Internet websites

The Internet provides teachers with an immense source of teaching materials and ideas, some examples of which are listed below:

- reading texts, either from 'authentic' sources (i.e. not originally designed to be used for teaching), or from English-teaching websites

- listening texts as *YouTube* videos, or audio podcasts

- tests, workpages, exercises and so on, from the various English-teaching websites, such as the British Council's *TeachingEnglish*, accessible from www.teachingenglish.org.uk

- self-access exercises and tests for students to use on their own. See, for example:

> Learn English: http://learnenglish.britishcouncil.org/en/
> Learn English Kids: http://learnenglishkids.britishcouncil.org/en/
> English Grammar Exercises: www.englisch-hilfen.de/en/exercises_list/alle_grammar.htm
> Guide to Grammar and Writing: http://grammar.ccc.commnet.edu/grammar/index.htm
> ESLflow: www.eslflow.com/index.html

Interactive digital tools

Email, obviously, can be used for many purposes in communication between teachers and students: submitting and correcting assignments, notifying of absences or changes in schedule and so on. Mobile phones are often seen as a nuisance in the classroom, but in fact they can be used to help learning: for example, students can use them to practise informal communicative writing, or to list new vocabulary which they can then review at odd moments.

Wikis and blogs

Wikis are a tool through which anyone can edit or comment on uploaded text: so they are useful for interactive editing and discussion of student-generated texts. They are increasingly used as a basis for class websites. *Blogs* are used as a way for students to comment on texts or respond to tasks: they often develop into full discussions, with 'comments' going back and forth.

Digital recording

Digital equipment, including most mobile phones, can be used to create both video and audio recordings. Students can create their own video clips or sound recordings; the teacher can record students' performance to play back later. Or live sound or video can be broadcast via the Internet ('streaming').

Production

Desktop publishing enables classes or individual students to create and design pages or whole booklets for publishing, either within the school or beyond. This is particularly useful for the presentation of research-based or creative projects done by students.

e-books

These may be used for the provision of extensive reading material; however, at the time of writing they are not systematically or widely used in English courses for this purpose. They may, however, answer the needs of more advanced students who can download novels for their own individual reading.

Digital tools are not a substitute for the face-to-face lesson or for direct interaction between teacher and student; rather, where available and well-used, they are a means of enriching it and making it more efficient. The combination of conventional and digital teaching/learning, known as *blended learning*, often using programs known as LMSs (Learning Management Systems), will be discussed further in Unit 16: Classroom interaction, p. 240.

Review

Answer as many as you can of the following questions, and then check answers by referring back to the relevant passages in this unit.

If you are working in a group, note down your answers first alone, and then share with the other members of the group. Finally, check the answers together.

How necessary is a coursebook?
1. Can you give at least three arguments in favour of using a coursebook in your teaching?
2. Can you suggest at least three disadvantages of using a coursebook in your teaching?

Coursebook evaluation and selection
3. Why is the layout of a coursebook so important?
4. Why are tests and reviews in a coursebook less important?
5. What other important criteria for textbook selection can you remember (20 are suggested in this section)?

Adapting course materials
6. What sorts of things can be done to improve a grammar exercise that is boring and does not provide enough practice?
7. What can be done to add more challenge to a too-easy text?
8. What might be done to make a difficult text easier for the class to cope with?

Supplementary materials (1): paper
9. What types of paper materials should be available to teachers for use in classes?
10. How can you make sure that teacher-made paper materials are available for later re-use?

Supplementary materials (2): digital
11. What is an IWB? How can it be used?
12. Can you suggest at least five other types of computer hardware or software that are useful to teachers today?

Further reading

Cooper, R., Lavery, M. and Rinvolucri, M. (1991) *Video*, Oxford: Oxford University Press.
 (Useful classroom activities for language learning using video)

Cunningworth, A. (1995) *Choosing Your Coursebook*, Oxford: Macmillan Heinemann.
 (Useful guidelines and checklists to help select coursebooks)

Dudeney, G. and Hockly, N. (2007) *How to Teach English with Technology*, London: Pearson Education.

    (A practical guide to the use of computers and web2 tools in the classroom, with plenty of actual activities clearly explained)

Erben, T. and Sarieva, I. (2007) *CALLing All Foreign Language Teachers: Computer-Assisted Language Learning in the Classroom*, Larchmont, NY: Eye on Education.

    (A comprehensive guide to the use of technology in language teaching: some chapters available online: http://sites.google.com/site/terben9397/callingallforeignlanguageteachers)

Tomlinson, B. (ed.) (1998) *Materials Development for Language Teaching*, Cambridge: Cambridge University Press.

    (A collection of articles about the design and composition of teaching materials, including materials targeting specific skills, purposes and populations)

Wright, A. and Haleem, S. (1991) *Visuals for the Language Classroom*, London: Longman.

    (A thorough discussion of the topic, exploring classroom procedures associated with the various types of materials)

15 Teaching content

15.1 Different kinds of content

By *content* I mean topics that texts are about, or that tasks relate to, as distinct from the target language itself. Look at the list of topics below: most or all of them are likely to come up in a general school course, although the amount of emphasis on different ones may vary widely. Courses of English for Specific Purposes (ESP) may be more limited, as described later.

- **Zero or trivial content.** Bland, fairly neutral characters and events; superficially interesting topics with no cultural or other information or connection with real-world issues. For example: sentences about a fictional 'John and Mary' doing everyday activities; stereotype family stories; some pop songs, trivial anecdotes.

- **The students themselves.** Exploration of students' own experiences, knowledge, opinions and feelings: for example, activities that ask students to write about someone they know, or compare tastes in food and drink.

- **The local environment.** Treatment of institutions, people, places, events, etc. from the students' own country or background. For example, Greek students might discuss places they would recommend that tourists should visit in Greece.

- **Moral, educational, political or social problems; cultural issues.** Presentation of issues showing different points of view, and encouraging students to express opinions: for example, an article describing a social conflict, or a dilemma to which students suggest a solution.

- **Another subject of study.** Topics based on other subjects on the school or university curriculum, such as science or history. In some cases, an entire school subject may be taught in English (for a more detailed discussion, see Section 15.3 below).

- **(Native) English-speaking countries.** Discussion of institutions, etc. from countries where English is spoken as a native language. Materials might cover British or American history, culture and customs, famous people, etc.

- **World or general knowledge.** Information or cultural artefacts from anywhere in the world: customs or festivals associated with another community, for example, or the history of a particular country, or world current events, or jokes, proverbs, etc. translated from other languages.

- **Literature.** To some extent a part of points 6 or 7 above, but important enough to be listed as a separate section: stories, novels, plays and poetry written in English or possibly translated into it (see Section 15.4 below).

- **Linguistics.** Aspects of English or language in general as topics of study in themselves. Some examples might be the history and development of the English language, the etymology or morphology of words, other interesting linguistic phenomena.

Why different courses emphasize some types of content and not others depends largely on the objectives of the course. If your students are immigrants whose purpose is to integrate into an English-speaking community, then topics that are based on that community will be very important. If, on the other hand, they are learning English as an international language for general communication purposes, then such content will be less prominent. If the course is ESP, then the content will focus on engineering, medicine, tourism or whatever the particular goal of the course is. If you are a schoolteacher and see yourself as an educator as much as an instructor in English, you may want to emphasize educational content: so you might prefer to choose a coursebook that emphasizes different educational issues or world or general knowledge.

Action tasks

1. Have a look at a coursebook for a course you are familiar with. How many of the topics above actually appear there? Which are missing? Which are predominant? Are there topics which you feel should have been given more, or less, emphasis?

2. Ask some students what kinds of content from the list they would like to see included in their own language courses, and which are most important in their opinion. Do their ideas agree, on the whole, with yours? (See Prodromou, 1992a for a description of a similar inquiry in Greece.)

15.2 Cultural content

The term *culture* may refer to a number of different things. It is a notoriously difficult and complex concept to define.

Task

What does the word *culture* include? Make a list for yourself, and then read on.

In its narrower sense (sometimes known as 'higher' culture, or Culture, with a capital C), the term includes only creative works that are seen as valuable: literature, art, music, etc. In its wider sense, it refers also to the behaviours, customs, attitudes and beliefs of a specific community. It would thus include things like dress, festivals, religion and conventions of acceptable and unacceptable behaviour. In this section I am using it in this wider sense. And in our case, it also includes the *culture of learning* in a specific community. For example, in some cultures of learning, it is expected that the students only respond to teacher questions or requests, while in others they are often expected to take the initiative; in some cultures, materials are expected to focus mainly on grammar teaching, while in others reading texts may be the priority.

Cultural content of teaching materials and classroom process

The cultural content in an English course may come from four main sources:

1. The home culture of the students
2. The culture of the English-speaking peoples
3. The culture of other communities in the world
4. Global, or international culture

1. **Home culture.** The topics relate to the native country, such as those suggested under *The local environment* in Section 15.1 above. They encourage students to discuss local issues and relate to their own experiences, beliefs, customs, etc. The way the materials deal with the content may also reflect the home culture: not only the actual texts, but also the design. For example, in some places it is unacceptable to show bare-armed or bare-legged women in illustrations due to religious beliefs. Both materials and classroom process will also conform to the culture of learning of the local community: they may, for instance, give more, or fewer, activities based on student initiative.

2. **The culture of the (native) English-speaking peoples.** For most of the twentieth century, most English language teaching materials, especially at more advanced levels, included a large component of British and American culture. They included not only literature (see Section 15.5 below), but also texts about British or American customs or institutions. The culture of other English-speaking countries was also occasionally referred to, but not very often. This is perhaps partly because the major ELT publishers were (and still are) British and American, and local publishers tended to follow their lead. In addition, it was assumed that the learner wanted to imitate a native speaker, not only in language proficiency, but also in cultural knowledge and behaviours. Today, in most institutions in non-English-speaking countries, the goal is the use of English as an international means of communication (see Unit 1: English

teaching today, pp. 4–6), and cultural knowledge of the native-speaking communities is therefore less important.

3. **The cultures of other speech communities.** This component is noticeably more important in modern materials. A typical coursebook today will include units on different countries and peoples, and customs and literature from various sources. One reason is simply that because of faster and more widely used communications and increasing travel, people are far more aware of events and cultures elsewhere. Another, related, reason is that today's students are likely to need English to communicate with other English speakers with a different L1 and a different culture, and so they need a high degree of *intercultural competence* (see below). A starting point for the development of such competence is awareness of the diversity of world cultures.

4. **Global cultural norms.** Culture with a capital C has for some time been international. Museums displaying Asian or African art, concerts of music by European composers, and libraries with translated books from authors of all nationalities can be found in most countries. But it is a relatively recent phenomenon that certain norms and conventions (culture with a small 'c') have begun to be accepted and used worldwide. These include things like dress, politeness norms and forms of communication. They are used in contexts where it is likely that different cultures may meet, for example at conferences, at airports, in international businesses, at higher education institutions and in tourist destinations. Note that the 'home' cultural norms are maintained in more local contexts: the home, the town or village, in basic education, and community meeting-places. But in more international social interaction, global cultural norms have taken over. For example, formal dress for a man is likely to be a suit, while informal dress for teenagers may mean T-shirts and jeans; and formal introductions will usually be accompanied by hand-shaking. In the area of written communication, internationally accepted norms are even more obvious: email conventions, for example, or the format of academic research papers or newspapers. All these are reflected in the content of modern coursebooks and English teaching.

Intercultural competence

The concept of *intercultural competence* has already been mentioned in Unit 1: English teaching today. It refers to a person's ability to function in a cultural context that is not his or her own, to be aware of and respect the cultures of other people, and to behave in a way that will be acceptable to them. The content of teaching materials has a crucial role to play here. It can teach students about a – necessarily limited – range of aspects of cultures different from their own and also raise cultural awareness and attitudes of tolerance and respect for people from different backgrounds. This means including texts and tasks that look at different cultural norms, as well as drawing students' attention to cultural implications in other texts that they might not otherwise notice.

Cultural awareness does not relate only to the cultures of other people. One useful by-product of attention to the cultures of other communities is the raised awareness of features of one's own culture in contrast. Linked to this is increased sensitivity to how one's own cultural norms might appear to others. It is important for our students to detach themselves from an ethnocentric point of view (which is perhaps inevitable in younger learners), see their own community as part of a worldwide mosaic, and to begin to learn about the differences and relationships between them.

15.3 Content and language integrated learning (CLIL)

Using texts which contain content which is useful to learn in itself, rather than just a medium to display language, has been around for some years. It began with CBI (content-based instruction), which has been taken a step further with CLIL (content and language integrated learning). CLIL refers to the teaching of school curriculum subjects such as mathematics or biology in a language other than the L1, in order to achieve the dual aims of improving the students' knowledge of this language and learning the subject. In these lessons there may be some language teaching through occasional error correction or explanation of new vocabulary, but in principle, the main focus is the subject being studied, and the language is used primarily as the means of instruction.

CLIL is an initiative which began and continues to develop mainly in Europe, though it has been implemented also in Asia and Latin America. The language of instruction is in the vast majority of cases English.

CLIL is seen as an important means of achieving the following goals of the European Commission:

- To increase **cultural and linguistic diversity** in the school
- To promote **multilingualism** among European students.

(Note that the second aim above, in principle, means enabling students to function in more than one European language; in practice, however, it relates primarily to the teaching and learning of English in addition to the local language(s).)

Applied to English specifically, CLIL is based on the following assumptions:

- **Language acquisition.** Learners will acquire English well when using it communicatively to understand content.

- **Authenticity.** Using English to learn subjects will imply real-life, authentic use of the language.

- **Integration of English into the curriculum.** English will be integrated into the curriculum in general, rather than treated as a separate subject.

- **Motivation.** Students will be motivated to learn English when they are using it to learn content that they are interested in.

- **Further education.** Students will need English in many cases for further studies after school: CLIL will provide a good basis for this.

- **Diversification of learning.** CLIL will add variety and diversity to lessons, teaching and learning.

- **Increase in exposure to English.** Students will get more hours of exposure to, and use of, English, which will promote acquisition.

- **Different perspectives.** Studying a subject through English will provide different cultural and educational perspectives.

- **Multicultural attitudes.** CLIL will promote multicultural, plurilingual interests and attitudes.

- **Increase in vocabulary.** CLIL will increase students' vocabulary, particularly that associated with the specific subject.

- **Improvement of oral skills.** Since lessons are primarily oral interaction, students' oral skills will be improved (particularly listening).

Task

Can you think of any possible problems with integrating CLIL into schools in a country where English is not commonly spoken outside the classroom? Note down your ideas, and then read on.

Problems

Where parents and educators have reservations about the introduction of CLIL (using English as the medium of instruction), these are based chiefly on the following points:

- **Lack of teacher expertise.** Teachers who are experts in their subjects may not know English very well and may not be able to teach effectively in that language. English teachers, on the other hand, may not have sufficient expertise in other subjects to be able to teach them.

- **Level of subject teaching.** Even if the above does not apply, the subject may be taught and learnt at a lower level than it would be in the L1, either because the students do not understand advanced English, or because the teacher is forced to simplify in order to be understood.

- **Lack of explicit English teaching.** Research indicates that learning of English in school-based courses is most effective when it includes explicit teaching.

Acquisition through communication is insufficient. (See Unit 5: Teaching vocabulary and Unit 6: Teaching grammar.)

- **Lack of teacher courses.** There are (at the time of writing) very few, if any, courses available that prepare teachers to teach school subjects through English.

Research findings

There is only limited research on the topic at the time of writing, but some tentative conclusions can be drawn (see Dalton-Puffer et al., 2010). There does not seem to be any evidence to support the claim that CLIL students will reach a lower level of achievement in the target subject. Their grades appear to be similar to those of students learning the same subject in their L1. As for English proficiency: CLIL students also show overall superiority, particularly in vocabulary knowledge (mainly, as one would expect, of items associated with the subject being studied) and listening comprehension. However, these findings are offset to some extent by the fact that participation in CLIL classes is very often voluntary, and participants tend to be those who are academically able and already at an intermediate (B1-B2) level in English or higher.

Conclusions and discussion

CLIL is increasingly being implemented, particularly in European countries, and particularly in subjects which are 'international', such as geography, mathematics, world history, art and science. It is less appropriate for subjects that relate to the students' own culture, such as (L1) literature and language.

However, it does not completely replace English lessons, for various reasons. For one thing, CLIL can only be used when the students' level of English is good enough to cope with it. At earlier stages there is no alternative to focused English lessons. For another, CLIL improves some aspects of students' English but has less effect on others: so English lessons are needed to compensate for this imbalance. Finally, there is evidence that optimal learning of English in school-based courses takes place when communicative use is supported by explicit teaching through explanation and focused practice. The best solution seems, therefore, to be the continued provision of English lessons alongside the teaching of selected subjects through English.

The implementation of CLIL in Europe has added momentum to the movement towards content-based instruction in English-teaching materials. Many of these materials now include an explicit CLIL orientation, expressed in their choice of texts and tasks.

If you are teaching, or likely to teach, a content subject in the school curriculum through CLIL, the following tips may help.

Practical tips

1. **Pause occasionally to focus on language.** Feel free to pause in your instruction of the subject in order to take occasional 'time out' to focus on a language point: to teach new words or focus on a student error.

2. **Present new items using L1.** Tell students what the L1 equivalents are for particular subject-linked terminology the first time you introduce them. After that use only the English words.

3. **Correct mistakes.** Correct students' errors of pronunciation, vocabulary and grammar as quickly as you can, but make sure they have 'noticed' them (see Unit 7: Error correction).

4. **Create opportunities for students to speak.** A lot of the lesson time will naturally be devoted to your own input of content information; however, make opportunities for students to produce language themselves: to answer questions at length, or to do group tasks.

5. **Create opportunities for students to write.** Require writing assignments in the target subject in English, not just reading. And again, correct language as well as content.

15.4 Literature as a component of the English course

It used to be taken for granted that the literature taught to learners of English should be classic British or American literature. Later this was expanded to include more modern English literature, and works written by authors from other countries where English is an official or major language such as Canada, Nigeria or India. More recently, the range has been widened still further to include translated literature.

Most of us are teaching English today as an international language, for purposes of global communication. It makes sense, therefore, to choose literature from as wide a range of sources as possible, including all the categories mentioned above.

However, even given this wider scope, the question arises as to whether literary texts and the tasks that go with them are an essential, or even a desirable, component of teaching materials. Literature is in a sense a 'luxury' item. It is not essential for social or work-related communication. If the main purpose of English teaching today is to enable our students to use English as an international language for practical purposes – to form personal relationships, to run a business, to engage in further study, etc. – why should they study literature?

Task

When you were learning a language in school, did you study literature? If so, what were the benefits and problems? If not, do you think you would have liked to? Why, or why not?

Below are some advantages and disadvantages of the study of literature in an English course.

Advantages
• It can be enjoyable and motivating.

• It can widen students' horizons by providing knowledge about the culture which is the background to the text.

- It encourages empathetic, critical and creative thinking.

- It raises awareness of different human situations and conflicts.

- Literature study has value in itself, like any other school subject.

- It provides examples of different styles of writing, and representations of various authentic uses of the language.

- It is a good basis for vocabulary expansion.

- It develops reading skills.

- It can provide an excellent starting point for discussion or writing.

Disadvantages and problems

- A lot of literature is written in language that may be difficult for students to read (we can use simplified versions, but these are inevitably inferior to the original).

- Many literary texts are long and time-consuming to teach.

- The culture on which the literature is based is alien to students and may be difficult for them to relate to.

- By using texts as a basis for language teaching, we may spoil students' enjoyment and appreciation of them as literature.

- Many students may feel that literature is irrelevant to their needs (e.g. students learning English for business or other specific purposes).

Task

If you are teaching, or likely to teach, a course in general English without any particular subject or skill orientation: do you think it appropriate to include a literature component in such a course? What are the main reasons for your decision?

If you are in favour of teaching literature, you will need to think about how to overcome some of the disadvantages listed above. The problems of length, difficulty and alien content are very real ones. They can be solved by careful selection of texts or by using only part of a long text. In some cases simplified or abbreviated versions can be used, if enough of the literary value of the original appears to be preserved.

Practical tips

1. **Choose literature you like.** If you can choose which literary works to teach, choose ones that are favourites of your own. You will probably teach them better and enjoy the process; students are also likely to learn and enjoy them more.

2. **Don't do much language work.** Use the literary text mainly for discussion of meanings and interpretations. Don't 'milk' it for grammar and vocabulary to teach, as we do with other kinds of texts (see Unit 3: The text). Doing so may reduce its literary value and students' enjoyment. This also means not worrying if the students don't understand every word.

3. **Don't over-analyse.** Let the literature make its own impact as much as possible. When doing discussion and analysis, try to involve the students and elicit their responses rather than telling them. Note that too much pre-reading work on themes and content can dilute the impact, as can detailed literary analysis later.

4. **Do teach style.** The exception to the above is the aspect of style. If there are stylistic features that contribute to the impact (drama, aesthetic impression, humour, etc.) of the work, then this is an ideal context for teaching about them.

5. **Reread at the end.** Finish your teaching of the work by rereading the entire piece (if it is short) or a significant section of it (if it is long). The students should be left with the literature itself echoing in their minds, not the comments!

6. **Look for other versions.** Enrich the study of a particular work by adding adaptations or different versions. Show them the movie of a book, or a video of a poem being read (try video-sharing websites such as *YouTube*). Alternatively, compare the literary text with a modern book or movie which adapts or reinterprets the plot and characters of the original.

15.5 Underlying messages

The content of a text often carries a 'hidden curriculum': underlying messages that go beyond factual information. These may be related to religious or political beliefs, or attitudes towards certain kinds of people, nationalities or cultures. It is very important to be aware of such 'subtext' for two major reasons. First, for your own professional integrity: you want to be sure you are teaching what you intend to teach, and not unconsciously expressing support for attitudes you do not approve of. Second, because students who identify with groups who are discriminated against in content may feel disadvantaged and learn less well: for example, female students using materials which consistently present the male as superior.

Favourable or unfavourable attitudes may be expressed in various ways. One is a hidden bias: for example, readers are asked to identify with people who belong to a particular group, or express opinions that reflect a particular political stance. Another is invisibility of opinions that are disapproved of, or of a discriminated-against group; for example, if only young adults are shown, with no representation of the middle-aged or elderly. A third – rarer, but easier to detect – is explicitly discriminatory statements: for example, implying that one language is 'superior' to another.

Many prejudices which we reject intellectually are very deeply ingrained in our thinking: so much so that we may betray them without realizing it. We may, for example, find ourselves using mainly 'he' in grammar examples, even if we are committed feminists. It often takes a conscious effort to counteract such tendencies. Indeed, both teachers and coursebook writers these days are far more aware of the possible hidden curriculum of course materials and make efforts to see that the underlying messages are acceptable.

Task

Take a coursebook – preferably one you are fairly familiar with – and try some or all of the following:

1. **Sexism**. Using either illustrations or texts, look at the occupations which men and women are shown doing. Was there a consistent 'type' of occupation given to either? If so, do you find such a division acceptable? Is there a reasonable balance between reflection of the real world and avoidance of stereotyping? For example, a book may portray a bus driver as a woman to avoid stereotyping, but in the real world bus drivers are mostly men. Do you think it is justifiable to present a distorted picture of normality in order to avoid discrimination? Does the book strike a reasonable balance?

2. **Ageism**. If your coursebook is illustrated, look through the pictures. Count the number of adults over the age of 40 compared with younger adults (not counting pictures of children or teenagers who will naturally predominate if the material is aimed at this age group). Does the division reflect your estimation of the proportion of young/older adults in society? If not, do you approve or disapprove of the book's distorted picture? If you approve, can you justify your approval?

3. **Cultural orientation**. Read a selection of texts and exercises. Are they appropriate for the social culture of your students? Do they include any material that your students would find totally alien? Embarrassing? Offensive? Or is it all fairly close to the culture of your students and would be comfortably accepted by them?

Classroom implications

If you have to use certain materials, but these display some kind of orientation that you do not find acceptable, what might you do about it?

Some possibilities regarding unacceptable cultural aspects are discussed in Unit 14: Materials, pp. 206–7. For the other types of discriminatory emphasis, you might:

- ignore them and try in your teaching to make sure that your own input and teacher-led activities are more balanced in content;

- compensate by adding extra material of your own which supplies the deficit and makes for a better balance;

- draw your students' attention to the bias, and lead an open critical discussion to raise their awareness of it.

Review

Answer as many as you can of the following questions, and then check answers by referring back to the relevant passages in this unit.

If you are working in a group, note down your own answers first alone, and then share with the other members of the group. Finally, check the answers together.

Different kinds of content

1. Can you remember at least seven different kinds of topics that are used in English courses?

Cultural content

2. What kinds of things does the term *culture* include?
3. What are the main sources of the cultural content we find in course materials?
4. What is 'intercultural competence'?

Content and language integrated learning (CLIL)

5. What is 'CLIL'?
6. Can you suggest some advantages and disadvantages of the implementation of CLIL in schools?
7. What are some research-based findings with regard to CLIL?

Literature as a component of the English course

8. What changes have occurred over the years in the selection of literary texts to be taught in English courses?
9. Can you list at least three arguments for and three against using literature in your English course?
10. Suggest two useful tips to help teach literature.

Underlying messages

11. How are underlying messages to do with cultural, social or political values conveyed through course materials?
12. What are some kinds of negative messages that might be conveyed by such means?

Further reading

Collie, J. and Slater, S. (1987) *Literature in the Language Classroom*, Cambridge: Cambridge University Press.
> (Discussion of some general issues followed by a variety of practical literature-teaching techniques, relating to various literary genres)

Cortazzi, M. and Lixian, J. (1999) Cultural mirrors: materials and methods in the EFL classroom. In E.Hinkel (ed.), *Culture in Second Language Teaching and Learning* (pp. 196–219), Cambridge: Cambridge University Press.
> (A readable summary of issues to do with culture, intercultural competence in English-teaching materials, with recommendations)

Lazar, G. (1993) *Literature and Language Teaching*, Cambridge: Cambridge University Press.
> (A good text to use to teach yourself how to teach literature: comprehensive, readable, with plenty of illustrative tasks accompanied by suggested answers)

Websites

European commission: language teaching: CLIL, accessible from http://ec.europa.eu/education/languages/language-teaching/doc236_en.htm

CLIL compendium: www.clilcompendium.com/clilcompendium.htm
> (These websites give some basic information on the aims and implementation of CLIL)

Classroom interaction

The sections in this unit are:

16.1 **Teacher questioning.** Some types of teacher questions and their purposes; effective questioning.

16.2 **Group and pair work.** Advantages and disadvantages of group and pair work; practical guidelines.

16.3 **Individual work.** Procedures that allow for varying levels of individualization.

16.4 **Blended learning.** Some ways in which digital tools and materials can be used together with conventional classroom interactions for optimal learning outcomes.

Unit 2: The lesson, pp. 18–21 provides a general overview of the range of classroom interaction patterns and their use for different teaching aims. This unit focuses on a more detailed discussion of the best way to run the four specific types of interaction shown in the list above.

16.1 Teacher questioning

Questioning is the most common and universally used activation technique in teaching, mainly within the Initiation–Response–Feedback pattern described in Unit 2: The lesson (p. 18).

Teacher questions are defined here as initiatives on the part of the teacher which are designed to elicit (oral) responses by the student. They may not always be worded as interrogatives, and conversely, interrogative forms are not always questions. For example, the question *What can you see in this picture?* may be communicated by a statement (*We'll describe what is going on in this picture.*) or a command (*Tell me what you can see in this picture!*), but it's still a 'teacher question', according to the definition provided at the beginning of this paragraph. On the other hand, an interrogative sentence like *Will you sit down?* is obviously not a question, but actually a request or command.

Task

What purpose do teacher questions serve in the classroom? Try to think of as many as you can, and then compare your list with the one below. Was there anything you had forgotten? Is there anything you can add?

Purposes of teacher questions

- To provide a model for language or thinking
- To find out something from the students (e.g. facts, ideas, opinions)
- To check or test understanding, knowledge or skill

- To get students to be active in their learning
- To direct attention, or provide a 'warm-up', to the topic which is about to be studied
- To inform the class through students' answers rather than through the teacher's input
- To provide weaker students with an opportunity to participate
- To stimulate thinking (logical, critical or imaginative)
- To probe more deeply into issues
- To get students to relate personally to an issue
- To get students to review and practise previously taught material
- To encourage self-expression
- To communicate to students that the teacher is genuinely interested in what they think.

Any specific question is likely to involve more than one of these; for example, it might review and practise while simultaneously encouraging self-expression.

Types of questions

We can classify and criticize teacher questions according to various criteria:

Communicative authenticity. Are they 'genuine' or 'display' questions? Does the teacher really want to find out the answer, or is he or she simply checking if the student knows it? 'Genuine' questions are authentic communication, because they involve a real transfer of information: and if we want to give students experience of using English for communication, there should be a place for these in classroom interaction. 'Display' questions are also important: indeed, they are essential for teaching. There are many occasions where we need to get students to demonstrate what they know, practise something, or speak or write in order to increase fluency. 'Display' questions are often the most effective way of achieving such aims.

Length of expected response. Do they elicit short responses (a word, phrase or short sentence) or extended ones? In general, questions that require longer responses (a long sentence or more) are better, because they create more student activation and lead to better learning. However, there is also a place for short ones where, for example, the aim is only to find out if a student has understood or not.

Number of expected responses. Are they closed-ended (with a single, right answer) or open-ended (with many possible answers)? Closed-ended questions usually have short responses and are useful for quick checks of knowledge or comprehension, or for testing. Open-ended ones may have short or long answers, but the point is that there are lots of them: each question leads to multiple responses. So they are good for situations where you want to get lots of practice of a particular language point, or of fluent speech or writing. Open-ended questions therefore lead to more activation. They also elicit more interesting responses (see Unit 4: The task, pp. 51–5).

Level of thinking required. Do they elicit lower-order or higher-order thinking? Lower-order thinking is simple recall or basic factual information (for example,

'What is the past tense of the verb *take*?'). Higher-order thinking involves deeper understanding, application, analysis, criticism, evaluation or creativity (for example, 'What are some differences between the opinions expressed in the two texts we have read?'). So I refer to the corresponding questions as 'lower-order' or 'higher-order' questions, respectively. Lower-order questions are mostly 'display', closed-ended and short-response, and vice versa – but not always.

There is a place for both higher- and lower-order questions in English language teaching. One difference is that you cannot do without lower-order questions for initial teaching and reviewing new material, whereas you can manage without the higher-order ones. As a result sometimes the latter are neglected. Higher-order questions are important for the cultivation of critical and creative thinking, and arguably lead to more challenging, interesting and richer language-learning procedures.

Action task

Choose one of the criteria above, observe a lesson and note down how many questions of each kind you hear: for example, how many 'display' questions did you hear and how many 'genuine'? Or how many short-response and how many long-response?

Which kinds were most common? Do you have any comments or criticisms?

If you are working in a group, each observer should focus on a different criterion, and then pool results later.

Most questions in most lessons are 'display', short-response, closed-ended and lower-order. In my experience, both teachers and course materials tend to under-use the genuine, long-response, open-ended and higher-order ones. This is partly because they are harder to formulate, and their responses are more difficult to monitor and correct. I am not claiming that all, or even most, questions should be from these under-used categories, but we should make sure that there are at least some of them in every lesson, for the reasons given earlier. They can be adapted to different levels, so can be used from the most elementary and youngest classes up to most academic adult ones.

Assuming, then, that classroom questioning should include all types of questions, what are some other criteria for 'effective questioning'?

Effective questioning

As language teachers, our motive in questioning is usually to get our students to engage actively with the language material and its content. So an effective questioning technique is one that elicits immediate, motivated, relevant and full responses. If most of our questions result in long silences, are only answered by the strongest students, obviously bore the class, or consistently elicit only very brief or unsuccessful answers, then there is something wrong. In such cases, the following checklist can help.

Checklist for effective teacher questioning

1. **Clarity.** Do the students immediately understand not only what the question means, but also what kind of an answer is required? Often it can help a lot if the teacher provides a sample acceptable answer or two first to give a model.

2. **Interest.** Do the students find the question interesting, challenging, stimulating?

3. **Accessibility.** Can most of the students at least try to answer it, or only the more advanced, confident and knowledgeable ones?

4. **Level of answer.** Are the answers demanded within the level of the students, both cognitively and linguistically?

5. **Learning value.** Does the question lead to, or effectively check, learning?

6. **Teacher reaction.** Are the students sure that the feedback to their responses will be respectful, that they will not be put down or ridiculed if they say something inappropriate?

Samples of teacher questioning

Below are some samples of actual classroom exchanges between teacher and students, showing different kinds of teacher questions, with following comment.

> **Task**
>
> Have a look at the exchanges below. Can you identify what the purpose of the teacher is in questioning, and comment on the way he or she did it, perhaps using the checklist above? Then read on.

Exchange 1: Discussing circuses

T: Now today we are going to discuss circuses. Have you ever been to a circus?

Ss: (immediately) Yes, yes.

T: Yes. Where you see clowns, and horses and elephants and acrobats. Our reading passage today is about a circus …

Exchange 2: The word *relief*

T: Yesterday we learned various words that express feelings. Let's review them. Can you tell me … What does 'relief' mean?

(pause)

Well, when might you feel relief?.

(pause)

Can you remember a time when you felt relief? Yes, Maria?

S1: When my friend was late, I thought she wasn't coming and in the end she came.

T: Right, a nice example: When Maria's friend was late, she thought she wasn't coming, but in the end she came. Good … Fran?

S2: I thought I will fail the exam, and then in the end I pass.

T: Good …

Exchange 3: What was the story about?

> T: Now: what was the story about? Can anyone tell me? Claire?
> S: Man.
> T: Yes, a man. What did this man do? Can you tell me anything about him?
> S: He ... married.

Exchange 4: Describe a picture

> T: Here's a picture, with lots of things going on. Tell me some of them. For example: the policeman is talking to the driver, perhaps he's telling him where to go. What else?
> S1: The little girl is buying an ice cream.
> S2: There's a woman, old woman, in the middle, she's crossing the road.
> S3: A man ... sitting ... on chair ...
> T: OK, a man is sitting on a chair, there in the corner ... What else?

Comment

Exchange 1: Discussing circuses. There is a problem of 'double messages' here, since the declared objective is contradicted by the questioning technique. The teacher says explicitly that the intention is to discuss; but the introductory question, though clear, actually discourages discussion. It is a yes / no question inviting a single, brief answer. However, it is both interesting and accessible to students. The fact that the students answer immediately and apparently enthusiastically indicates that they probably have something to say. However, they are given no opportunity to do so. The teacher gives information that could have easily been elicited from them and then moves on to the reading passage. Either the teacher did not really intend to 'discuss' at all and prefers to hold the stage him- or herself, or he or she is not aware of the inappropriate form of his or her questions; perhaps a combination of the two.

Exchange 2: The word *relief*. The aim is to review vocabulary learnt the day before, and it is clear from what they say later that the students do in fact know the meaning of the word. The obvious question: *What does X mean?*, though apparently clear, is unsuccessful in eliciting answers. This is probably because it is too abstract and difficult. Even an advanced speaker of English might find it difficult to give a definition. So the question is simply not accessible to the students. This teacher, however, quickly realizes his or her mistake and rephrases, twice. The question that demands a concrete example from experience is much better, and predictably receives immediate and full responses.

Exchange 3: What was the story about? There do not seem to be any pauses after the questions, and the answers are basically correct in content; the questions also seem fairly clear, interesting and available to most of the class. But their learning value is lowered because of the difficulty the students have in expressing their answers. The teacher might have been able to help by giving some hints or modelling answers in his questions: *Was it about a man, a woman, an animal ...? It was ... Yes, Claire?*

Exchange 4: Describe a picture. Here the teacher makes it very clear what kinds of responses are required by providing examples, and also indicates that a number of different answers is expected. The combination of these two strategies makes the question far more accessible and easy to answer than something like *What can you see in the picture?* (compare to the previous exchange). The number of student responses to the single cue looks as if it will be relatively large, and S3, who is more hesitant and sounds as if he or she is not as good at English as the others, attempts a response based on the examples (of the teacher and of previous speakers) which he or she might not have done without these models.

Practical tips

1. **Wait-time.** When asking questions in class, remember to wait a little before nominating a student to answer. This increases the number of students who might be able to answer it. But don't overdo it: too much wait-time slows down the process, and might lead to boredom and lack of attention.

2. **'Echo'.** In many cases it's a good idea to 'echo' student responses, like the teacher in Exchange 2 above. This is a confirmation of the response, and an indirect compliment to the responding student. It also makes sure that the rest of the class hears the response, as not all students speak clearly or loudly enough to be heard by everyone. Echoing is also an opportunity to correct and extend the student's response for the benefit of the rest of the class, as provided by the teacher at the end of Exchange 4.

16.2 Group and pair work

Both group (three or more students working together) and pair work involve collaborative activity, but may be used for slightly different purposes and in different situations.

Group work is more difficult to organize, because it usually involves moving students, and sometimes their chairs and tables. Pair work is easier, because students are often sitting in pairs anyway, and simply turn towards each other. For this reason, pair work is more appropriate for the shorter collaborative tasks, for example comparing answers to an exercise. Also, group work is often more difficult to control with an undisciplined class: some students are inevitably sitting with their backs to you, focusing on each other, and will be less ready to pay attention to you.

However, group work has some advantages. More students can contribute ideas to a discussion task; there are more participants if the activity is a game; groups can often work as teams in a competition; and the mere fact that students get up and move in order to form, or re-form, groups can provide a welcome break from the routine of sitting in the same place all the time.

But most collaborative activities can be done either in groups or in pairs. In this section from now on, the term *group work* includes pair work.

Advantages

Group work has a number of advantages as a component of classroom interaction:

- It fosters learner autonomy. Students working in groups are not directly controlled by the teacher, and they make their own choices about how they do the group task. If they are collaborating on gapfill grammar exercises, then their choices will be limited to the pace at which they work, the amount of work they do, and perhaps the order in which they do different items. If they are discussing something, then the language they are using will be determined by them, not the teacher. If they are working together on a project, then the content itself may depend on their own decisions.

- Although collaborative work does not suit the learning style of some students, for many group work is very motivating. It is pleasant to cooperate with others to produce a joint result, and students enjoy the sense of group solidarity and warmth that often results.

- It is particularly important for practising oral fluency. Students in a class that is divided into five groups get five times as many opportunities to talk as in a full-class discussion (see Unit 9: Teaching speaking, pp. 118–19).

Problems

Both teachers and students may have reservations about doing group work.

Teachers

Some teachers fear that by moving out of the role of manager and leader, and fragmenting the class, they may lose control, particularly with young or adolescent groups in schools. Students might start using the L1 too much, make a lot of noise, and may not in fact be engaged in the task at all. Even if they are engaged, there is the nagging question: how much learning is actually going on? Would they have learnt as much, or more, in full-class or individual interaction? There is in fact some basis in the research for this concern (see Seedhouse, 1997). For these reasons, many teachers – particularly new teachers, and/or where the class is an unruly one – avoid group work completely, in spite of its advantages.

Students

Some students do not like group work. They prefer a teacher-led classroom, or working on their own. Some may simply not be used to it if it is not part of their 'culture of learning'. Others think that working with other students does not result in serious learning: they feel they should be learning from the teacher, not from each other. Another reason is individual learning style. Some students simply learn best when working on their own, and working in groups does not suit them.

Addressing the problems

Some of the problems described above can be solved or at least reduced. Here are some suggestions.

The problem of students going off-task, over-using the L1, making a lot of noise, etc. during group work is a very real one in some classes. There are two points to be made here.

First, some of these events may not be as negative as they seem. If the task involves talking, there will be a lot of noise – which is not necessarily a bad thing! And using L1 is not necessarily counterproductive either. In many cases some L1 use can help students perform the task more effectively, and it can save time during instruction-giving which can then be used for engaging with English. It is true that it can get out of hand: so you need to keep an eye on what is happening and limit L1 use as you feel necessary. Student monitors within the group whose job it is to check the use of the L1 can be useful here (see Unit 9: Teaching speaking, p. 119).

Second, you can often prevent clearly counterproductive developments such as students misinterpreting the task or failing to do it altogether through carefully organized presentation, management and closing of group tasks (this is discussed in detail in Unit 4: The task, pp. 49–51).

The fact that some group work does not produce much learning may be due to faulty task design (see Unit 4: The task, pp. 43–51). With many classes, the exact process of the task, including the outcome, needs to be carefully structured. For example, if the groups have been set the goal of reaching a decision on a controversial topic in order to get practice in talking, you need to make sure that both objectives are achieved, and that they do not just all agree with the first person who suggests a decision! You could, for example, make it a rule that everyone has to express an opinion; or give each member of the group a role to play; or provide some extra issues or facts that they need to relate to in their discussion; and so on.

But even with the best organization and task design, some classes may not enjoy group work, for any of the reasons listed above under *Students*. In such cases, it might help to explain to the class why it is important to do occasional group tasks, give them opportunities to express how they feel about it, and agree together with them how much, or how little, you will do it.

Summary

Group work is only valuable when it motivates and enables good learning. In some classes it may be really difficult to do successfully, so you do not need to feel guilty if you use it only rarely! A lot of classroom learning depends on full-class work led by the teacher; and individual work is also important, as discussed in Section 16.3 below. However, make an effort to include some group work, even if only occasionally. It adds variation, it provides opportunities for students to talk in English, it suits the learning style of many students, and it promotes learner autonomy.

16.3 Individual work

Individualization means adapting texts and tasks to the individual student's level, speed of work, needs, personal learning styles and so on. It implies varying degrees of learner choice and autonomy, as the student him- or herself decides what to learn and how, within a range of options provided by the teacher or course materials.

Self-access centres

The concept of 'individualized learning' in education is sometimes identified with the provision of a self-access centre (SAC). In an SAC, different materials are available: audio and video equipment, computers with language-learning software and internet access, a library of books, worksheets, games and puzzles, areas where people can simply sit and chat in English and so on. The students themselves choose where to work and how to engage with the tasks they have selected.

SACs are more common in universities and colleges, less so in primary or secondary education. One problem is expense. SACs cost a lot, in terms of both money and work, to set up; they also need constant maintenance, tidying and replenishing. Another problem is the fact that most students need a structure to their learning: without a clear programme, deadlines, goals and set tasks, many students feel uncomfortable, lose motivation and find it difficult to concentrate and get things done. To solve this, the teacher can set up a programme during class time. For example, each student has to work on a certain number of specific types of tasks (they can choose exactly which one) and keep a record of what they have done. But then the teacher needs to monitor who does what, make sure that not too many students are trying to use the same resource at the same time, and check that they actually complete the tasks: it is a lot of work! In short, SACs are only likely to be successful in institutions that have the necessary financial resources, and where there are motivated students and dedicated teachers.

Individualization in the regular classroom

A more moderate, and perhaps easier to implement, version of individualization might be defined as follows: a situation where individual students have some freedom to choose how, what or how much they learn within the conventional classroom framework. The teacher no longer dominates interaction but invites students to choose what to do from a range of tasks provided, or how they tackle a particular task. This is the opposite to what is known as 'lockstep' learning, where everyone in the class, in principle, is expected to do the same thing, at the same time, in the same way.

So this version of individualization means that you do not need to set up lessons based entirely on self-access tasks. However, it does mean a serious attempt to provide for different learner needs within a class and to give the students themselves more responsibility for guiding and organizing their own learning.

Below is a list of classroom procedures that allow for differing degrees of individual learner choice within a regular classroom.

1. **Worksheets.** The teacher distributes worksheets which all practise the same language point but contain various sections with different kinds of practice tasks and topics. The students choose which sections they want to do and complete as much as they can in the time given.
2. **Questions for homework.** The class has been given a set of questions based on a reading text from the coursebook to answer in writing, some of which have been done in class. They are asked to finish them for homework.
3. **Varied tasks.** The teacher sets up different areas in the classroom with different materials or equipment: computers with language tasks to complete or web-based searches for information; worksheets or work cards;

DVD equipment with headsets; a range of simplified readers; and so on. Alternatively, if each student has access to a computer with an internet connection, the teacher prepares the addresses of a number of different websites with different tasks: reading texts with comprehension work, grammar exercises, webquests, vocabulary work, dictionary work and so on. In either case, the students work in the different areas according to individual choice.

4. **Computerized exercises**. The students work on individual computers, doing sets of grammar practice exercises from a CD-ROM, or from a website specified by the teacher. They can choose from three levels and can check their own answers, but they are all working on the same target grammatical feature. They do as much as they can in half an hour.

5. **Readers**. Students choose individual simplified readers, of varied level and topic, from a school library, and are asked to read at home for at least twenty minutes every day, more if they can.

6. **Writing**. Students are given 20 minutes to write as much as they can on a given topic.

These activities are individualized to different extents, depending on what aspect of the task can be varied. The main such aspects are:

A. **Speed**. Each student works at his or her own pace.
B. **Level**. Tasks are available at different levels, so each student can choose the one they find appropriate.
C. **Quantity**. Each student may choose how much or how little they actually produce or complete.
D. **Task**. Each student works on a task of his or her choice, but all the tasks are focused on a similar aspect of language: vocabulary, for example, or grammar, or reading comprehension.
E. **Teaching/learning focus**. The student can choose what he or she does from a wide variety of tasks focusing on different aspects of language learning.

Task

Look at the list of classroom procedures listed above. In the margin next to each one, write which aspects are individualized (speed, level, quantity, task, teaching/ learning focus). Then compare your answers to my own, shown below.

Comment

1. **Worksheets**. These provide individualized **speed, level, quantity** and **tasks**. They are all focused on the same teaching/learning point. Note that the fact that the worksheet contains a variety of task-types is likely to enhance individualization but does not guarantee it. If the students had been told that they all had to do the entire worksheet, the demands would have been fairly uniform. So the level of individualization here is mainly a result of the teacher instructions rather than the material itself.

2. Questions for homework. Here, the only aspect which is individualized is **speed**: each student takes as much time as he or she needs. Otherwise, everyone in the class is doing the same kind of work and the same amount. It might lead to more real individualization if the teacher fixed an amount of time ('take 20 minutes, do whichever questions you can and as many as you can'). In that case each student would be able to choose what and how much to do, and the task as a whole would be better adapted for different ability levels. This, however, only works if you can trust students to keep to the time limit at home as instructed!

3. Varied tasks. The provision of varied tasks leads to a very high level of individualization: in **speed**, **level**, **quantity**, **task** and **teaching/learning focus**. In fact the variety here is similar to that provided in an SAC. Students are able to work at their own speed, choose the level and the amount of work to do, and choose from a range of tasks using different skills and with different learning goals.

4. Computerized exercises. These provide for individualization in **speed**, **level** and **quantity**, but not in teaching/learning focus. The task-types cannot be very varied, because self-checking computerized exercises have to be based on a limited number of closed-ended items such as multiple-choice or gapfills.

5. Readers. The use of student-chosen readers ensures individualization of **speed**, **level** and **quantity**, but not of task or teaching/learning focus. Note that the instruction 'read for at least 20 minutes' rather than 'read for 20 minutes' makes sure that everyone spends at least a minimum time reading, but allows flexibility as to how much more each student chooses to do. This kind of reading is probably one of the most useful individualized activities (see Unit 10: Teaching reading, pp. 145–6).

6. Writing. The writing task described here obviously does not provide for variation in speed, task or teaching/learning focus, but it does allow for varied **level** and **quantity**. It is a useful exercise, fun to do and easy to set up. The resulting pieces of writing can later be rewritten and edited and developed into longer written assignments.

Task

Now go back to the list of classroom procedures, and note how much teacher work you think is necessary in each case in order to prepare or set up the individualized procedure and check results: w = little or no work, ww = some work, www = a lot of work, wwww = an enormous amount of work.

Some conclusions

If your answers are similar to mine, then the obvious implication is that the more choices the student has (in other words, the more opportunities for individualization), the more work it means for the teacher. More individualized tasks may also mean more work in feedback later. If everyone has done the same task, then the results can be quickly checked in full class; however, if each student has done something different, then each piece of work needs to be checked individually. In other words, the fact that the student takes more responsibility for his or her choices does not reduce the amount of work that the teacher has to do: quite the reverse!

To summarize: total individualization and learner autonomy, in an SAC centre or self-access areas in a classroom, are probably not feasible in most teaching contexts. Some degree of individualization within a normal classroom is, however, practicable, and it is important to provide it wherever possible. Some possibilities have been listed above, but there are many more (see some more suggestions in Unit 19: Learner differences (2): teaching heterogeneous (mixed) classes, pp. 276–80).

16.4 Blended learning

Some different types of digital materials used in language teaching were described in Unit 14: Materials, pp. 211–12. This section looks at the way these function within classroom interactions through what is known as *blended learning*. This term is usually taken to refer to the kind of learning that combines conventional teacher–student interaction in a face-to-face classroom situation, with computer-mediated interaction when students and teacher are not in the same place at the same time. A wider definition includes the use of computerized equipment as it functions:

- within the lesson

- outside the lesson (asynchronous teaching/learning)

- instead of the lesson (synchronous teaching/learning)

This section looks at these three implementations of the concept of blended learning as they affect classroom interaction and learning outcomes.

Within the lesson
The interactive whiteboard (IWB)
The IWB is an attractive and increasingly widely used tool. However, the fact that it is so attractive and flexible in its use should not blind us to its limitations as regards classroom interaction. Like the white-or blackboard it replaces, it directs students' attention towards a centralized, teacher-controlled focus, and so moves the class towards teacher-led interactions. We need, therefore, to be careful how, and how much, we use it.

Computers
Again, many classrooms are now equipped with computers, or students bring them to class for use during the lesson. If there are not enough for all students to use them simultaneously, they can be used collaboratively. Individual computers can be used as both notebook and coursebook, as well as allowing students to take advantage of various internet-based facilities. Like the IWB, they influence the kind of interaction that can take place in the classroom – though in a totally different direction. They attract and focus attention, and their use, therefore, moves the class towards individual and personalized learning, and away from cooperative or teacher-led classroom process – far more so than the conventional books that they may to some extent replace. So again, we need

to be aware of where and why computers are useful and where they might be counterproductive.

Finally, there is the problem of control: it is very easy for students using computers that are connected to the Internet to access websites that are irrelevant to the work in progress and/or do not facilitate learning. Some classes may need careful direction and monitoring to make sure that the equipment is being used as intended.

Outside the lesson

Asynchronous teaching through computer-mediated communications means that teacher input is not immediately followed by student response, and vice versa. Responses are given in the participant's own time, when convenient. So, for example, you may ask the class a question which each student answers when they log in at home: this may be a day, a week, or maybe more, later. This can be done through email, wikis, blogs or LMSs (see below).

In asynchronous interaction with students, you can do all or any of the following:

- provide explanations or other written input; students indicate that they have read and understood
- upload reading texts, audio or video: students read, listen to or view them and do comprehension or other tasks related to them, which you can check
- start a discussion through a 'forum', and invite student contributions, responding and contributing further yourself as appropriate
- set tasks (with a time limit for submission if you wish)
- receive, comment on and assess tasks the students have done
- give final grades for the course.

There are various digital tools which enable some or all of these functions: the most common are email, wiki, blog and LMS.

Email

Email enables far more individual communication between teacher and students than was possible previously. It is used by students to submit individual written assignments, as well as by the teacher to check and return them and give grades. It is also useful if the teacher wants to correspond with individual students about any particular issues that need to be discussed personally.

Wiki

A wiki can be used to engage in interactive editing of written assignments (see again Unit 14: Materials, p. 212), so it enables collaborative work between students, with the teacher monitoring and making suggestions as necessary. It can also be used for online discussion. Like email, it enables more interaction between teacher and students outside the lesson, but in this case everything written on the wiki is seen, and edited and commented on, by the entire class. Some teachers, indeed, use a wiki as their class website, with a new 'page' for each lesson or learning unit. In principle, the wiki is a tool which leads to a more collaborative, student-centred type of interaction, with the teacher assuming the role of facilitator, monitor and adviser rather than instructor or assessor.

Blog

Blogs are more teacher-led than wikis. Students do not edit each other's writing, but add comments as requested by the teacher in the main blog entries, or as responses to each other's comments. Blogs can be used as the class website in the same way as wiki. Neither wiki nor blog, however, are appropriate vehicles for the displaying of grades, since they are open to the entire class, and students normally prefer to receive grades privately (for a tool which solves this problem, see *Learning Management System* below).

Learning Management System (LMS)

An LMS is a platform or multiple-facility program which enables a large number of classroom teaching and management functions to be carried out online. Its advantage is that it can provide all the functions of email, wikis and blogs in one 'package', as well as tasks and exercises for the students. It also enables you more easily to share texts or links to websites, or even an entire coursebook, for students to refer to; to keep track of the assignments and assessments given to a group during the course; and to ensure that in a list of final grades each grade is seen only by its recipient.

LMS homepage

Asynchronous teaching/learning can be used for courses based on distance learning, when there is no possibility of face-to-face lessons and the entire course is done online. However, it is more widely, and perhaps effectively, used within the blended learning model as described here, where it functions as a supplement, rather than a substitute, for ordinary lessons. Many English courses these days are taught through regular lessons, enriched and supported by any of the tools described above. The most obvious result of the use of such tools is to make the management of a course easier and more organized, and students' performance easier to monitor. It has the important side effect of maintaining regular and ongoing interaction between teacher and students, even if the two sides do not actually have any face-to-face contact between lessons.

Some LMSs include tools that enable actual online lessons carried on in real time, as described below.

Instead of the lesson

Computer programs such as *Ellumination Live!* enable the teacher to teach a lesson synchronously, i.e. interacting in real time with students even though they may be miles away. The students all sit at their computers at home, log in at a pre-set time, register their attendance and participate in a lesson for a set period of time. The teacher may lecture and show slides or other visual material. Students watch and listen but may also respond: raise their hands and then, when called on, contribute a question or comment; send a note to the lecturer or to other participants; express their feelings through smileys; vote in polls.

In my experience, online synchronous teaching of this type can be useful and productive – and fun! – particularly if the lesson is based primarily on information provided by the teacher. However, it is not a substitute for face-to-face interaction, which is the primary and most effective mode of teaching and learning. Like the asynchronous teaching described previously, it is therefore best used together with and as a supplement to conventional lessons, rather than as the sole basis for a course.

Review

Answer as many as you can of the following questions, and then check answers by referring back to the relevant passages in this unit.

If you are working in a group, note down your own answers first alone, and then share with the other members of the group. Finally, check the answers together.

Teacher questioning

1. Teacher questions may have various purposes: can you recall at least five?
2. Can you think of one example of a 'lower-order' question? One example of a 'higher-order' question?
3. What are some of the characteristics of effective teacher questions?

Group and pair work

4. What are the main advantages of using group work in the English classroom?
5. Can you suggest three problems associated with group work?
6. Suggest some ways these problems can be addressed.

Individual work

7. What is an SAC?
8. What five different aspects of learning can be individualized?
9. Suggest some practical ways in which the teacher can allow for individualized choices in the classroom.

Blended learning

10. What is *blended learning*?
11. What is the difference between *asynchronous* and *synchronous* computer-mediated interaction?
12. What sorts of things can be done using an LMS?

Further reading

Questioning

Brualdi, Amy C. (1998) Classroom questions. *Practical Assessment, Research & Evaluation, 6*(6) (http://PAREonline.net/getvn.asp?v=6&n=6).

> (A brief, useful summary of the main issues in teacher questioning)

Tsui, A. (2001) Classroom interaction. In R. Carter and D. Nunan (eds.), *The Cambridge Guide to Teaching English to Speakers of Other Languages* (pp. 120–5), Cambridge: Cambridge University Press.

> (A discussion of the various aspects of classroom interaction, focusing particularly on teacher questioning processes)

Group work and individualization

Jacobs, G. M., and Hall, S. (2002) Implementing cooperative learning. In J. C. Richards and W. A. Renandya (eds.), *Methodology in Language Teaching* (pp. 52–8), Cambridge: Cambridge University Press.

> (Some very practical tips on the organization of group work in English lessons)

Mcdonough, J. and Shaw, C. (2003) *Materials and Methods in ELT: A Teacher's Guide* (2nd edn), Malden, MA: Blackwell.

> (See chapters 11 and 12 for some useful discussion of group and pair work, and of individualization, focusing on self-assess facilities)

Blended learning

Martin, D. (2009) *Activities for Interactive Whiteboards*, London: Helbling Languages.

> (A set of ideas for how to use the interactive whiteboard in order to involve and activate students)

Sharma, P. and Barrett, B. (2007) *Blended Learning*, Oxford: Macmillan.

> (A practical guide to the use of technology combined with traditional teaching, with an emphasis on the development of learner autonomy)

The sections in this unit are:

17.1 **What is classroom discipline**? A definition and description of some aspects of a disciplined classroom.

17.2 **What teachers can do to create a disciplined classroom**. General guidelines and practical tips for making sure lessons run smoothly.

17.3 **Dealing with discipline problems**. Some practical ideas for how to deal with teacher–student conflicts and discipline problems in the classroom.

17.4 **Discipline problems: episodes**. A number of scenarios illustrating different kinds of problems, analysed and discussed.

This unit is about classroom discipline and (potentially or actually) misbehaving students. For discussion of general classroom management and organization, see Unit 2: The lesson and Unit 4: The task.

17.1 What is classroom discipline?

Task

Can you define the term *classroom discipline*? You might begin: 'Classroom discipline exists when …'. Then look at a possible definition below and compare it to your own.

Defining terms

For most teachers the phrase *classroom discipline* has an immediate and clear meaning, but in fact it is quite a complex concept, and hard to define.

A possible definition might be:

> Classroom discipline exists when teacher and students accept and consistently observe a set of rules relating to classroom behaviour in order to facilitate smooth and efficient teaching and learning.

What does a disciplined classroom look like?

Below are some possible characteristics of a well-disciplined classroom.

Task

Imagine a classroom that is well disciplined. Then look at the statements below, and note by each one how true it is of the situation you imagine. Add any comments or questions in the margin. Then read on.

1. Learning is taking place.
2. It is quiet.
3. The teacher is in control.
4. Teacher and students are cooperating smoothly.
5. Students are motivated.
6. The lesson is proceeding according to plan.
7. Teacher and students are aiming for the same objectives.
8. The teacher has natural charismatic authority.

Comment

1. **Learning is taking place.** The question of the relationship between discipline and learning is crucial. It seems fairly clear that in a disciplined classroom it is easier to activate students in the way you want, and that time will be probably spent on-task, rather than wasted on organizational problems or disruptive behaviour. However, I have seen well-disciplined classes in which little or no learning was taking place, simply because the tasks had themselves little learning value (see Unit 4: The task, p. 43). So a disciplined classroom does not, in itself, necessarily cause learning to take place. On the other hand, the converse is probably nearer the truth: there is unlikely to be much learning in a totally undisciplined classroom.

   We might sum up by saying that discipline is a necessary, but not sufficient, condition for good learning to take place.

2. **It is quiet.** It is easy to claim that this is irrelevant. What about well-disciplined classes where noisy pair- or group work is going on? However, think about the following points. First, cooperative work involving talk takes up only a part of lesson time, probably a minority – what about the rest? Second, imagine walking down the corridor of a school, listening at the door of each classroom, and hearing noise in some and quiet in others. If you had to guess which were the better-disciplined ones, what would you say?

   The bottom line is that disciplined classes may or may not be quiet, but undisciplined ones are always noisy. Therefore, there is arguably a positive association between quietness and discipline. The teacher needs to ensure that the class is quiet enough for students to hear the teacher and each other, and to complete tasks without being disturbed.

3. **The teacher is in control.** Yes, definitely. However, the fact that a teacher is in control does not necessarily mean that he or she is standing in front of the class telling everyone what to do. The students may have been given the initiative in a particular activity. Nevertheless, it was the teacher who took the decision about the handover of initiative, and he or she may, at any point, take it back. As it is often said, 'The classroom is not a democracy.' The underlying responsibility for the control of any disciplined classroom has to be in the hands of the teacher. How authoritarian or liberal, rigid or flexible he or she is in using this control is another question.

4. **Teacher and students are cooperating smoothly.** A smooth-running lesson is the main evidence of discipline in the classroom, and the participants have to cooperate to produce this. Such smooth cooperation may occur because

it is part of the culture of learning; or it may be because of the personality of the teacher; or because the students fear punishment if they do not cooperate. Whatever the reason, smooth ongoing cooperative work is a clear indication of a disciplined classroom.

5. **Students are motivated.** It is fairly easy to imagine a class of unmotivated students which is disciplined, or a class of motivated students which is, perhaps temporarily, out of control. So this feature is not as clear or necessary as the previous one. The association between motivation and discipline is one of probability: if the class is motivated to learn, it is more likely to be easy to manage (on motivation in general, see Unit 1: English teaching today, pp. 10–11; on making tasks interesting, see Unit 4: The task, pp. 51–5).

6. **The lesson is proceeding according to plan.** Again, we have a case of probability rather than certainty. It is true that some lessons that are improvised or changed as they proceed may be disciplined, but on the whole a lesson which is going according to plan is more likely to be so. The teacher knows where he or she is going, activities are well prepared and organized, and the awareness that the sequence of events is clearly organized boosts teacher confidence and student trust, which in their turn also contribute to good discipline.

7. **Teacher and students are aiming for the same objectives.** Obviously, if students are aware of the objectives of a lesson and accept them (or occasionally even help to plan them), the lesson is far more likely to be disciplined. On the other hand, the students may be totally unaware of the objectives of the lesson and still happily cooperate with the teacher. But if they have their own agenda that contradicts the teacher's, the result is likely to be conflict. A shared knowledge of and agreement on lesson objectives is not absolutely necessary for a disciplined classroom, but it probably contributes to it.

8. **The teacher has natural charismatic authority.** There is no doubt, in my opinion, that the quality of charismatic authority exists, that some teachers have it and others do not, and that teachers who do have this quality find it much easier to control classes. The good news is that the classes of teachers who do not possess natural 'authority' (and I speak as one myself!) can be equally disciplined: we just have to work at it harder. The rest of this unit is devoted to some guidelines which can help.

17.2 What teachers can do to create a disciplined classroom

There are various teaching skills, attitudes and activities which help achieve a disciplined classroom.

Classroom management skills. Such skills include things like knowing how to organize the beginning of a lesson, for example, or how to get students to raise their hands instead of shouting out answers, or how to get students smoothly in and out of group work.

Selection of an appropriate methodology. If students feel that they are learning through procedures that are 'right' and useful for them, they will be willing to cooperate. If they feel they are being made to do activities that they feel irrelevant, too childish or too sophisticated, then the immediate result will be discipline problems.

Good interpersonal relationships. This does not mean that you have to love – or even necessarily like – your students! But it does mean that you need to maintain an attitude of respect and goodwill towards them, and try to encourage similar attitudes between the students themselves.

Good planning. A carefully and clearly organized lesson is likely to contribute to good discipline, as described above. It is not enough just to mark the sections of the coursebook you intend to do! (See Unit 2: The lesson, pp. 21–6.)

Student motivation. This is a key factor, and one that can be enhanced by teacher action. The more interesting and motivating the learning activity, the more likely it is that students will be cooperative and stay on-task (see Unit 4: The task, pp. 51–5).

Task

Have a look at the advice for beginner teachers below. Can you find at least one example that is related to each of the factors discussed above?

Advice for beginner teachers

This list is adapted from one in *Classroom Management and Control* (Wragg 1981, p. 22), based on responses from new teachers to the question 'What advice on classroom discipline did you find most helpful?' So they are probably all useful tips. The question is which are more, or less, important, and why.

1. Be firm with students at the start: you can relax later.
2. Get silence before you start speaking to the class.
3. Know and use the students' names.
4. Prepare lessons thoroughly and structure them firmly.
5. Be mobile: walk around the class.
6. Start the lesson with a 'bang' and sustain interest and curiosity.
7. Speak clearly.
8. Make sure your instructions are clear.
9. Have extra material prepared (e.g. for slower-/faster-working students).
10. Look at the class when speaking, and learn how to 'scan' (keep an eye on what is going on in all parts of the room).
11. Make work appropriate (to students' age, ability, cultural background).
12. Develop an effective questioning technique.
13. Develop the art of timing your lesson to fit the available period.
14. Vary your teaching techniques.
15. Anticipate discipline problems and act quickly.
16. Avoid confrontations.
17. Clarify fixed rules and standards, and be consistent in applying them.
18. Show yourself as supporter and helper to the students.
19. Don't patronize students; treat them with respect.
20. Use humour constructively.
21. Choose topics and tasks that will activate students.

Task

Read through the list and decide which are the ten most important for you. You can, of course, add any you think are missing. If you are working in a group, compare your answers with those of other participants. If you are working alone, try to find an experienced teacher to compare notes with.

The first 20 items above are listed in order of importance, according to the original respondents' opinions. In other words, the most useful ten tips for them were items 1–10. I personally agree with most of the original respondents' priorities, but not all. Your own list, if you did the task, was also probably different. The choices made by an individual depend very much on personal experience and an awareness of one's own strong and weak points as a teacher.

I added item 21 (the activation value of tasks) as particularly relevant to language teaching, and worth discussing. But I would not include it in my top ten. Activation of students (particularly in a task involving talk and/or physical movement) is important for learning, but it is a double-edged weapon for classroom discipline as such. It may get students involved and cooperative, but it can also get them overexcited and unsettled.

The next step: student self-discipline

Although the teacher has responsibility for classroom discipline initially, the ultimate goal is for students to take on or at least share this responsibility. Self-discipline depends on the maturity of the student to some extent, but it can be promoted by the teacher. The way to do this is not simply to try to hand over responsibility to the students for running the lesson – this teaches little, and can be disastrous. First get them used to the 'feel' of an organized lesson, and then gradually begin to share decision-making based on this. For example, once they have had plenty of experience of individual and group work initiated and organized by you, you might ask them how they would like to do a particular task. See also some discussion of autonomous individual work in Unit 16: Classroom interaction, pp. 234–8.

17.3 Dealing with discipline problems

Like Section 17.2, this section deals with practical recommendations, but this time the focus is on the prevention and treatment of discipline problems as they arise, rather than the creation of a disciplined atmosphere in the first place.

Below are some useful practical principles for dealing with problems with student behaviour in class. These are based on my own experience as a teacher who had to learn the hard way how to teach unruly classes of adolescents in a country to which I was an immigrant, and whose language I did not speak very well. They are, therefore, most relevant to this age group, but they may also be found useful when dealing with younger or older students.

Task

As you read, can you recall incidents from your own experience as a student or as a teacher of the use of strategies similar to the ones described here?

Before the problem arises

The teachers who are most successful in maintaining discipline in class are not those who are good at dealing with problems, but those who know how to prevent them from arising in the first place. I suggest four main strategies for this:

- **Make an agreement.** At an early stage, work out a written agreement, or 'contract', with the class stating clearly what is and is not acceptable. It should describe student participation during lessons, and the penalties for unacceptable behaviour. You can start by suggesting yourself what the rules and penalties should be, but give the class an opportunity to discuss and change them before finalizing.

- **Plan the lesson carefully.** When a lesson is clearly planned and organized, there is likely to be constant momentum and a feeling of purpose, which keep students focused on the current task. This prevents gaps when nothing particular is going on, which may be filled by distracting or counterproductive activity. Moreover, the awareness that there is a clear plan contributes a great deal to your own confidence, and to your ability to win the trust of the students.

- **Instruct clearly.** Problems often arise due to student uncertainty about what they are supposed to be doing. Even though instructions take up a very small proportion of lesson time, they are crucial. You need to clarify precisely what the task involves and what the options are (see Unit 4: The task, pp. 49–51). This is not incompatible with student–teacher negotiation about what to do. However, too much hesitation and mind-changing can distract and bore students, and reduce their confidence in the teacher's authority, with obvious implications for discipline.

- **Keep in touch.** You need to be sensitive to what students are doing. 'Scan' the classroom constantly so that you can immediately pick up any lack of attention on the part of individual students. This achieves two things. First, students know you are aware of them all the time, which encourages participation and personal contact on the one hand, and discourages deviant activity on the other. Second, you are able to notice immediately if a student loses interest or gets distracted and do something about it before it becomes a problem.

When the problem is beginning

Students are beginning to chat quietly between themselves; one student is obviously not listening, another is starting to do something that is not connected to the task ... Inexperienced teachers often ignore minor problems like this, in the hope that they will go away by themselves. Occasionally they do, but more often they escalate. In principle, it is advisable to respond promptly and pro-actively to any emerging problem you detect.

- **Deal with it quickly and quietly.** The best action is a quiet but clear-cut response, keeping the problem as low-profile as possible. For example, if a student has not opened his or her book in response to an instruction from you, it is better quietly to go up to them and open the book yourself than draw the attention of the whole class by a reprimand or loud, repeated instruction. Over-assertive reactions can lead to the very escalation you wish to avoid.

- **Don't take it personally.** This is a difficult instruction to follow sometimes, but an important one. Inexperienced teachers of adolescents are often upset by remarks that were not intended personally, or allow unpleasant conflicts to continue annoying them long after the student has forgotten they ever happened. Try to see the problem, not the student, as the object to be attacked and dealt with. Even if you are quite sure the criticism was meant personally, do your best to behave as if it was not: don't let the student pull you into personal conflict.

- **Don't use threats.** Threats are often a sign of weakness; use the formula 'if you ... then ...' only as a real, factual option that you are ready to put into practice, not as a weapon to make an impression or intimidate.

When the problem has 'exploded'

The 'explosion' may be an unacceptable level of noise in the classroom, a confrontational, rude comment by a student, or a refusal by the class to do something you have asked them to do. In some cases it may take the form of unacceptable behaviour between students: bullying, or humiliation of a vulnerable student, or even physical violence. The priority here is to act quickly in order to get the class to return to smooth routine as fast as possible. Often it is preferable to take a decision fast, even if it is not the best one, than to hesitate or do nothing. Don't allow yourself to be drawn into a public confrontation. Confrontations mean time-wasting arguments that are likely to complicate rather than solve the problem. Stop the problem in its tracks with one of the ideas below.

- **'Explode' yourself.** Often a quick, loud command will do the trick, with a display of anger. This is provided, of course, that you do not really lose your temper or become aggressive! The trouble with displaying anger is that you cannot do it too often, or it loses its effect.

- Give in. For example, if students refuse to do homework you might say, 'All right, don't. Instead, let's …' This is a perfectly respectable option, which is unfortunately rejected by many teachers who feel they risk losing face. Its advantage is that it immediately defuses the situation and, if done quickly and decisively, will not be seen as dishonourable surrender! It also puts you in a position to demand something from them in return! But again, it cannot be used too often.

- Make them an offer they can't refuse. Sometimes you find that students are pushing you into a confrontation, and you cannot give in but do not wish to impose your decision by assertive commands. You need to look for a way of avoiding the confrontation by one of the following strategies: **postponement** ('Let's come back to this tomorrow at the beginning of the lesson. Remind me.'); **compromise** ('I'll tell you what: you have to do all the assignments, but I'll give you extra time to finish them …'); or **arbitration** ('Let's discuss this with the class teacher, and accept his or her decision …').

- Call in assistance from a higher authority. Calling in the class teacher, school principal or other authoritative figure may appear to lessen your own authority. However, if none of the previous strategies have worked, then it is better to call for help than to let the situation escalate. This is particularly true if you have a situation of bullying or violence between students. If you do this, then make sure that later you hold a follow-up discussion with the class in order to come to an agreement with them on measures to prevent the problem from happening again.

17.4 Discipline problems: episodes

This section applies practical principles from the rest of the unit to critical discussion of actual classroom incidents.

> **Task**
>
> Read through the descriptions of episodes and think about or discuss the following questions with colleagues:
>
> – What caused the problem?
>
> – What could the teacher have done to prevent it?
>
> – Once it had arisen, what would you advise the teacher to do?

Episode 1
The teacher of a mixed-level class of 13-year-olds is working through a class reader in an English lesson. He asks Terry to read out a passage. 'Do we have to do this book?' says Terry. 'It's boring.' Some members of the class smile, one says 'I like it', others are silent awaiting the teacher's reaction.

(Wragg, 1981, p.12)

Episode 2
The teacher is explaining a story. Many of the students are inattentive, and there is a murmur of quiet talk between them. The teacher ignores the noise and speaks

to those who are listening. Finally she reprimands, in a gentle and sympathetic way, one student who is talking particularly noticeably. The student stops talking for a minute or two, and then carries on. This happens once or twice more, with different students. The teacher does not get angry, and continues to explain, trying (with only partial success) to draw students' attention through occasional questions.

(Adapted from Sarah Reinhorn-Lurie, unpublished research project on classroom discipline, Oranim School of Education, Haifa, 1992.)

Episode 3

The teacher has prepared a worksheet and is explaining how to do it. His explanation has carried on so long that John, having lost interest, begins to tap a ruler on his desk. At first the tapping is occasional and not too noticeable, but John begins to tap more frequently and more noisily, building up to a final climax when he hits the table with a very loud bang. The class, startled by the noise, falls silent and looks at both John and the teacher to see what will happen.
(Adapted from Wragg, 1981, p.18.)

Episode 4

The teacher begins by giving out classroom books and collecting homework books.

Teacher (to one of the boys):	This book's very thin.
Boy 1:	Yeah, 'tis, isn't it.
Boy 2:	He's been using it for toilet paper, sir.
(Uproar)	

(Adapted from Wragg & Wood, 1981, p. 32.)

Episode 5

The students have been asked to interview each other for homework and write reports. In this lesson they are asked to read aloud their reports. A few students refuse to do so. The teacher tells these students to stand up before the class and be interviewed by them. They stand up, but do not take the questions seriously. They answer with jokes, or in their L1, or not at all. The teacher eventually sends them back to their places and goes on to the next planned activity, a textbook exercise.

(Adapted from Sarah Reinhorn-Lurie, unpublished research project on classroom discipline, Oranim School of Education, Haifa, 1992.)

Comment

Episode 1 (Terry refuses to read, says the book is boring). The causes of this were, possibly, that the book is indeed boring; Terry is looking for a way to avoid reading aloud; or he simply wants to challenge the teacher and take a break from work. It is difficult to see how the teacher could have foreseen or prevented the incident. Now the priority is to neutralize the challenge and get the class back on task. The most appropriate answer to Terry's question is a postponement: 'Yes, we do have to do this book; we'll discuss whether it's boring later. Please read.' This commits the teacher to discussing the book later with the class, allowing also those students who like it to express an opinion. But this discussion will be initiated and managed by the teacher, which is a totally different situation from what would have happened had the teacher allowed him- or herself to be drawn into an argument in the original lesson.

Another secondary question arises here, and that is whether we should insist on a student reading aloud if he or she doesn't want to. In this case, Terry did not actually say he didn't want to read, but this may have been the underlying reason for his comment. You may, as suggested above, insist on the nominated student reading, with no exceptions. But there may be very good reasons for allowing students not to read aloud if they don't want to (and reading aloud is of questionable learning value; see Unit 10: Teaching reading, p. 135). This has to be part of the 'ground rules', a legitimate choice for the student as to whether he or she reads aloud or not. It may be better to adopt such a ground rule than to face constant battles with those students who hate reading aloud and try to refuse to do it.

Episode 2 (students keep chatting during teacher explanation). This situation is very common and is probably caused by a lack of firm and consistent rules in the classroom, or by the teacher's failure to insist on them. As a result a number of students are learning little or nothing from the lesson. The teacher should have insisted on quiet and attention from the start, and stopped each murmur as it began. Possibly she is afraid of losing popularity, as her reprimands lack 'attack' and are quickly ignored; the result being that constant inattention and chat become an acceptable and normal situation for the students.

To reverse the situation when it has got this far is extremely difficult. It may be necessary to hold a serious discussion with the class at the beginning of the next lesson, agree on new ground rules and insist on them strictly from then on.

Episode 3 (John bangs a ruler while teacher is explaining). Here, the incident was caused by the teacher's over-lengthy explanation, the child's impatience, and the failure of the teacher to notice and stop the disturbance when it started (perhaps by going to John and quietly removing the ruler, promising to return it later). Most people's intuitive reaction when the class has fallen silent would be to reprimand John. However, a more effective response would probably be to use the silence to instruct the class firmly to start work on the worksheet, promising to deal with any further problems in response to raised hands. Once the class is working, the teacher could talk to John, make it clear that his behaviour is unacceptable, but that the incident is now over and he should be working. A further word or two with him after the lesson may make it less likely that he will repeat the behaviour.

Episode 4 (student is cheeky to teacher about a notebook with pages missing). The immediate cause of this incident, given the confident and cheeky character of members of the class, was the teacher's mistake in getting into a public argument with one boy in the middle of an organizational routine involving all the class. The argument then escalated rapidly into a full-class crisis. The teacher should have finished distributing and collecting books and dealt with the notebook problem later, privately. Now that the class is in uproar, the priority should be to abandon the individual problem, and concentrate on regaining order and finishing the book collection and distribution as quickly as possible.

Episode 5 (students refuse to read aloud their reports). The cause of this was the refusal of the students to read out their work, and the mistaken response of the teacher. It was fairly obvious that if these students refused to read out their work from where they were sitting, they would also not cooperate if standing before the class. The fact that they were a group, reinforcing each other's responses, only made things worse. Only one student should have been nominated to stand up and answer questions, and it should have been the one who was least likely to make fun of the task. Given the very uncomfortable situation of students actually making fun of a teacher-directed task, the reaction of stopping it and going on to the next bit of the lesson was the right one, although late. However, the teacher should talk to each student later, alone, in order to make it clear that this behaviour was unacceptable and to try to prevent it from happening again. As with Episode 1, there is also the problem of students not wanting to read aloud. Again you need to decide whether this type of reading is compulsory or optional. Either way, if the reading text is a composition by the student, it is often a good idea for you to read it out yourself. You can make it sound much better than the student can, and the fact that you are presenting the composition to the class is a subtle compliment to the author.

Review

Answer as many as you can of the following questions, and then check answers by referring back to the relevant passages in this unit.

If you are working in a group, note down your own answers first alone, and then share with the other members of the group. Finally, check the answers together.

What is classroom discipline?

1. Can you remember, more or less, how *classroom discipline* is defined here?
2. What are three or four characteristics of a disciplined classroom?
3. Does a disciplined classroom mean that learning is taking place?

What teachers can do to create a disciplined classroom

4. What, apart from classroom management skills, should the teacher work on to ensure that the classroom will be disciplined?
5. List as many of the short tips under *Advice for beginner teachers* you can remember. (There were 21 in all.)
6. Recall three which you think are particularly important.

Dealing with discipline problems

7. What things can you do in advance to try to ensure that discipline problems do not arise?
8. What should you do when you see that a discipline problem is beginning during the lesson?
9. What are some options when you have a discipline crisis in the classroom, such as students rudely refusing to do what you ask?

Discipline problems: episodes

10. If a student doesn't want to read aloud – what are some things you can do about it?
11. Some of the discipline problems described in the episodes were partly caused by the teacher's mistakes: can you think of two examples?
12. There were some recommendations to the teacher as to how to deal with the problems described in the episodes: can you recall two of them?

Further reading

Charles, C.M. (2010) *Building Classroom Discipline* (10th edn), Boston: Pearson Education.
> (Practical and readable, written for trainee or practising teachers; a summary of various models of classroom discipline and guidelines for practical application)

Cohen, L., Manion, L. and Morrison, K. (1996) *A Guide to Teaching Practice*, London: Routledge.
> (A valuable practical guide to all aspects of school teaching)

Maclennan, S. (1987) Integrating lesson planning and class management. *ELT Journal, 41*(3), 193–7.
> (On alternating lively and quiet activities in the lesson process)

18 Learner differences (1): age

The term *young learners* refers here to pre-adolescents: pre-school and primary schoolchildren.

18.1 Differences between younger and older learners
Do younger learners learn languages better?

Action task

Interview at least two experienced teachers of school classes who have taught different age groups. In their experience, do younger classes learn better?

A lot of people believe that young children learn languages more easily and more effectively than older ones, and that school-based language teaching should therefore start as early as possible. This is based on the observation (confirmed by research) that in immigrant families, young children tend to learn the new language to a higher level than their parents, often becoming indistinguishable from native speakers. It is supported by the *critical period hypothesis* (CPH): the idea that young children naturally and quickly acquire language up to a certain age, and lose that ability later. The CPH is based on studies of children who did not have the opportunity to acquire language at an early age and found it very difficult to learn it later.

However, the CPH research has been done mainly in the context of the acquisition of a first language, and may not apply to second language learning. Similarly, results of research on immigrants learning a new language in an immersion situation may not apply to the learning of English in courses in places where the students' L1 is the one normally used outside the classroom. Indeed, if you have done the task above, you have probably found that teachers find their older students better learners than the younger ones. Some of the reasons for this are the following.

- **The main reasons for good learning by immigrant children cannot be replicated in the English classroom in schools.** Young children learn well in immigrant situations for a number of reasons which are unconnected to natural language-learning ability. For one thing, they are extremely motivated: for a child entering a kindergarten or school in a new country, learning the language is a matter of survival. For another, once they enter the education system of the new country, they will have a huge number of hours of exposure to the target language (probably more than eight hours a day). Finally, their engagement with the language is largely through one-to one communication with native speakers, most often children of their own age. These conditions are significant factors in successful language learning in immigrant situations; however, none of them apply to schoolchildren studying English in a country where English is not the main language.

- **The research evidence indicates that older students in school learn better.** Early research on children learning an additional language showed that, *given the same amount of exposure to the foreign language*, the older the child the more he or she learns (Snow & Hoefnagel-Hoehle, 1978). More recently, Muñoz (2007) looked at two groups of students who received the same total number of hours of English instruction in school, but one group started much younger than the other. When tested, the late starters performed better than the early ones. This result corresponds to the findings of Swain and her colleagues in extensive studies of students in immersion courses in Canada (Swain, 2000).

- **Success in English learning in school depends largely on the student's general cognitive ability.** It is commonly observed that school students who are best at English also tend to be good at other subjects. The conclusion has to be that language learning in school does not depend very much on a specific and independent talent for learning languages, but is associated rather with the cognitive ability that enables students to learn all sorts of subjects successfully: how well they can understand, remember, problem-solve and think critically and creatively. Moreover, these abilities increase with age, up to adolescence. In other words: the older and/or more intelligent the child, the more likely he or she is to be able to learn English well in school.

So the answer to the question 'Do younger learners learn languages better?' is no, they don't, in the context of school-based lessons. On the contrary, the older they are, the more they will benefit from instruction. So it is probably unwise to insist on children starting English in the early stages of primary school, and preferable to invest the hours at a later stage, when they can make better use of them.

However, given that in many places children do start to learn English early in school – most commonly from the age of eight or nine, but sometimes earlier – we do need to explore how young students learn, and to consider how best to teach them.

Do young children learn differently from adolescents and adults?

In this case the answer is definitely yes, they do.

Implicit versus explicit learning

Children learn best through implicit learning: imitating, memorizing, acquiring intuitively through repeated exposure and production in enjoyable or interesting activities (see Section 18.2 below for some examples). However, this kind of learning, though effective in the long term, takes a lot of time. (This is why immigrant children in situations where they have extensive and continuous exposure to the target language learn so well.) The older a student gets, the more explicit the learning processes he or she will use: accessing and applying explanations, deliberate learning of lists of vocabulary, testing hypotheses, focused practice (Dekeyser, 2001). These are efficient, time-saving strategies; this is why adolescent and adult students are likely to learn faster given the limited number of hours available in a school course.

Discipline and cooperation

Adult classes tend to be more disciplined and cooperative – as anyone who has moved from teaching children to teaching adults, or vice versa, will have found. This may be because as they get older, people learn to appreciate the value of self-restraint and disciplined cooperation in order to achieve long-term gains. Younger learners are more impatient, and intolerant of tedious practice or difficult tasks with no immediate reward.

Concentration span

Teachers often notice that they cannot get young children to concentrate on certain learning activities as long as they can get older learners to do so. However, the problem is not the attention span itself – children will spend long periods of time on activities that really interest them – but whether the individual is willing to continue doing something of no immediate interest to them, as noted in the previous point. One implication for teaching is the need to give careful thought to the (intrinsic) interest value of learning activities for younger learners (see Section 18.2 below).

Motivation

Adults are usually learning voluntarily, have chosen the course themselves, and have a clear purpose in learning (work, travel, higher study, etc.). They are therefore likely to feel motivated and committed to their studies. Most young learners and adolescents, on the other hand, have English lessons imposed on them. The younger ones have little awareness of the reasons for learning, and neither young nor adolescent students have much choice as to where, how or by whom they are taught. So their motivation is likely to depend on extrinsic factors such as test results and grades, or intrinsic ones such as the interest-value of the texts and tasks.

18.2 Teaching young learners

Action task

If you learnt a foreign language in school at primary level, what do you remember about the lessons? Do you think you learnt well? What did you enjoy and what did you dislike?

If you did not have the experience of early language learning in school, find someone who did and ask them these questions.

Write down the answers, and compare with the ideas below.

These practical guidelines for the teaching of younger learners are based on the general principles described in Section 18.1 above.

- Use learning tasks that help implicit learning. This means providing lots of exposure to meaningful language, with opportunities to learn such language by heart, play with it or use it to convey messages. Try not to use abstract explanations, language analysis, or exercises based on application of rules.
- Motivate the students through activities and materials that will grab and maintain their interest. Don't rely on long-term motivation to learn English!
- Plan lessons with a variety of components, and make sure each activity does not last too long. Activities can vary in different ways: 'stirring' (more exciting) activities versus 'settling' (calmer) ones; tasks that demand physical activity versus ones done sitting down; collaborative versus individual or teacher-led interaction. They also vary as to the skill being used: listening, speaking, reading and writing.

Some practical ways in which we can implement the principles listed above are through using pictures, stories, games and enjoyable 'language play' activities. Below are some ideas for using each of these in the classroom teaching of young learners.

Pictures

Lack of aural stimulus is relatively easy to tolerate: even young learners will work for a while in silence without needing something to listen to. However, this is not true of visual stimuli. Sight is a very dominant sense, so much so, that if young learners are not given something to look at that is relevant to the current learning task, they will probably find and be distracted by something that is not.

The most obvious type of visual material for children is a picture, and the more clearly visible, interesting and colourful the better. Pictures are very useful as the basis for language tasks and can be used for describing, interpreting, dictating, comparing. See, for example, the third game below.

On the whole, professionally drawn pictures or photographs are most commonly used: those in the textbook, or coloured posters, or pictures downloaded from the Internet and projected on a screen or IWB. Note that there may be a problem of copyright with some internet pictures. In order to make sure your downloading is legal, use Creative Commons, which shows where you can find pictures that are free to use (usually provided you acknowledge the source and don't try to sell them on). See www.Flickr.com/creativecommons.

Videos, particularly brief video clips, are also very attractive to children and can be shown if you have a computer and projector or IWB in your classroom (see *Practical tip 5* below). Make sure you watch the clip in advance to make sure it is suitable.

But there is also a place for the teacher's own quick drawings on the board. Don't be discouraged from drawing because you feel you are not good enough! Even untidy and inartistic drawings by the teacher are appreciated by young learners, and there is guidance available through books such as Andrew Wright's *1000 Pictures for Teachers to Copy* (1984).

Finally, young learners enjoy drawing their own pictures, to illustrate written compositions or in response to activities like 'Picture dictation' (students draw, instead of writing, the meanings of words or phrases that the teacher dictates). They can also draw on the board. This not only provides student-created visual stimuli, but also gets them on their feet for some welcome physical movement (see *Practical tip 1* below).

Stories

Stories are one of the simplest and richest sources of language input. Young children both enjoy and benefit from stories told in language they can understand.

Folk tales are particularly appropriate for younger learners. It doesn't matter if they already know the plot: they will enjoy hearing and understanding the English version. Folk tales often involve repetition of similar phrases or sentences in a series of similar events that build up to a climax, as in 'The Gingerbread Man', or 'Goldilocks and the three bears'. (See Taylor, *Using Folktales* (2000), for a collection of folk tales with suggestions for how to use them in teaching.) Many modern stories for children include the same kind of repetitive cycles (Eric Carle's *The Very Hungry Caterpillar*, for example). This kind of repetition is very good for language learning, and the students can themselves after a while join in and chant the key phrases with you as you get to them.

A very effective combination in teaching is pictures and stories together, so tell stories from picture books whenever you can. Use the IWB, if you have one, to show the pictures as you narrate the story. The problem is that many picture books are intended for native speakers, and the language of the stories is usually far too difficult for our students. The solution is to tell the story in your own words, based on the pictures, rather than reading aloud.

Even if the original text is about the right level, it is usually better to improvise the text of a story in your own words than to read the stories aloud from the book. You can base your story on the written version, but use it only as a guide. Improvise the actual text yourself, adding, repeating, paraphrasing or occasionally even translating to make sure that your students are following. Narrating in this way also allows you to maintain more eye contact with the students so that the storytelling becomes – as it should be – a form of personal interaction between storyteller and listeners, rather than a top-down lecture. It also makes it easier to stop and elicit active responses.

Use pictures, realia (actual objects) and of course your own facial expression and movement, or those of students, to bring the story alive and add interest. Stories are also an excellent basis for activities involving movement: students can move around the class as they act out the stories or mime actions of the characters.

Action task

Try telling a story in the way suggested above to a group of young learners.

Once your students are able to write and have reached an appropriate level of proficiency, they can start writing and illustrating their own stories in the form of booklets or presentations to share with the rest of the class.

Games

Children in general learn well when they are active; and when action is channelled into an enjoyable game, they are often happy to invest a lot of time and effort in playing it. However, games in a language lesson need to be carefully designed so that they do contribute to language learning as well as being fun. Some games are largely a waste of time: see, for example, the description and criticism of the game Hangman in Unit 4: The task, pp. 45,47. Others use such a lot of materials (cards, dice, counters, boards and so on) that as much time is spent setting them up as playing them. Nevertheless, there are hundreds of games that are easy to set up, learning-rich and enjoyable. Here are three of my own favourites.

1. **Doodles.** Draw an abstract 'doodle' on the board and invite students to say what they think it represents. The idea you think most interesting or original 'wins', and that student gets to draw the next doodle and judge the suggestions.

2. **Association dominoes.** You need a collection of small pictures – about three times as many as there are students in the class. Give each student two. These are their 'dominoes'. Stick one in the centre of the board, and leave the rest in

a 'pool' on your desk. Students may suggest adding one of their pictures next to the first one if they can think of a convincing link between the two. For example, a camel may be put next to a table because they both have four legs. The aim is to make the longest possible line of pictures, or to make the line reach the sides of the board. Students who run out of pictures may take another from your pool. An additional rule is that the same link may not be used twice. So if a student wants to put a zebra by the camel, he or she cannot say *They both have four legs* but perhaps *They are both animals*. Then if another student wants to put a cow by the zebra, he or she may not say *They are both animals*, but has to find another argument: for example, *They both eat grass*.

Note that this activity does not have the aim of getting rid of all your dominoes. This is for two main reasons. First, because allowing students to take new dominoes whenever they run out means that the game can go on for much longer and many more students can participate. And second, so that the task is cooperative rather than competitive; there is no single winner, and participation is more relaxed and enjoyable.

3. **Decide on names.** Students are put in pairs and each student is given a copy of the picture shown below. In turn, each student chooses a character, decides on a name for him/her, and tells the other student what it is ('you see the man in the black hat, he's smiling … his name is Peter'). The condition is that students are not allowed to look at their partners' pictures. They can write in the names on their own pictures, but the identification of the character to be named has to be done entirely through talking. After a certain time, stop them. Students lay their pictures on their desks and check that they have given the same names to the same people. As an optional follow-up, ask them to tell each other what colour the faces, clothes and other things in the picture are, and colour in accordingly.

Enjoying the English language: language play, songs, chants, rhymes

There are many very useful activities that are based on the enjoyment of the sound of the language rather than serious communicative purpose (see Cook, 2000). So, for example, we might introduce young learners to the onomatopoeic noises animals make in English, as compared to the noises the same animals make in their own language. Or play with rhyming phrases ('a blue shoe', 'Silly Billy') or alliterative ones ('a happy hippopotamus', 'a lonely lion'). Or write acrostic poems (poems where each line begins with a letter of a word written vertically down the left-hand side of the page). (See Holmes & Moulton's *Writing Simple Poems: Pattern Poetry for Language Acquisition* (2001) for this and other good ideas for poetry writing by younger learners.)

Other enjoyable uses of language involve learning sequences of language by heart and then performing them: songs, chants, rhymes and so on.

The most obvious of these uses is songs. Like stories, songs are enjoyed by younger learners and are a rich source of language. However, unlike stories, the enjoyment of songs is not dependent on understanding. Children can enjoy hearing and singing songs that make no sense to them, so you do need to make sure that they know what they are singing about! If you are singing songs regularly, check every now and again that they remember the meanings of problematic words or phrases. A useful strategy is to get them occasionally to say or chant the words of the song rather than singing it. This will focus them on the spoken rhythm of the lyrics and make it easier to transfer the words and phrases learnt through the song into their own speech.

For the reason given above, I find that chants are actually more useful for language learning than songs, and can be very enjoyable. Look at Carolyn Graham's 'Jazz chants' books (e.g. Graham, 2006). Jazz chants are designed to replicate the sound of natural speech, but because of the rhythmic quality are enjoyable to perform. They can be done in different ways: very loudly, very softly; very fast, very slowly; starting softly and getting louder (*crescendo*), or the reverse (*diminuendo*); in a high or low tone; and so on.

Here is an example:

> •   •
> Little baby monkeys.
> •   •
> One, two, three.
> •   •   •   •
> I like them and they like me.
> •   •
> Little baby crocodiles.
> •   •
> One, two, three.
> •   •   •   •
> I like them but they don't like me.
>
> (Graham, 2006, p. 90)

Traditional or modern rhymes, tongue twisters, brief dialogues or other 'chunks' of language involving pleasing, humorous or dramatic combinations of words or phrases can be taught and used in the same way as chants.

Task

On your own or with colleagues, try to list as many songs, rhymes or chants as you can that you know of or have used and that are appropriate for younger learners. If you can't think of many, try searching online or in children's books.

Practical tips

1. **Have more than one student at the board at the same time.** If you are doing something that requires students to draw or write on the board, ask three or four children to do so simultaneously. This means more students can participate, and creates more drawing or writing for the rest of the class to look at.

2. **Use choral work.** Elicit answers from all the class together instead of one at a time, not only for songs, chants, etc., but also during question–answer interactions. This activates the entire class and makes it easier to participate.

3. **Do plays.** Dramatize a story the students have heard, integrating as far as you can texts they have learnt by heart (songs, rhymes, dialogues, chants). The resulting play can then be performed to another class or to parents. These plays, if they are well rehearsed, usually result in the whole class being familiar with, or even memorizing, the entire text. This is a good investment for them, as well as being very enjoyable for both performers and audience.

4. **Read aloud student compositions.** If the students have written simple stories on their own, read them aloud to the class (correcting mistakes as you go) rather than asking the students to do so. You can make them sound much better, and encourage both the author and other students to write more.

5. **Prepare video clips in advance.** If you intend to use a video clip from the Internet, play it to the end on your computer before the lesson, and then just 'replay' in the lesson. Otherwise the sequence will be interrupted by irritating 'buffering' (when the screening pauses every now and then to upload the next bit). Note that actually downloading rather than 'streaming' a video clip may involve copyright problems: see the note on *Creative Commons*, p. 258 above.

18.3 Teaching adolescents

The learning potential of adolescents is greater than that of young children (see Section 18.1 above), and they are beginning to use more conscious, explicit strategies for language learning. For example, you can start to use explanation of grammatical rules with them. However, most of them are still learning because they have to rather than because they want to, and may therefore be reluctant to invest effort. There is the added factor of adolescent-specific problems of identity, relationships, physical change and so on, which make it more difficult for them to concentrate. So adolescent classes may be more difficult to motivate and manage, and it takes longer to build up trusting relationships.

One useful and reliable source about how to teach adolescents is the adolescents themselves. Their opinions can be elicited through questionnaires, such as the one shown below, which I gave to my own students.

Task

Look at the questionnaire below, writing down for each item which responses you would expect.

Student opinions

Write a tick in the appropriate column.

	Very much agree	Agree	Undecided	Disagree	Totally disagree
1. It is important for a teacher to dress nicely and look good.					
2. It is important for a teacher to care a lot about his/her teaching.					
3. A good teacher controls the class firmly.					
4. A good teacher treats his/her students with fairness and respect.					
5. A good teacher is warm and friendly towards students.					
6. A good teacher knows and uses students' names.					
7. A good teacher is interested in each student as a person.					
8. A good teacher will change the lesson plan and do something else if that is what the students want.					
9. A good teacher lets students mark their own tests.					

	Very much agree	Agree	Undecided	Disagree	Totally disagree
10. I like it when the students take over and run the lesson.					
11. A good teacher makes sure students have fun in lessons.					
12. A good teacher gets students to work hard.					
13. A good teacher always gives interesting lessons.					
14. If we need help, a good teacher finds time to talk outside the classroom.					

(Questions 1, 8, 9, 11, 15 are adapted from a questionnaire in 'Pupil appraisals of teaching' by E. C. Wragg & E. K. Wood, in Wragg (1984, pp. 230–2).)

Action task

If you can, give the questionnaire to a class of adolescents, and then compare their answers with your own before reading on.

Comment

The comments below are based on responses from two classes of 15-year-olds in the school where I taught, and may differ to some extent from those you found yourself if you did the task above (however, they are likely to be similar in most cases).

Statement 1: It is important for a teacher to dress nicely and look good. There was agreement, but it was not unanimous. On the whole I found that students care a lot less about their teachers' appearance than I would have expected. Moreover, in the Wragg and Brown survey referred to above, it was found that only a very small minority expected the teacher to be very smartly dressed. So we probably do not need to worry too much about appearance. On the other hand, this would depend also very much on the surrounding culture and what is expected in the institution.

Statement 2: It is important for a teacher to care a lot about his/her teaching. Most of my respondents agreed, some strongly. It seems that our professional commitment is very clearly communicated to students, through how well we prepare lessons, how quickly and thoroughly we check assignments, how much attention we pay to the progress of individual students, etc. So we should not be deceived by superficial displays of indifference or cynicism!

Statement 3: A good teacher controls the class firmly. This was strongly agreed with. Most students like to feel that the teacher has authority and is clearly in control. Interestingly, you may feel a contradictory message coming across in many classes: the students may appear to be opposing you, but in fact they are relieved if you are consistently firm with your demands. There is a subtle distinction between being 'bossy' (which students do not like) and being firm (which they do). See Unit 17: Classroom discipline.

Statements 4 and 5: A good teacher treats his/her students with fairness and respect / A good teacher is warm and friendly towards students. These two statements both relate to the kind of relationship students expect to have with you, and were both predictably agreed with by most adolescents. The interesting point here is that the first of the two scored significantly higher than the second. Most adolescents think it is more important for you to respect them than for you to be their friend. The one, of course, may sometimes lead to the other, but what needs to be established first is respect and fairness as the basis of a teacher–student relationship.

Statements 6 and 7: A good teacher knows and uses students' names / A good teacher is interested in each student as a person. These two statements apparently relate to the same teacher characteristic, and were both agreed with. My respondents, however, were noticeably less enthusiastic about the second than about the first. Adolescent students certainly want you to identify and relate to them as individuals. However, they do not necessarily want you to be too interested in what may be seen as private territory. Be careful with adolescents when dealing with personal matters. Sometimes they may welcome your interest, but at other times it may be embarrassing or distressing.

Statements 8, 9 and 10: A good teacher will change the lesson plan and do something else if that is what the students want / A good teacher lets students mark their own tests / I like it when the students take over and run the lesson. All three of these statements relate to the idea that students should themselves take responsibility for some learning decisions. Although many of my respondents were used to being consulted in classroom affairs, their responses to statements 8 and 10 were very mixed, and to 9 there was complete disagreement. In the Wragg and Brown survey referred to earlier, students actually identified statement 8 as a characteristic of a **bad** teacher. My own conclusion would be that adolescent students expect you to take the decisions. This does not mean that they should not be consulted and their opinions taken into account, but the ultimate responsibility for decisions about classroom management, lesson planning and assessment is yours.

Statements 11 and 12: A good teacher makes sure students have fun in lessons / A good teacher gets students to work hard. These two questions relate to how serious and learning-focused the students think lessons should be. My students agreed with both statements, but they gave a higher score to the second. Students like to have fun but are very aware that they are in lessons to learn English. They judge us, ultimately, by how much they learn from us, not by how much they enjoy our lessons. Furthermore, as they get older, they understand more clearly that good learning requires effort.

Statement 13: A good teacher always gives interesting lessons. Predictably, most respondents agreed with this one fairly enthusiastically. This is all very well, but the students do not stop to consider whether it is reasonable to demand that all lessons be consistently interesting! Both teachers and students need to be realistic in their expectations.

Statement 14: If we need help, a good teacher finds time to talk outside the classroom. This was agreed with almost unanimously. Your responsibility is not just to give lessons but to do all you can to make sure that the students learn English. If this means setting up brief meetings to chat to or advise individual students outside lesson time, then it is important to try to make the time to do so.

18.4 Teaching adults

The teaching of English to adults has in recent years increased, as more and more people realize how vital it is for them to know English. In theory, the number of adult learners should decrease in coming years, as English is now taught in most schools worldwide as a compulsory subject and required for many school-leaving exams. But in fact many students leave school with a relatively low level of proficiency in the language. This could be for various reasons: they may not have learnt well, or they may have been badly taught, or they may have had to leave school early to get a job, or perhaps they, or the school, could not afford the necessary materials. The bottom line is that the demand for adult classes in English seems unlikely to fall in the foreseeable future: on the contrary.

The teaching of adults is in some ways easier than the teaching of children and adolescents. As mentioned earlier in this unit, adults are usually learning voluntarily and are very aware of the need to make progress. This means that they are likely to be disciplined, motivated and willing to invest effort in both class- and homework. All of this makes it much easier for the teacher, who does not usually have to worry about discipline or motivation problems. They are also able to learn through more sophisticated conscious learning strategies, such as finding and applying explanations, making their own lists of vocabulary to learn and so on.

On the other hand, adults are also likely to be more critical and demanding, and ready to complain to the teacher or the institution if they feel the teaching is unsatisfactory. This critical attitude is reinforced if they are paying for the lessons themselves, in which case they want to feel that they are getting their money's worth. To put it another way, a teacher of adults, particularly in private language schools, may be seen as a hired coach rather than an authority or educator as they are in school.

Some tact may be needed in activating and giving feedback to adults, particularly those who are in management posts and are used to having authority over others. They may find the role of 'student', acknowledging the authority of the teacher, difficult to cope with, especially when they make mistakes and are corrected, or when their work is assessed and criticized. And they may find it very stressful speaking in English in class, where they are suddenly less able to express themselves as fluently and authoritatively as they can in daily life. Make sure you treat these students respectfully and supportively when giving feedback or inviting participation.

Teaching methods and materials

As mentioned earlier, adults tend to learn the language well through conscious learning strategies. They benefit from explicit descriptions of language, explanations of grammar, and detailed definitions of meanings. They appreciate opportunities to apply language rules in focused exercises. Many are also interested in learning 'about' the language: for example, the etymology of particular words, comparisons between American and British English, or contrasts with their own language. However, they also need plenty of communicative practice, in all four skills.

Many adult classes are relatively advanced. This means that you are likely, even with a monolingual class whose L1 you know, to be able to conduct the entire lesson in English. Their level, combined with high motivation, means that you can normally get through much more in a session than with younger learners. Make sure you prepare plenty of material, including a reserve that you can use if you finish everything you had planned.

The choice of materials will usually be determined by the type of course you are teaching: see below.

Types of classes

The main types of adult English classes which you may be required to teach are listed below.

General English

Most courses for adults are aimed at improving general proficiency: the students have found that the amount of English they learnt at school is inadequate for their present needs. Such courses are often run by private language schools or institutions such as the British Council, and might prepare students for one of the international exams (such as the Cambridge English: First (FCE) exam).

English for Academic Purposes (EAP)

These are the classes that are run in universities or other institutions of higher education. The students may be learning English because the university is itself located in an English-speaking country, and so all the courses are run in English. Or they may be studying at a university in a non-English-speaking country but need a high level of academic English, both written and spoken, in order to access the research literature, to write papers for international journals, hear and understand lectures given by experts from abroad, or participate in international conferences. The emphasis is on the acquisition of academic vocabulary, and on the development of a formal and correct English written and spoken style, rather than communicative informal conversation.

Business English (BE)

This is another field which is on the increase. Most university business management programmes worldwide will include BE courses, and many large international corporations run in-house courses for their employees. Teachers of such courses are expected not only to teach English to a high level, but also to be knowledgeable about the principles, practice and terminology of modern international business, including information technology (IT).

English for Specific Purposes (ESP)

These are courses that are often run in language schools or vocational training courses that focus on English for a particular occupation: English for tourism, English for hotel management, English for medicine and so on. Their materials are based on tasks and situations that are typical of the target occupation and provide useful vocabulary and phrases. The emphasis is less on the production of accurate, formal English and more on effective communication in situations that the students are likely to encounter in their professional practice.

Other

There is a wide range of other types of specific-focus courses available to adults today: conversational English; written English; translation; and of course English for the teachers of English themselves!

Review

Answer as many as you can of the following questions, and then check answers by referring back to the relevant passages in this unit.

If you are working in a group, note down your own answers first alone, and then share with the other members of the group. Finally, check the answers together.

Differences between younger and older learners

1. Suggest three reasons why immigrant children learn the language of the new country so well.
2. What are some practical implications of the research showing that older students in school-based courses of English learn faster than younger ones?
3. List some differences between the way young children learn a new language and the way older students do.

Teaching young learners

4. Suggest some important principles to remember when teaching younger learners.
5. Why are pictures important in the teaching of younger learners?
6. Why is it preferable to tell children stories in your own words rather than reading aloud to them?
7. What are 'chants', and how are they used?
8. What should you take care to check when choosing or designing a game for young learners?

Teaching adolescents

9. What are three or four clear preferences expressed by teenagers about the way they like to be taught?

Teaching adults

10. What are some common characteristics of adult learners that make it easier, or more difficult, to teach them than younger learners?
11. What is EAP?
12. What is ESP?

Further reading

Teaching younger learners

Brewster, J., Ellis, G. and Girard, D. (1992) *The Primary English Teacher's Guide,* Harmondsworth: Penguin.
> (A systematic and sensible guide to the teaching of English as a foreign language to younger children, with a rich, well-organized selection of teaching ideas, and suggestions for teacher development)

Ellis, G. and Brewster, J. (eds.) (1991) *The Storytelling Handbook For Primary Teachers*, Harmondsworth: Penguin.
> (On using children's picture stories for foreign-language teaching; clear, basic and practicable ideas)

Moon, J. (2005) *Children Learning English*, Oxford: Macmillan.
> (Some very practical ideas for lesson planning and task design in younger classes)

Nixon, C. and Tomlinson, M. (2001) *Primary Activity Box*, Cambridge: Cambridge University Press.
> (A set of games based on simple vocabulary for young learners, with plenty of photocopiable materials)

Phillips, S. (1993) *Young Learners,* Oxford: Oxford University Press.
> (A collection of suggested activities for young learners, sensibly classified under listening, speaking, grammar, etc.)

Ur, P. and Wright, A. (1991) *Five-Minute Activities*, Cambridge: Cambridge University Press.
> (A collection of very short, easily prepared and administered game-like activities)

Wright, A. (1989) *Pictures for Language Learning*, Cambridge: Cambridge University Press.
> (A large number of pictures and ideas how to use them; also provides guidance to teachers on how to produce their own pictures)

Teaching adolescents

Puchta, H. and Schratz, M. (1993) *Teaching Teenagers,* Harlow: Longman.
> (Suggestions for fluency activities with teenagers, based on humanistic self-expression; accompanied by interesting accounts of how similar activities worked when tried with German teenagers)

Teaching adults

Guse, J. (2011) *Communicative Activities for EAP,* Cambridge: Cambridge University Press
> (Ideas for teaching adult academic classes, with ready-made photocopiable material)

Lewis, M. (ed.) (1997) *New Ways in Teaching Adults,* Alexandria, VA: TESOL. Teaching adults, retrieved from www.writing.colostate.edu/guides/teaching/esl/adults.cfm
> (A useful set of tips for the teaching of adults)

19 Learner differences (2): teaching heterogeneous (mixed) classes

19.1 Differences between individual students in the heterogeneous class

The *heterogeneous* class is often called 'mixed level', but its population is inevitably mixed in more than just level of knowledge of English. The opposite is *homogeneous*: classes where the students are all similar. There is, of course, no such thing as a completely homogeneous class; all students are different, even if they have been put into groups according to ability or level.

Task

In how many ways are students different from each other? Make a list of all the ways that they are different which would have an effect on teaching. (For example, eye colour or height would not be important, but personality would be.) Then compare your list with the one below.

Gender and age

- **Gender.** In some mixed-gender classes you may find differences between students that are gender-linked. This to a large extent depends on the surrounding culture, and how differently boys and girls are educated.

- **Age or maturity.** Adult classes may be composed of students of widely varying ages. Even in school classes where students are usually all the same age, they may have different levels of maturity, particularly in adolescent classes. This will make a large difference to the way they prefer to learn, how motivated they are and so on (see Unit 18: Learner differences (1): age).

Knowledge

- **English.** Students vary a lot in their knowledge of English. This may be because of their success or failure in previous learning, or because they have had more, or less, exposure to English outside the classroom.

- **Other languages.** Students may know only the dominant language of their own country, or they may also know other languages spoken by a local community, or in the home, or learnt in school.

- **General.** Students also vary as to the amount of general world knowledge they have, based on their own life experience and the information they have learnt either in school or through extra-curricular activity.

Ability

- **Intelligences.** According to Gardner's (1983) theory of multiple intelligences, each student has a different combination of various types of intelligence (mathematical, spatial, linguistic, etc.). This is a useful way to look at and value the various talents and abilities of different students.

- **Cognitive ability.** Some students are simply better at learning things than others. They get higher grades in a variety of subjects, understand explanations more quickly and so on. Cognitive ability is thought to be age-linked up to late adolescence. A 16-year old, for example, normally learns better than an 11-year-old.

Personal characteristics

- **Personality.** Students vary a lot in their personality: shy or confident, friendly or withdrawn, dominant or submissive, talkative or quiet, and so on. This will influence not only the way they learn but also the way they relate to you and to other students.

- **Learning style.** Individual students are very different in the way they prefer to learn. For example, some prefer to learn on their own, others like to work with classmates; some are more visual, some more aural; some learn through doing, others are more reflective and receptive (see Kolb, 1984).

- **Attitude and motivation.** Some students come to the classroom with a positive attitude to language and studying, others do not, and for many different reasons. For example, they may (not) feel it is important to know English; they may (not) have had bad experiences with learning it in the past.

- **Interests.** Students enjoy different kinds of television programmes, movies or books. They have different leisure-time activities. They are interested in different school, or extra-curricular, subjects.

Background and experience

- **Cultural and linguistic background.** In many places you may find yourself teaching students who come from different countries, or different cultural groups within the country where the school is located. In some cases individuals may have different L1s.

- **Learning experience and culture of learning.** The way students behave in the classroom will depend on their previous experiences learning English, which may vary widely. They may be used to rather different cultures of learning (see Unit 15: Teaching content, p. 217).

When teaching a heterogeneous class, catering for different abilities and levels is the main problem, and so this is inevitably the focus of much of the material in this unit. But it is important to remain aware of the other differences between the individual students in our class, as listed above, and take them into account in teaching.

19.2 Problems and advantages

Problems

Below are five teacher statements describing the problems they have with their heterogeneous class.

Task

Which of the problems below do you think are the most important? With which teacher do you personally most sympathize?

Mark: 'I can't make sure they're all learning effectively; the tasks I provide are either **too difficult or too easy** for many of them.'

Sara: 'The **material is unsuitable**: the texts and tasks in my coursebook are targeted at students at a particular level, and some of my students need easier or more difficult material.

Tania: 'I **can't activate them all**: only a few students – the more proficient and confident ones – seem to respond actively to my questions.'

Peter: 'They get **bored**: I can't find topics and activities that keep them all interested.'

Ella: 'I have **discipline problems** in these classes; I find them difficult to control.'

Perhaps the most crucial problem is Mark's. Our main job is to make sure the students are learning: if some of them are not, then we have a major professional challenge, which we need to address immediately. In principle, the solution to the problem is what is called 'differentiated instruction': providing individualized teaching appropriate to different students. This is often interpreted as preparing different tasks appropriate to the varying abilities of the members of the class, which is fine in theory, but not very practical for teachers who are already working hard to prepare all their lessons! It simply is not reasonable to expect us to prepare separate tasks for a number of individuals. See Section 19.3 below for some alternatives.

Sara's problem of materials is a very real one. Many of the exercises in coursebooks are clearly aimed at a particular level (see *Open-ending* in Section 19.3 below), and the texts are also often presented with very few options or ideas for making them more, or less, challenging (see Unit 14: Materials, pp. 202–8). This means adapting the materials ourselves, or looking for new ones.

Active participation is also a challenge in heterogeneous classes, as Tania says. Inevitably, the moment we ask a question, it will be the more advanced and confident students who volunteer answers, and it is sometimes difficult to involve the others as well. We need to think of ways to provide opportunities for the less able or confident students to participate without competing with their more assertive classmates.

Peter raises the issue of students getting bored. There are two main reasons for student boredom in these types of classes. One is the varied interests of different students and their different learning styles: a topic and task that are fascinating for some members of the class may be totally uninteresting for others. The second problem is associated with the different levels. In order to help the less able students, a teacher must occasionally provide easier tasks, or take time to explain things that the rest of the class already know. In either case, the students who need more challenge or already know the material may get bored and will consequently learn little.

The discipline problems which worry Ella arise as a direct result of the boredom discussed above. When students are waiting for slower workers to finish a task, or to understand what the teacher is explaining, they are very likely to start talking or otherwise disturbing the class. The lower-level students may also start disturbing the class because they don't understand what is going on or are unable to participate in a class activity because they do not know the necessary language.

The advantages

Heterogeneous classes are seen mostly as problematical; however, they have their advantages as well, and some of these can be used to help solve the problems.

Task

What positive aspects of heterogeneous classes can you think of that might help teaching? Make a quick list (if you are working with others, share ideas with them). Then look at my suggestions below and compare: can you add more?

Human resources. Heterogeneous classes provide a richer pool of human resources than more homogeneous ones. Between them the individuals have far more life experience and knowledge, more varied opinions, more interests and ideas – all of which can be used in classroom interaction.

Educational value. There is educational value in the close contact between very different kinds of people: classmates get to know each other's cultures, experiences, opinions and so increase their own knowledge and awareness of others as individuals. If there are people from very different cultures in the group, then this contact may go some way towards challenging stereotypes and helping students to understand and respect each other's cultures.

Cooperation. The fact that the teacher is less able to pay attention to every individual in the class means that for the class to function well, the students must help by teaching each other and working together. Peer-teaching and collaboration are likely to be common, contributing to a warm and supportive classroom climate.

Teacher development. These classes can be seen as very much more challenging and interesting to teach, and provide greater opportunity for creativity, innovation and general professional development on the part of the teacher.

19.3 Practical principles

The practical principles described in this section may not be able completely to solve the problems described earlier. But they can go some way towards addressing them. They do not necessarily involve a large amount of preparation or the creation of new materials. Rather, they are based on a slight 'tweak' in the way tasks are designed or presented, or simple adaptation of coursebook materials.

Variation

In a heterogeneous class – particularly a large one – you cannot possibly be actively teaching all the students all the time. There will be times when you are neglecting the students who like to work in groups in order to provide activities that allow for individual work. There will be others when you are neglecting more advanced students in order to concentrate on helping the others to catch up. As discussed earlier, such situations may lead to boredom, lack of learning for some of the class, and sometimes discipline problems. But you cannot avoid them completely. What you *can* do is make sure that you give time and attention to the different groups of students in a balanced way, so that the inevitable occasional neglect of individuals is fairly distributed. You can achieve balance by ensuring that you vary your lessons in the following ways:

Level and pace. You can sometimes use more demanding texts and tasks, at other times easier ones; and similarly work sometimes at a faster pace, sometimes more slowly.

Type of classroom organization. Some students really like working with their classmates; some like working alone; others prefer to interact directly with the teacher. Try not to get into a routine of doing a lot of teacher-led work and very little individual work; or a lot of individual but very little group- or pair-work. Make sure that there are opportunities for all three types of interactional organization.

Skill. Vary the focus on listening, speaking, reading and writing. Some students are more visually oriented and prefer written material. Some are more oral/aural and prefer spoken. Some function better when being active and productive and prefer speaking and writing; others are more reflective and receptive, and prefer listening and reading. Again, it is a question of maintaining a balance.

Topic. Usually the topics will be determined by the coursebook, but if you notice that the coursebook tends to use just one kind of topic, and some of the class are getting bored, try to find out what they are interested in and bring in new topics to supplement the book.

Task. Vary the tasks, not only in the skill used, but also in the kind of mental activity they demand: applying rules, analysis, creativity, puzzle-solving, game-like challenge and so on.

Interest

Inevitably, as mentioned above, we will be sometimes working at a speed or level which is inappropriate for some of the students. These students may then become bored and stop participating, or even start misbehaving. The trick is to try to keep them all engaged, so that even if the task is inappropriate for their level, preferences or interaction style, they will continue to participate because they find the task *interesting*.

An interesting topic does not help very much, because there are not many topics that all the class will find interesting. It is also, unfortunately, very easy to 'kill' an interesting topic by using a boring task. However, the opposite is also true: the most boring topic can be made interesting by using it in a stimulating task. Bottom line: it is the task rather than the topic which usually provides for interest in the classroom.

To take a brief example: the topic of cardinal numbers (one, two, three …) is fairly boring. However, suppose we do the following: ask students each to choose a number which is significant for them (for example, the year of an important event in their lives, the number of brothers and sisters they have or their phone number), and then to tell their classmates what the number is and invite them to guess its significance (revealing the right answer later if it isn't guessed). This activity is likely to be interesting for everyone, including students who already know the numbers and do not need to practise them.

In this case the interest is based on **personalization** (which I will discuss in more detail later); but there are other task-design features which also help to maintain interest. See Unit 4: The task, pp. 51–5 for a more detailed discussion of this topic.

Individualization

Individualization is not the same as personalization. It does not involve things like personal experiences, opinions, etc. It relates to students' learning level and includes strategies which enable students to learn at an appropriate pace and level, even when they are doing a routine teacher-led or coursebook exercise. Here are two simple ideas:

- **Start wherever you like.** In a conventional exercise with numbered items, give students a minute or two to skim through the exercise, and then invite them to raise their hands and answer any one of the items they like: they don't have to start at the first one. This gives weaker students the chance to try first for the easier items, and in general allows more choice and flexibility.

- **Set time, not quantity.** Instead of saying 'Do exercise six', tell students: 'Do as much of exercise six as you can in five minutes.' The same can be done for homework: 'Work on this task for twenty minutes' rather than 'Finish this task.' The slower-working students will do less, faster-working ones will do more, but all are working according to their own pace and ability.

For more on individualization, see Unit 16: Classroom interaction, pp. 234–8.

Personalization

Personalization is not only a way to arouse interest; it is also a very basic aspect of task design in heterogeneous classes. Students have a vast range of different backgrounds, experiences, personalities, tastes and so on, and we should design activities that allow them to express these. For example, we might, at a very simple level, provide a list of foods, ask students which are their three favourites, and invite them to try to find classmates with the same tastes. At a more advanced level, we might, as suggested on p. 14, give them a selection of metaphors for the English lesson (is it like a football match? a symphony concert? shopping? a conversation? a medical consultation? a variety show? climbing a mountain?), ask students to choose the one they feel is most appropriate and to explain why.

Collaboration

Allowing students to work together on completing a task encourages peer-teaching. Students learn from one another and are enabled to perform the task better as a result. The problem is that if you put a stronger student with a weaker one, the stronger student may wonder 'what's in it for me?' The answer is to use collaboration mainly for tasks where a larger number of students will always get better results, regardless of their level. Brainstorming or memorizing activities are ideal for this: two or more students are likely to be able to think of or remember more items than a single individual. See, for example, *Recall and share* as described in Unit 11: Teaching writing, p. 163.

Open-ending

Closed-ended cues have one right answer: for example, in order to practise the present perfect, you might give the sentence-completion cue:

> Sue is really worried! (She … lose … purse)

The students are required to write the response: 'She has lost her purse.' Students who are at a lower level and have not yet mastered the relevant verb forms will either not respond at all, or are likely to get the answer wrong. Correcting them may help them get it right next time, but they will have got no useful practice from the present item. The more advanced students are also neglected, because the item is easy and boring, and provides them with no opportunity to show what they can do or to engage with language of an appropriate level.

Open-ended cues, on the other hand, provide opportunities for responses at various levels. In this case, we might rephrase the cue as follows:

> Sue is really worried. What do you think has happened?

The more advanced students can make up more sophisticated and longer answers. The less advanced can listen to other learners' responses and use them as models before volunteering simple ideas of their own. Moreover, even a basic exercise like this allows for expression of personal experience and opinion. Finally, the increase in the number of learner responses to one teacher cue means an increase in the amount of learner talk. This means there will be a significant rise in the proportion of students who can make active contributions.

Closed-ended textbook exercises can often easily be adapted to make them open-ended. For example, you can delete the cues in a gapfill or sentence-completion exercise so that students can fill the gaps with whatever they like (as long as it makes sense and is grammatically acceptable!). Or you can delete one of the columns in a 'matching' exercise and ask students to invent the 'matches' themselves (see some examples of such adaptation in Unit 14: Materials, p. 206).

Compulsory plus optional

The idea here is to have a compulsory 'core' task which is easy enough to be successfully completed by all members of the class, and also an extra component which is longer and more challenging, but clearly defined as optional. In this way, all members of the class can succeed at the basic task, while there is enough extra content to keep the more advanced or faster-working students busy, challenged and learning at an appropriate level.

Almost any classroom task to be done by individuals can be presented in this way. The key phrase in the instructions is *at least*: 'Do at least five of the following questions (more if you can)'; 'Find at least five vocabulary items to put in each column (more if you can)'; 'Write a story of at least 100 words: if you can, then longer.' Sometimes an extra task can be added explicitly, with the instruction *if you have time*: 'Finish this exercise for homework; if you have time, do the next one as well.'

This can easily be done with listening comprehension, for example. Instead of giving the class comprehension questions on a spoken text, ask them to listen to a description or report containing quite a lot of factual material (you could, for example, describe members of your own family!) and tell them that their task is to write down at least four facts they have learnt from their listening. At the end, ask them if they have at least four facts. In my experience they almost all have more, and are eager to tell you what they are.

The main problem that teachers usually bring up at this point is 'How do I get students to work according to their full potential? Given the choice, surely they will opt for the easier "compulsory" work?'

In my experience they don't. On the contrary: if I have a problem, it is that the less advanced students try to do too much. I am not sure why this is. Perhaps they prefer challenge and interest to easiness and boredom. It may also be partly from considerations of self-image ('I wish to see myself as the kind of student who does more advanced work'). In any case, usually these motives seem to be more powerful than the wish to take easy options.

The 'compulsory plus optional' principle also applies to tests. One of the problems with classroom tests is that not only are they too easy for some and too difficult for others, but also that some students finish early and are left with nothing to do. They can, of course, be asked to read or get on with some other learning task. However, it is simpler to add an extra optional item, which is more challenging and flexible in the amount of time it may take. They could be asked to compose more questions on a reading text and answer them, to write a story, to express their opinion on a text and so on. The problem is then how do you grade this extra item? It is only fair to allow 100% of marks on the 'compulsory' components. The optional ones would then receive a 'bonus' of 10 or 20 marks. This sometimes produces grades of, for example, 110%, but I don't think this matters. The main point is to give the students who invest extra work some kind of acknowledgement of their effort and achievement.

Summary

To recap, teaching large heterogeneous classes is a challenge, and there are no perfect solutions. However, there are some simple techniques that can help:

- **Vary** activities, so that different learning-styles and levels are addressed
- Make them **interesting**, so that more advanced students won't be bored by lower-level activities
- **Individualize choice**, in order to allow flexibility in level and pace
- **'Personalize'** activities to allow room for self-expression of different individual students
- Encourage **collaboration**, to take advantage of possibilities of peer-teaching and - learning
- **'Open-end'** activities to create opportunities to respond at different levels
- Design activities whose basic task is fairly easily done successfully, plus **further optional extensions** for faster or more advanced students.

Task

Choose a task from a coursebook you know, and plan how to adapt it for a heterogeneous class using any of the principles listed above.

Action task

Implement at least one of the ideas suggested in this section in a class you are teaching, and note the results.

19.4 Teaching high and low achievers

High achievers

Some students are 'high-fliers': they complete tasks easily and to a high level, and are in danger of feeling bored and frustrated when working on material which is below their level or with other students who are less proficient. These may be native speakers of English, or simply talented students with plenty of exposure to English outside the class. Often the two last strategies suggested in Section 19.3 above (*open-ending* and *compulsory plus optional*) can help to keep such students on-task and learning. However, you might find that you need occasionally to give them extra, or alternative, work to do, such as projects or extensive reading of books of their choice.

The high achievers, however, are normally very much less problematic than the low achievers, to whom most of this section will be devoted.

Low achievers

If students are not doing very well in your class, this could be for a number of reasons.

- They have learnt badly before joining your class and are unable to catch up in spite of their best efforts.
- They are unmotivated: see no point in learning English and refuse to invest effort in it.
- They have done badly in most subjects up to now and are convinced that they cannot do well in English: a problem of self-image.
- They are below the rest of the group in cognitive ability and simply find it difficult to learn as fast as the others.
- They suffer from a clinical condition that limits their functioning in some way: they are sight- or hearing-impaired, or find it difficult to control and coordinate physical movement.
- They have a specific learning disability, such as reading disabilities of various kinds, or attention deficit hyperactivity disorder (ADHD).
- They have personal emotional problems based on their home background or social conflicts.

Most of us are not qualified to diagnose specific disabilities. Nevertheless, if you see that a member of the class is not doing very well, is disturbing the lesson a lot or otherwise behaving abnormally, you need to try to find out why. If a child is hearing-impaired, for example, you need to know that he or she needs to sit near the front, and you need to speak very clearly, facing him or her. You may need expert advice on how exactly to relate to students with specific psychological or physical problems. Consult the classroom teacher if you are in a school, or the parents, or any previous teachers of the individual student, or the school counsellor.

Under-achieving students who are likely to hold back other students if working in the same class are sometimes taught in separate groups. Teaching such groups is very challenging: not only are the individual students having difficulties, but also the group itself is very heterogeneous. The tips below can help, and you may be able to apply some of them to under-achieving students who are studying in a general class.

Practical tips

1. **Find time to relate to students individually.** This includes checking and commenting on their written work regularly, and having occasional chats outside the lesson. These are important for any class, but particularly for one of this kind. Moreover, here they are more feasible, because these classes tend to be quite small in size. Students need to know you are aware of them as individuals, care about them and are monitoring their progress.

2. **Make sure the tasks are success-oriented.** Adapt coursebook tasks and texts, or add your own, that are clearly doable by the students. This may mean providing differentiated tasks and tests (see *Compulsory plus optional* in Section 19.3 above), but the principle is to make sure that the students can, with a bit of effort, succeed. Having done that, you will be justified in making demands, as described in the next tip.

3. **Make demands.** Keep your expectations high. One of the main problems with under-achieving students is that they have often simply accepted that they are failures and don't expect anything else. So an important teaching goal is to convince them that they can succeed. You will quickly learn what they are capable of. Demand that they perform according to the highest level they can. Don't just say 'oh, it doesn't matter, don't worry about it' when they fail to do a task. When designing tasks and tests, set a standard for success that is appropriate for the students, as described in the previous tip, and then insist that they achieve it.

4. **Give praise where it is deserved.** It is of course important to boost the students' confidence by praising them often, but make sure this is not indiscriminate. Over-frequent, unearned compliments soon lose their value and are ignored by students. Only give a compliment when the students have actually succeeded as a result of effort, and when both they and you know that the praise is deserved.

5. **Use a coursebook.** You may think that it is better to write or select specific materials for such groups rather than using a coursebook. However, the students may interpret this as discrimination: 'Other classes get coursebooks, why don't we? The teacher obviously doesn't think we're up to it.' The use of a coursebook conveys the message that you expect the students to complete a programme and syllabus and make systematic progress. You can always supplement the coursebook with extra materials or skip bits of it as necessary.

Review

Answer as many as you can of the following questions, and then check answers by referring back to the relevant passages in this unit.

If you are working in a group, note down your own answers first alone, and then share with the other members of the group. Finally, check the answers together.

Differences between individual students in the heterogeneous class

1. Why is 'heterogeneous' a better way to describe these classes than 'mixed-level'?
2. Recall at least seven ways in which individual students differ from one another in a heterogeneous class.

Problems and advantages

3. Suggest at least three problems in teaching heterogeneous classes.
4. What is 'differentiated instruction'?
5. List some advantages of heterogeneous classes.

Practical principles

6. What kinds of variations can the teacher make in the way he or she teaches the lesson in order to cater for students' different learning styles, interests and so on?
7. What kinds of tasks are suitable for collaborative work?
8. What does 'open-ending' mean? How can you transform a closed-ended classroom exercise into an open-ended task?
9. What does 'compulsory plus optional' mean? Can you give an example?

Teaching high and low achievers

10. How might you address the needs of high achievers in your class?
11. Suggest at least three reasons why some students might be performing below the expected class level.
12. List four practical things you can do to help low achievers make progress.

Further reading

Hadfield, J. (1992) *Classroom Dynamics*, Oxford: Oxford University Press.
  (Ideas for mixed-skills activities to foster good relationships, awareness of others, group solidarity)

Hess, N. (2001) *Teaching Large Multilevel Classes*, Cambridge: Cambridge University Press.
  (A practically oriented handbook providing ideas for teaching large heterogeneous classes)

Prodromou, L. (1992a) *Mixed Ability Classes*, London: Macmillan.
  (Thought-provoking and readable, with suggestions for activities and tasks to stimulate learning and teacher thinking)

Teacher development

20.1 The first year of teaching

My first year of teaching English in a country to which I had recently immigrated was in a primary school. I had two classes, of 10- and 12-year-olds. I had a fairly hard time. Lessons rarely went smoothly, I had trouble getting the students to do what I wanted, and they were often cheeky. There were, it is true, some positive aspects: an end-of-year play that children and parents enjoyed; the awareness that the students were progressing; the occasional sparkle in the eyes of a child who had succeeded in a task or suddenly become aware how much he or she knew. However, I also remember investing an enormous amount of time and effort in preparing lessons and materials, much of which was, I felt, wasted; feelings of disappointment and sometimes humiliation.

The turning point was an event at the end of that first year. I went to the class teacher of one of the classes I had been teaching and told him I thought I was unsuited to be a teacher and wished to leave. He told me to think less about my own feelings and to look at the students. 'Ask yourself,' he advised me, 'what they have got out of your teaching. Not only how much English they have learnt from your lessons, but also whether their motivation and attitude to the language have improved.' He said that if I honestly thought they had not progressed and that they didn't like learning English, I should leave.

I stayed.

Action task

Ask an experienced colleague what he or she remembers from his or her first year of teaching: key events and learning experiences.

For many teachers the first year is hard (but it always gets better later!). If your first year is smooth and easy, you are one of the lucky ones. Moreover, the need to overcome a variety of professional problems results in a great deal of learning, perhaps the most effective learning there is. What you can learn from courses or books like this one is limited; there are some abilities and professional knowledge that you learn only from experience.

What can help?

It is easy for experienced teachers to give good advice such as: be patient and don't give up if lessons don't seem to be going well; believe in yourself; focus on the students and their learning, not on your own behaviour; prepare lessons carefully. This is all good advice, but it is also pretty obvious – you could have worked it out on your own. When you are starting out, practical suggestions like the ones below can be more useful.

A mentor

Your school should allocate an experienced teacher to you as a mentor for your first year. If they do not, ask for one. A mentor's job is to keep in touch with you continually, and be ready to meet you regularly to chat and discuss any problems. The problems may be practical, such as how to register grades or make photocopies. Or they may be about classroom management or difficulties with particular students. Some mentors actually observe lessons of new teachers and give feedback, or invite the new teachers to see theirs. In any case, having a mentor means that you are not alone, and it can considerably reduce stress to know that there is someone available to consult and share with.

Reflect and talk it over

Take time at the end of the day to think about things that went particularly well or badly, or any particularly interesting events or experiences. Some teachers actually keep journals, which helps a lot to structure thinking and get the most out of it. It is even better if you have someone to talk to. This could be your mentor, but it is perhaps better to talk to someone you feel comfortable with: another new teacher who is going through similar experiences, a friend, your partner or a family member.

Staff meetings

Make sure you participate in staff meetings. The topics discussed may be administrative matters (whether to buy a new interactive whiteboard or not, cover for a colleague who is going to be away on maternity leave, etc.). However, they may also discuss issues you can learn from: criticisms from parents, for example, or particularly problematic classes. And your participation, even if at first you do not actively contribute, will be appreciated and will help you feel part of the teaching team.

20.2 Lesson observation

Lessons may be observed for various reasons and by various people:

- **Observation for appraisal.** The appraiser observing your class may be an inspector representing the ministry of education, checking teaching standards in the school. He or she may be a senior member of staff representing your employers, who are considering whether to extend your teaching contract or to promote you. Appraisal will probably take into account the opinions of your immediate superior, other members of staff, and perhaps the exam record of the classes you have taught. Less commonly, students might be asked for their opinions of your teaching. But almost always the major consideration is your actual teaching as evaluated by an observer of your lessons.

- **Observation for teacher development.** In this case, lesson observation and evaluation is a source of learning and development for the observing or observed teacher. You may be observed by a trainer, mentor or colleague and then get feedback that will contribute to your professional development. Or you may yourself observe an experienced teacher in order to learn from their professional abilities in action.

Asking a colleague to observe one of your lessons and give feedback is an excellent strategy for development, but there are some difficulties to be overcome: most of us feel uncomfortable about being observed and cannot function naturally when we know an observer is in the room. It takes some courage to deliberately open yourself to criticism in this way. Nevertheless, it is worth doing. One possibility is to make a mutual arrangement with a like-minded colleague: 'I'll observe your lesson, you observe mine, and we'll share feedback.'

For the same reasons it is sometimes difficult to find an experienced teacher who will be willing to let you come in and watch their lessons. If you are on a teacher-training course, then this may be arranged by your trainer or mentor.

Criteria for lesson evaluation

Whether you are observing another teacher, or someone else is observing you, it is important to be aware of the major features the observer may be looking for. The following are some possible criteria for evaluation:

1. The learners are active all the time.
2. The learners are attentive all the time.
3. The learners enjoy the lesson, are motivated.
4. The students are clearly learning English.
5. The lesson goes according to plan.
6. English is used communicatively throughout the lesson.
7. There is a good relationship between teacher and students.

> **Task**
>
> Note by each item above ✓✓✓ (essential), ✓✓ (very important), ✓ (quite important), ? (not so important, or not sure). Then read on.

If we analyse the items above, we can divide them into processes which are likely to lead to good learning (1, 2, 3, 5, 6, 7) and the objective, the learning itself (4). The essential criterion has to be the learning: if a lesson does not result in learning, then it is not a good lesson. The problem is that it is sometimes difficult to assess whether students are actually learning or not. This is why many lesson observation forms are based on more easily observable factors such as whether the students were enjoying themselves, or whether the language was used communicatively. However, it is possible that all these aspects may be observed and the students are still not learning very well. For example, they may be active, attentive, using English, enjoying the lesson, etc. but not learning very much if they are spending their time on 'fun' tasks which are far too easy for them. On the other hand, they may learn a lot from doing things which are not enjoyable, or not communicative.

An observer must attempt, therefore, to evaluate the most fundamental concern: whether the students were in fact progressing in their knowledge of English. The fact that this is difficult and the conclusions may not be absolutely certain is not an excuse for not trying to do it. An observer can usually make a fairly accurate assessment of learning, based on whether the tasks the students are being asked to do are learning-rich (see Unit 4: The task), and how they are doing them.

The observer may then look at the other aspects, which may clarify why learning was, or was not, taking place.

Lesson observation forms

In some cases, detailed lesson observation forms are used with lists of aspects of the lesson to assess. For example:

The lesson started and ended on time.	☐
Objectives of the lesson were made clear to students.	☐
The teacher spoke and wrote clearly.	☐
The teacher was well prepared.	☐
Explanations were clear.	☐
The teacher asked questions at both lower and higher levels of thinking.	☐
etc.	

(See 'Classroom observation' at, www.shambles.net/pages/staff/classroom/ for some complete examples.)

There are problems with these forms. First, if the observer tries to complete them during the lesson, they are distracting. While considering how to fill in one section, they may miss something going on in the classroom that may be relevant to another. Second, this type of form, however long, cannot be entirely comprehensive. It may not direct attention to some significant or interesting points: for example, how the teacher opened and closed the lesson. So the best way to use them is probably as extra, helpful checklists after the lesson rather than during it. Finally, of course, they do not directly address the point stressed earlier: whether there was good learning.

During the lesson it is most convenient to make notes on a more open form, such as the one shown below. It simply asks for the events, their timing and any comments or questions that occur to the observer at that point in the lesson.

Time	Events	Comments or questions

Sometimes there may be a specific focus to the observation. If you are being observed by a colleague, you could ask him or her to focus on a particular aspect of your teaching that you find problematic (e.g. how you move around the classroom, or your use of the board). Or your trainer may ask you to focus on a similar specific feature, or set of features, when observing an experienced teacher (see Wajnryb, 1993 for a wide range of focused observations and accompanying observation forms).

Feedback

Observer feedback is a vital source of teacher development, so it is important to schedule a feedback session after the lesson. This does not have to be immediately after, if the observer has to rush off to another lesson, but it should certainly be on the same day.

Feedback sessions need to involve two main components: frank criticisms, both positive and negative, from the observer; and input by the teacher being observed, concerning his or her own performance. Some observers focus too much on one or the other so that the session may be limited either to a lecture by the observer, or an unhelpful elicitation session ('What did you feel about your teaching …?'). So whether you are observer or observed, try to make sure that both kinds of input are included.

The feedback should include substantial and detailed, not vague, comments. Comments such as 'A well-planned lesson' or 'you need to improve your questioning skills' are not very helpful to the teacher who has been observed. Ask for actual examples of what they mean, and if it is a negative criticism, then also ask for practical, specific suggestions for change.

Practical tips
If you are being observed …

1. **Tell the class.** Remember to tell the class in advance that an observer is coming, and that they are going to observe your teaching, not their learning. This is a courtesy, but it also may work to your advantage, as the class is likely to cooperate in presenting a good lesson to the observer.

2. **Plan a routine lesson.** Don't try to do unusual things that you think will impress your observer. Include familiar lesson components that you feel confident that you know how to manage.

3. **Thank the observer.** If the observer is giving you feedback in order to contribute to your own development, remember to thank them at the end of the feedback session.

If you are observing …

4. **Take notes.** You won't remember everything you have learnt or want to discuss after the lesson, so you need to take notes and look through them later.

5. **Sit at the side of the class.** If you sit at the front, you will find it difficult to observe the teacher, and you will distract the class. If you sit at the back, you won't be able to see clearly what the students are doing.

6. **Thank and chat to the teacher afterwards.** Even experienced teachers find it stressful to be observed! Thank them, share with them what you have learnt from the observation, and ask them about anything that was not clear to you.

20.3 Ongoing development

Ongoing teacher development during work at school is important not only for your own sense of progress and professional advancement; in some cases it may even make a crucial difference between job satisfaction on the one hand and burnout on the other. Observation and feedback (see Section 20.2) can help, and so can further study (see Section 20.4 below). However, the main tools for professional development are available within your own teaching routine: your own teaching experience and your reflections on it; discussion with other teachers in your institution; feedback from students.

Personal reflection

The first and most important basis for professional progress is simply your own reflection on daily events. This mostly takes place inside the classroom, but also occasionally outside it. Often this reflection is spontaneous and informal, and happens without any conscious intention. Travelling to and from your classes, or at other odd moments when you have nothing particular to occupy you, things that happened in the classroom come to mind and you start puzzling about what to do about a problem, work out why something was successful or rethink a part of your lesson plan. This sort of spontaneous reflection is the necessary basis and starting point for further development.

Spontaneous reflection, however, can help you only up to a certain point. Its limitations are rooted in its unsystematic and undisciplined nature. You will find your thoughts are easily diverted into less productive channels (irritation at an argument with a colleague or student, for example, and what you should have said if you had thought of it!). Also, you may not have access to all the information you need to draw useful conclusions, and even if you have a brilliant idea, you may not remember it later!

In order to address these problems, you will need at some stage to write something down. This may be a brief note on a piece of paper or on your mobile phone, calendar or 'tasks' list: a reminder to yourself when you start preparing the next lesson. For many teachers, systematic journal writing is even more productive: entries are made regularly in a notebook or in a computer document, recording events, plans, reminders, thoughts or ideas. Journals can be reread later to contribute to further reflection and learning.

Another advantage of writing is that putting things into words forces you to work out exactly what you mean. E. M. Forster famously said: 'How can I know what I think until I see what I say?' This can be applied also to writing: 'How do I know what I think until I see what I've written?' Many people (myself included) only discover what they really think when they have to express it in writing. In a sense, writing *is* thinking, but thinking that must be disciplined, rational and able to be communicated to a reader, even if that reader is only oneself.

Action task

If you have not done it before, try writing down your thoughts twice or three times a week about lessons you have taught. This can be very rough – it doesn't matter if other people can't read it! After a week or two, reread your notes. Do you find them interesting? Useful? Thought-provoking?

Collaborative discussion with colleagues

Another problem with the personal reflection described above is that it means you can only use your own experience. Your own experience is indeed the main source of professional learning, but there comes a point when it is not enough. Even the most brilliant and creative of us can learn from others things we could not learn on our own.

Informal discussions with a colleague you feel comfortable with can contribute a lot to your own development, as well as boosting morale. What you share may be negative or positive. You may want to find a solution to a problem, admit a failure or get an idea for how to teach something; or you may wish to tell someone about an original solution you have found to a problem, share your pleasure at a success or discuss a new teaching idea you have had.

Sharing problems

Unfortunately teachers often feel uncomfortable about sharing problems: perhaps because of a sense of shame, or inhibition, or a fear of losing face. However, once such feelings are overcome, the results are likely to be rewarding. Colleagues will rarely criticize you; they are far more likely to be sympathetic, recall similar incidents from their own experience and suggest solutions. Even if they cannot provide solutions, the act of sharing and the awareness that other people have similar problems relieves tensions.

Sharing successes

In some schools there is a feeling of rivalry between teachers which stops them revealing professional 'secrets' to one another for fear of being overtaken in some kind of professional race. And sometimes you may feel shy of 'boasting' about things that went well. However, sharing good ideas is helpful to everyone, so find opportunities to do so. Colleagues are unlikely to feel you are boasting if your goal in telling them is frankly stated, and they are given the choice whether to listen or not: 'I had a marvellous experience today – I've got to tell someone about it. Have you got time to listen?'; or 'You remember that problem we were talking about the other day? I think I have an idea about how to solve it – can we find time to talk?'

Task

If you have teaching experience, can you recall informally sharing problems or successes with a colleague? What was it like, and what were its results?

Student feedback

It is fairly unusual for teachers to ask their students for feedback on their teaching: maybe because teachers have a fear of undermining their authority or of losing face. This is a pity. Students, even younger learners, are an excellent source of feedback on your teaching: arguably the best. Their information is based on a whole series of lessons rather than on isolated examples, and they usually have a fairly clear idea of how well they are learning and why. Moreover, they appreciate being consulted and usually make serious efforts to give helpful feedback. In my experience the process tends to improve rather than damage teacher–student relationships.

Underline the option, or options, that you choose

1. On the whole I feel I am learning *very well / fairly well / don't know / not very well / badly*

2. I find the lessons *interesting / moderately interesting / boring*

3. Things I would like to do MORE of in our course: **pronunciation practice / vocabulary / grammar/ listening / speaking / reading / writing / homework / group or pair work / individual work / other (say what)**:

4. Things I would like to do LESS of in our course: **pronunciation practice / vocabulary / grammar / listening / speaking / reading / writing / homework / group or pair work / individual work / other (say what)**:

5. In order to get the most out of the course, I need to try to …

6. In order to make the course better, my suggestions to my teacher are …

7. Further comments and suggestions:

Questions to students should be phrased so as to direct their appraisal towards themselves as well as to you, and should encourage positive suggestions rather than negative criticisms. A structured, written questionnaire, such as the one above, ensures that students will respond to the questions you are interested in. (With less advanced students whose language you know, the questionnaire can be written in their L1.)

Another less structured method, which is useful with more advanced or older classes, is to write the students a letter. Give them your own feedback and your opinion about how the course is going, and ask for their responses and suggestions in an answering letter.

Either way, the results are not always clear-cut. There are sometimes contradictory messages from different students due to differing student personalities and needs, and some responses may be confusing or unhelpful. Nevertheless, I have found when doing this myself that there is usually enough consensus to provide useful and constructive feedback that I can use to inform and improve my teaching.

20.4 Development through reading and further study

As you develop as a teacher, it is important to start looking for sources of further professional knowledge outside your own school. One of the characteristics of the expert, in any profession, is that they never stop learning and progressing. In contrast, the phenomenon of burnout is strongly linked with lack of further learning. Sooner or later, you will start looking for ways to learn more, to broaden your knowledge and, start thinking about the teaching of English outside the immediate resources of your own school.

Reading

The first and perhaps best way to learn more is to access both theoretical and practical information through reading.

Most schools have a basic library of professional literature, and this is where you will probably start. Professional journals, available in print and digital form in university libraries, are an excellent and convenient source of reading material. Their articles are easier to cope with than a full book, and recent issues will have up-to-date news and ideas. Also, the bibliographies at the end of most articles and book reviews will give you ideas for further reading. See *Further reading* at the end of this unit for a list of references related to English teaching in general, and similar lists at the ends of other units for more specific areas.

Information on a variety of subjects is, of course, easy to access through the Internet, but there is so much that it can be rather time-consuming trying to find what you want. The other problem is that the information or opinions you will find there may not be very reliable. Check the credentials of the authors or the institution carefully.

The most useful way to use the Internet is probably to find books and articles which may have been recommended by colleagues, lecturers or teacher trainers, or mentioned in the bibliographies of literature you have read (this book, for example). Increasingly, full texts of articles and books are provided free online; and abstracts (short descriptions) of articles are always available. Many schools and universities have online subscriptions to journals, which enable you to see full texts of articles, so check what is available at your institution.

Reading is also a necessary accompaniment to formal study, and hopefully continues after it. It may be, for some, a substitute for courses and conferences – but the opposite is not true: courses and conferences are no substitute for reading.

Action task

Ask two or three experienced teachers what book(s) they would recommend: ones that have had substantial influence on their professional thinking, or have been most useful for their teaching.

University study

If you have the opportunity, it is worthwhile to take further courses of study. This usually means a degree, or another academic course at a university, in foreign-language teaching or an associated subject: pure or applied linguistics, the various branches of education, psychology or sociology. Or, if you do not yet have a formal qualification, you may wish to take a course that gives you one. The attraction of such studies is not only the satisfaction of the learning itself and its contribution to your professional expertise, but also an internationally recognized qualification, with its associated prestige and aid to promotion.

These courses provide a valuable opportunity to take a step back from the demands of everyday practice, reflect quietly on what you do, and rethink your own principles and practice in the light of other people's theories and research. However, you will find that you need to approach academic theories and research cautiously and critically, checking the ideas you are learning against your own experience and if possible applying and testing them in practice.

Conferences and in-service courses

Conferences are being organized by English teachers' organizations with increasing frequency in many countries. They offer a rich selection of lectures, workshops, seminars, panel discussions and so on. They enable you to update your knowledge on the latest research and controversies, learn new techniques and methods, find out about the latest published materials and meet other professionals. A wide variety of such conferences take place ranging from the very large international ones such as IATEFL and TESOL, to the national conferences such as BrazTESOL in Brazil, or the smaller regional ones such as APAC in Catalunya, Spain.

The strength of conferences (the huge number and variety of sessions and materials available to participants) is, however, also their weakness. Usually the schedule is based on a number of concurrent sessions, so you can attend only a small proportion of them. Moreover, they vary widely in level and effectiveness as well as in topic. The sessions you select may or may not satisfy you, and it is unlikely that

you will find everything worthwhile. In fact, if each day you feel that one or two of the events you attended were of real value to you, you are doing well!

Conferences cannot supply the systematic coverage of topics that you get from formal courses, but you may well come across new materials or ideas which trigger insights or ideas of your own. Their other major advantage is the opportunities they provide for meeting teachers from other places, exchanging ideas and learning about each other's problems and solutions. Arguably, at least as much interesting learning takes place between sessions as during them.

Action task

Find out what national or international English associations there are that are holding conferences for English teachers in your part of the world in the coming year. Check out also 'virtual' events held by English teachers' associations worldwide.

20.5 Further development: your own contribution

This section suggests ways in which you yourself can make a contribution to the field through sharing your own ideas, innovations or research with others.

Sharing techniques and methods

Very often the first step in this direction for practising teachers is sharing a practical classroom innovation: a technique, a bit of material, an idea that worked. You describe it to a colleague and he or she is enthusiastic. So why not let other teachers benefit as well? Organizers of conferences (both national and international) are likely to welcome your contribution. Moreover, conference-goers often prefer attending this kind of session to the more theoretical lectures given by international experts who often have not taught an English lesson for years, if ever. Workshops are probably the best format for practical topics of this type: a clear explanation followed or preceded by trying something out (such as an example of the target activity type) and plenty of opportunity for the audience to participate and discuss.

Practical ideas can reach a wider audience if described in an article. If your local English teachers' association has its own journal, start with this. Or you could try ones with a more international circulation. Keep your article short, and make sure ideas are clearly expressed in straightforward language and illustrated by practical examples. It is a good idea to ask colleagues to read through your article and make comments before finalizing it and sending it off.

Don't be discouraged if your first article is not accepted. Take note of any constructive criticisms, and keep trying.

Your own ideas can also be published online. First there is the possibility of a blog, where there is no problem with getting your article accepted, and you can reach a wide audience. There are many successful English teachers' blogs on the Internet, and it is easy to start up your own. If you do not want the commitment of regular updates to a blog, have a look at some of the major English teacher's websites: many of them invite readers to contribute ideas. See, for example, www.teachingenglish. org.uk/. Finally, *Twitter* is an increasingly popular way for teachers and ELT experts to exchange brief teaching ideas and references to useful reading or websites.

Materials writing

Another way of contributing to the profession is by writing English-teaching materials. This often means coursebooks, but not always. Today there is a need – and a market – for a wide range of supplementary materials: books or websites aimed at students, providing texts or tasks focused on one or more aspects of language learning; simplified readers; teaching materials or handbooks suggesting ideas for classroom procedures or lesson plans. The best materials are undoubtedly those written by authors who are themselves practising teachers or have had extensive teaching experience.

The way into this kind of writing is producing material for local consumers: worksheets for your own class, and texts and tasks for use in your own institution. If you get positive feedback, you could offer your services to a commercial publisher. Publishers, both local and international, are constantly looking for new authors with teaching experience and interesting and original ideas, but they do demand, obviously, a high standard of good, clear and organized writing. Don't expect them to publish your ready-made material. If the publisher thinks they might be able to employ you, they will ask for a sample of your work, and will then decide whether to commission further work on the basis of this sample.

Classroom research

The term *research* may be defined, after Stenhouse, as 'systematic, self-critical enquiry' (Hopkins & Rudduck, 1985: 8). So it does not have to be based on complicated statistics or long, detailed observation or experiments. Furthermore, the results do not necessarily have to apply to other situations. It does, however, have to be disciplined and accurate, and to apply objective criteria. It also has to state clearly its own limitations. Some simple small-scale research projects are often an integral part of pre-service training. A number of the tasks in this book labelled 'Action task', for example, could be defined as mini-research projects.

Research on foreign-language teaching and learning does not need to be the monopoly of the academic establishment. As in medicine, any practitioner may do research in his or her field. However, not many practitioners have the knowledge, time or money to do the ambitious research that academics can. We are usually limited to small-scale projects, based on classrooms and resources which are easily available to us. Our research is therefore nearly always context-specific and of limited generalizability. Nevertheless, as long as this is made clear, the results can be interesting and valuable, both to professionals working in other contexts and to professional researchers. A bit of research on your classroom may inspire an examination of similar topics in mine or someone else's, stimulate new thinking, and lead to significant innovation or further research

One model that has been suggested as feasible for practising teachers is known as 'action research': research carried out by teachers on phenomena in their own classrooms. It is based on a systematic process of investigation, action, conclusions and possibly re-investigation according to the following stages:

1. A problem is identified.
2. Relevant data are gathered and recorded.
3. Practical action is suggested that might solve the problem.
4. A plan of action is designed.
5. The plan is implemented.
6. Results are monitored and recorded.
7. If the original problem has been solved, the researchers may begin work on another; if not, the original problem is redefined and the cycle is repeated.

For example, a teacher may be wondering whether it is better to read aloud a story or tell it in his or her own words. The teacher may try out these methods in different classes on different occasions, and ask a colleague to observe and compare the students' behaviour during the two types of storytelling. He or she then draws conclusions which will be implemented in future teaching. The teacher's results should also be shared with other teachers: first within his or her own school, and later, possibly, through conference presentations and published articles.

How much effort you can put into your research will depend on your own circumstances. But the point I am trying to make here is that classroom research can and should be done by teachers. The results are valuable not only for your own learning and development but also because they can contribute to the advancement of professional knowledge as a whole.

Action task

Plan and carry out a research project of your own. Most of the modules in this book include at least one inquiry-oriented task: look at them for some ideas or create your own. When you have finished, share your results with colleagues.

Review

Skim through the unit again.

Which recommendations are most relevant and useful to you, in your present teaching or pre-teaching situation?

Further reading

Books

Brown, H.D. (2001) *Teaching by Principles: An Interactive Approach to Language Pedagogy* (2nd edn), London: Longman.

> (A readable guide to language teaching, covering a wide selection of topics and including discussion questions and suggestions for further reading)

Cohen, L. and Manion, C. (2007). *Research Methods in Education* (6th edn), London: Routledge.

> (A clearly written and comprehensive guide to research on learning and teaching)

Harmer, J. (2007a) *The Practice of English Language Teaching* (4th edn), Harlow, Essex: Pearson Education Limited.

> (A readable and comprehensive treatment of the topic: provides extensive information on both practice and underlying theory)

Lightbown, P. M. and Spada, N. (2006) *How Languages Are Learned* (3rd edn), Oxford: Oxford University Press.

> (A not-too-long, readable summary of theories and research on first and second language learning)

Richards, K. and Edge, J. (eds.) (1993) *Teachers Develop Teachers Research,* Oxford: Heinemann.

> (A collection of conference papers: discussion of the concept of teacher research, and descriptions of particular projects)

Wajnryb, R. (1993) *Classroom Observation Tasks*, Cambridge: Cambridge University Press.

> (A very useful resource book of focused observation tasks, with worksheets and comments)

Wallace, M. (1991) *Training Foreign Language Teachers: A Reflective Approach*, Cambridge: Cambridge University Press.

> (A rationale of the reflective approach to teacher training and development)

See also

The Cambridge Handbooks for Language Teachers series: a set of handbooks on a variety of practical procedures and skills in English Language Teaching. The list is available from: www.cambridge.org/gb/elt/catalogue.

Some useful journals

English Teaching Professional

> (Practical teaching ideas and photocopiable material for a variety of teaching contexts)

Language Teaching

> (Regular overviews on specific areas of English language teaching, up-to-date information on issues and research)

TESOL Quarterly

> (The main journal of the US-based organization TESOL: mainly research-based articles)

The ELT Journal

> (Articles are often research-based but have clear practical implications; includes discussions of controversial teaching issues)

Glossary

antonym: a word which means the opposite of another word, for example *big* is the antonym of *small*

asynchronous: not at the same time

aural: relating to hearing

bottom-up reading: reading by understanding the meanings of all the words of a text (contrasted with **top-down reading**)

CALL: Computer-Assisted Language Learning

CEFR: Common European Framework of Reference: a document describing the standards by which different levels of language proficiency are defined in the European Union

CLIL: Content and Language Integrated Learning: learning academic subjects through a language which is not the students' L1

closed-ended: a question or cue which has one right answer

coherence: the way the different parts of a text hang together to make a logical whole

co-hyponym, or co-ordinate words: that belong to the same lexical set, for example *red*, *yellow*, *green* and *blue*

collocation: the tendency of words to occur together with certain other words, for example *make* goes with *mistake*, but not *do*

corpus: a large database of written and/or spoken texts in a language

critical period hypothesis: the theory that the ability to learn languages declines after a certain age

deductive (grammar-teaching process): students learn a rule and then apply it in practice exercises (see also **inductive**)

differentiated teaching: teaching different levels in a class through giving more/less difficult tasks and texts to different students

digraph: a pair of letters that are pronounced as one sound, for example 'sh' is pronounced /ʃ/

discourse: a complete text composed of connected sentences

drill: a simple exercise, usually of grammar, that focuses on repeated production of correct sentences

EAP: English for Academic Purposes

elision: the disappearance of a word or sound in informal speech, for example 'fith' for *fifth* or 'You coming?' for *Are you coming*?

ELT: English Language Teaching

ESP: English for Specific Purposes (for example English for nursing, or English for tourism)

etymology: the origin or history of a word

explicit (language acquisition): learning or teaching language through deliberate explanations and definitions (see also **implicit**)

formative assessment: assessment whose aim is to improve learning (see also **summative assessment**)

global method: teaching reading by getting learners to recognize full words at sight (see also **phonic method**)

gloss: explanatory note

higher-order thinking skills: thinking skills such as analysing, prioritizing, deducing and associating (see also **lower-order thinking skills**)

homonyms: words that sound and are spelt the same, but have different meanings, for example *bear* the animal, and *bear* to tolerate

hyponym: a word that is one of the items covered by a general term, for example *dog* is a hyponym of the word *animal* (see also **superordinate**)

immersion: a situation where the learner is exposed for most of his or her waking time to the language being learnt

implicit (language acquisition): learning or teaching language without any actual explanations, but through exposure or communicative use only (see also **explicit**)

inductive (grammar-teaching process): a procedure in which the teacher provides students with language data, from which they work out the rule themselves (see also **deductive**)

inferencing: a strategy by which learners work out the meaning of words from their context

IWB: Interactive Whiteboard

L1: a learner's first language (mother tongue)

L2: a learner's second language

lexical: relating to vocabulary

LMS: Learning Management System: a computer program composed of various tools which allow teachers to provide texts and exercises, hold online discussions, receive, check and grade assignments, etc.

lower-order thinking skills: thinking skills involving only simple recall or basic comprehension (see also **higher-order thinking skills**)

metalanguage, metalinguistic: terminology that defines aspects of language, for example *noun*, *verb*, or *the present perfect*

minimal pairs: two words which differ from one another in one sound (phoneme) only, for example *ship* and *sheep*

mnemonic: a strategy to help you remember something, for example connecting the French word *blanc* (white) to a 'blank' white sheet of paper

morpheme: a component of a word that has meaning, for example the word *unbreakable* has three morphemes: *un + break + able*

morphology: the study of how words are formed, for example the addition of prefixes and suffixes (see also **morpheme**)

'noise': (when applied to listening comprehension) chunks of text that we do not 'perceive or understand' because they are unclear or incomprehensible

open-ended: question or cue that has more than one right response

peer-teaching: a situation where students teach each other

phoneme: a sound (vowel or consonant) used in a specific language

phonemic awareness: a pre-reading stage where the students become aware of the separate sounds in the language for which they will later learn the corresponding letters

phonic method: teaching reading through teaching first the separate letters and their sounds, and later putting them together (see also **global method**)

phonology: all the phonemes (sounds) of a language

plosives: consonants whose pronunciation involves a brief stop and release of the flow of air: for example, /p/, /k/, /t/

PPP: Presentation, Practice, Production: a model of language teaching based on skill theory

prefix: a morpheme added to the beginning of a word, for example *sub-* in the word *subway* (see also suffix)

realia: real-life objects or toy representations used in the classroom to illustrate new vocabulary, or as the basis for a task

redundancy: a situation where a section of a text is not essential for the communication of its meaning

schwa: the neutral vowel sound /ə/; for example in the word *away*, pronounced /ə'weɪ/

suffix: a morpheme added to the end of a word, for example *-ment* in the word *government*

summative assessment: assessment that provides a final evaluation at the end of a course or period of study (see also **formative assessment**)

superordinate: a general term which covers a number of actual items, for example *furniture*, *animal* (see also **hyponym**)

synchronous: happening at the same time

synonyms: two (or more) words that mean more or less the same thing, for example *big* and *large*

syntax: the study of the structure of sentences

target language: the language being taught or learnt

top-down reading: the use of real-world knowledge to assist the understanding of a text (contrasted with **bottom-up reading**)

unvoiced: see voiced

voiced: consonants that are pronounced using the vocal cords, as opposed to unvoiced ones which are pronounced in a whisper; for example /z/ is the voiced version of /s/

Bibliography

Bachman, L. (1990) *Fundamental Considerations in Language Testing*, Oxford: Oxford University Press.

Baddeley, A. (1997) *Human Memory*, Hove: Psychology Press.

Bartram, M. and Walton, R. (1991) *Correction: Mistake Management – A Positive Approach for Language Teachers*, Hove: Language Teaching Publications.

Bilbrough, N. (2007) *Dialogue Activities*, Cambridge: Cambridge University Press.

Bogaards, P. and Laufer-Dvorkin, B. (2004) *Vocabulary in a Second Language: Selection, Acquisition and Testing*, Amsterdam/Philadelphia: John Benjamins.

Brewster, J., Ellis, G. and Girard, D. (1992) *The Primary English Teacher's Guide*, Harmondsworth: Penguin.

Brown, H.D. (2001) *Teaching by Principles: An Interactive Approach to Language Pedagogy* (2nd edn), London: Longman.

Brualdi, Amy C. (1998) Classroom questions. *Practical Assessment, Research and Evaluation, 6*(6). Available from http://PAREonline.net/getvn.asp?v=6&n=6

Brumfit, C. J. (ed.) (1984) *General English Syllabus Design (ELT Documents 118)*, Oxford: Pergamon Press/British Council.

Byram, M. (1997) *Teaching and Assessing Intercultural Communicative Competence*, Clevedon: Multilingual Matters.

Cambridge Advanced Learner's Dictionary, Cambridge: Cambridge University Press.

Carter, R. and McCarthy, M. (1997) *Exploring Spoken English.* Cambridge: Cambridge University Press.

Chandler, J. (2003) The efficacy of various kinds of error feedback for improvement in the accuracy and fluency of L2 student writing. *Journal of Second Language Writing, 12*(3), 267–96.

Chang, A.C. and Read, J. (2006) The effects of listening support on the listening performance of EFL learners. *TESOL Quarterly, 40*(2), 375–97.

Chapelle, C.A. and Douglas, D. (2006) *Assessing Language through Computer Technology*, Cambridge: Cambridge University Press.

Charles, C.M. (2010) *Building Classroom Discipline* (10th edn), Boston: Pearson Education.

Chomsky, N. (1957/2002) *Syntactic Structures*, The Hague: Mouton de Gruyter.

Cohen, A.D. (1994) *Assessing Language Ability in the Classroom* (2nd edn), Boston: Heinle & Heinle.

Cohen, L. and Manion, C. (2007) *Research Methods in Education* (6th edn), London: Routledge.

Cohen, L., Manion, L. and Morrison, K. (1996) *A Guide to Teaching Practice*, London: Routledge.

Collie, J. and Slater, S. (1987) *Literature in the Language Classroom*, Cambridge: Cambridge University Press.

Common European Framework of Reference for Languages (2001) Cambridge: Cambridge University Press.

Concise Oxford English Dictionary, Oxford: Oxford University Press.

Cook, G. (2000) *Language Play, Language Learning*, Oxford: Oxford University Press.

Cooper, R., Lavery, M. and Rinvolucri, M. (1991) *Video*, Oxford: Oxford University Press.

Cortazzi, M. and Lixian, J. (1999) Cultural mirrors: materials, and methods in the EFL Classroom. In E. Hinkel (eds.), *Culture in Second Language Teaching and Learning* (pp. 196–219), Cambridge: Cambridge University Press.

Coxhead, A. (2000) An academic word list. *TESOL Quarterly, 34*(2), 213–28.

Crystal, D. (2006) *Language and the Internet*, Cambridge: Cambridge University Press.

Cunningworth, A. (1995) *Choosing Your Coursebook*, Oxford: Macmillan Heinemann.

Dalton-Puffer, C., Nikula, T. and Smit, U. (2010) *Language Use and Language Learning in CLIL Classrooms*, Amsterdam: John Benjamins.

Davis, F. and Rimmer, W. (2010) *Active Grammar 1*, Cambridge: Cambridge University Press.

Davis, P. and Rinvolucri, M. (1988) *Dictation: New Methods, New Possibilities*, Cambridge: Cambridge University Press.

Day, R. and Bamford, J. (1998) *Extensive Reading in the Second Language Classroom*, Cambridge: Cambridge University Press.

Day, R. and Bamford, J. (2004) *Extensive Reading Activities for Teaching Language*, Cambridge: Cambridge University Press.

Dekeyser, R. M. (2001) The robustness of critical period effects in second language acquisition. *Studies in Second Language Acquisition*, 22(4), 499–533.

Dekeyser, R. M. (2007) Introduction: situating the concept of practice. In R. M. Dekeyser (ed.), *Practice in a Second Language: Perspectives from Applied Linguistics and Cognitive Psychology* (pp. 1–18), Cambridge: Cambridge University Press.

Dörnyei, Z. and Ushioda, E. (2009) *Teaching and Researching Motivation*, Harlow: Longman.

Driscoll, L. (2004) *Reading Extra*, Cambridge: Cambridge University Press.

Dudeney, G. and Hockly, N. (2007) *How to Teach English with Technology*, London: Pearson Education.

Edge, J. (1989) *Mistakes and Correction*, London: Longman.

Ellis, G. and Brewster, J. (eds.) (1991) *The Storytelling Handbook for Primary Teachers*, Harmondsworth: Penguin.

Ellis, R. (1993) The structural syllabus and second language acquisition. *TESOL Quarterly, 27*(1), 91–113.

Ellis, R. (2001) Grammar teaching: practice or consciousness-raising? In J. C. Richards and W. A. Renandya (eds.), *Methodology in Language Teaching* (pp. 167–74), Cambridge: Cambridge University Press.

Erben, T. and Sarieva, I. (2007) *CALLing all Foreign Language Teachers: Computer-Assisted Language Learning in the Classroom*, Larchmont, NY: Eye on Education.

Ferris, D. and Hedgcock, J. (2005) *Teaching ESL Composition: Purpose, Process, and Practice* (2nd edn), Mahwah, NJ: Lawrence Erlbaum Associates.

Field, J. (2008) *Listening in the Language Classroom*, Cambridge: Cambridge University Press.

Fitzgerald, A. and Milner, J.O. (2007) Words in the air: do read-alouds engage the high school English classroom? (Studies in Teaching – 2007 Research Digest). Available from www.wfu.edu/education/gradtea/forum07/proceedings07.pdf

Gammidge, M. (2004) *Speaking Extra: A Resource Book of Multi-Skills Activities*, Cambridge: Cambridge University Press.

Gardner, H. (1983) *Frames of Mind: The Theory of Multiple Intelligences*, New York: Basic Books.

Gardner, R.C. (1991) Attitudes and motivation in second language learning. In A.G. Reynolds (ed.), *Bilingualism, Multilingualism and Second Language Learning* (pp. 43–64), Hillsdale, NJ: Lawrence Erlbaum Associates.

Gorsuch, G. and Taguchi, E. (2010) Developing reading fluency and comprehension using repeated reading: evidence from longitudinal student reports. *Language Teaching Research*, *14*(1), 27–59.

Grabe, W. (2009) *Reading in a Second Language*, Cambridge: Cambridge University Press.

Graham, C. (2006) *Creating Chants and Songs*, Oxford: Oxford University Press.

Guse, J. (2011) *Communicative Activities for EAP*, Cambridge: Cambridge University Press.

Hadfield, J. (1992) *Classroom Dynamics*, Oxford: Oxford University Press.

Hallam, S. (2004) *Homework: The Evidence*, London: Institute of Education, London University.

Harmer, J. (1984) How to give your students feedback. *Practical English Teaching*, *5*(2), 39–40.

Harmer, J. (2007a) *The Practice of English Language Teaching* (4th edn), Harlow, Essex: Pearson Education.

Harmer, J. (2007b) Planning lessons. In *The Practice of English Language Teaching* (4th edn) (pp. 364–78), Harlow, Essex: Pearson Education.

Harmer, P. (2005) How and when should teachers correct? *Research News: The Newsletter of the IATEFL REsearch SIG*, *15*, 38–9.

Hess, N. (2001) *Teaching Large Multilevel Classes*, Cambridge: Cambridge University Press.

Hewings, M. (2004) *Pronunciation Practice Activities*, Cambridge: Cambridge University Press.

Hinkel, E. (2004) *Teaching Academic ESL Writing: Practical Techniques in Vocabulary and Grammar*, Mahwah, NJ: Lawrence Erlbaum Associates.

Holmes, V.L. and Moulton, M.R. (2001) *Writing Simple Poems*, Cambridge: Cambridge University Press.

Hopkins D. and Rudduck J. (eds.) (1985) *Research as a Basis for Teaching: Readings from the Work of Lawrence Stenhouse*. London: Heinemann.

Hughes, A. (2003) *Testing for Language Teachers* (2nd edn), Cambridge: Cambridge University Press.

Hyland, K. (2003) *Second Language Writing*, New York: Cambridge University Press.

Jacobs, G. M. and Hall, S. (2002) Implementing cooperative learning. In J. C. Richards and W. A. Renandya (eds.), *Methodology in Language Teaching* (pp. 52–8), Cambridge: Cambridge University Press.

Janzen, J. (2002) Teaching strategic reading. In J. C. Richards and W. A. Renandya (eds.), *Methodology in Language Teaching* (pp. 287–94), Cambridge: Cambridge University Press.

Jenkins, J. (2002) A sociolinguistically-based empirically researched pronunciation syllabus for English as an international language. *Applied Linguistics, 23*(1), 83–103.

Johnson, K. (1996) *Language Teaching and Skill Learning*, Oxford: Blackwell.

Kirkpatrick, A. (2007) *World Englishes*, Cambridge: Cambridge University Press.

Klippel, F. (1985) *Keep Talking: Communicative Fluency Activities for Language Teachers*, Cambridge: Cambridge University Press.

Kolb, D. A. (1984) *Experiential Learning: Experience as the Source of Learning and Development*, Englewood Cliffs, NJ: Prentice Hall.

Krashen, S. (1982) *Principles and Practice in Second Language Acquisition*, Oxford: Pergamon. Available from: www.sdkrashen.com/Principles_and_Practice/Principles_and_Practice.pdf

Krashen, S. (1999) Seeking a role for grammar: a review of some recent studies. *Foreign Language Annals, 32*/2, 245–54.

Kroll, B. (2003) *Exploring the Dynamics of Second Language Writing*, Cambridge: Cambridge University Press.

Laufer, B. (2003) Vocabulary acquisition in a second language: do learners really acquire most vocabulary by reading? Some empirical evidence. *Canadian Modern Language Review, 59*(4), 567– 87.

Laufer, B. and Nation, P. (1995) Vocabulary size and use: lexical richness in L2 written production. *Applied Linguistics 67,* 307–22.

Lazar, G. (1993) *Literature and Language Teaching*, Cambridge: Cambridge University Press.

Lewis, M. (ed.) (1997) *New Ways in Teaching Adults*, Alexandria, VA: TESOL.

Lightbown, P. M. and Spada, N. (2006) *How Languages Are Learned* (3rd edn), Oxford: Oxford University Press.

Lynch, T. (2009) *Teaching Second Language Listening*, Oxford: Oxford University Press.

Lyster, R. (2004) Differential effects of prompts and recasts in form-focused instruction. *Studies in Second Language Acquisition, 26*(3), 399–432.

Mcdonough, J. and Shaw, C. (2003) *Materials and Methods in ELT: A Teacher's Guide* (2nd edn), Malden, MA: Blackwell.

McKay, P. (2006) *Assessing Young Language Learners*, Cambridge: Cambridge University Press.

Maclennan, S. (1987) Integrating lesson planning and class management. *ELT Journal*, *41*(3), 193–7.

Maley, A. (1993) *Short and Sweet: Short Texts and How to Use Them*, London: Penguin.

Martin, D. (2009) *Activities for Interactive Whiteboards*, London: Helbling Languages.

Moon, J. (2005) *Children Learning English*, Oxford: Macmillan.

Muñoz, C. (2007) Age-related differences and second language learning practice. In R.M. Dekeyser (eds.), *Practice in a Second Language: Perspectives from Applied Linguistics and Cognitive Psychology* (pp. 229–55), Cambridge: Cambridge University Press.

Nation, I.S.P. (2001) *Learning Vocabulary in Another Language*, Cambridge: Cambridge University Press.

Nixon, C. and Tomlinson, M. (2001) *Primary Activity Box*, Cambridge: Cambridge University Press.

Norris, J.M. and Ortega, L. (2001) Does type of instruction make a difference? Substantive findings from a meta-analytic review. *Language Learning*, *51, Supplement 1*, 157–213.

Nunan, D. (2004) *Task-Based Language Teaching*, Cambridge: Cambridge University Press.

Nuttall, C. (1996) *Teaching Reading Skills in a Foreign Language* (3rd edn), Portsmouth: Heinemann.

Papathanasiou, E. (2009) An investigation of two ways of presenting vocabulary. *ELT Journal*, *63*(4), 313–22.

Phillips, S. (1993) *Young Learners*, Oxford: Oxford University Press.

Pienemann, M. (1984) Psychological constraints on the teachability of language. *Studies in Second Language Acquisition*, *6*(2), 186–214.

Pinker, S. (1995) *The Language Instinct*: *The New Language of Science and Mind*, London: Penguin Books.

Prodromou, L. (1992a) *Mixed Ability Classes*, Oxford: Macmillan.

Prodromou, L. (1992b) What culture? Which culture? Cross-cultural factors in language learning. *ELT Journal*, *46*(1), 39–50.

Puchta, H. and Schratz, M. (1993) *Teaching Teenagers*, Harlow: Longman.

Read, J. (2000) *Assessing Vocabulary*, Cambridge: Cambridge University Press.

Richards, J.C. (2001) *Curriculum Development in Language Teaching*, Cambridge: Cambridge University Press.

Richards, J.C. and Rodgers, T.S. (2001) *Approaches and Methods in Language Teaching*, Cambridge: Cambridge University Press.

Richards, K. and Edge, J. (eds.) (1993) *Teachers Develop Teachers Research*, Oxford: Heinemann.

Rivers, W. (1980) *Teaching Foreign Language Skills*, Chicago: University of Chicago Press.

Roget's Thesaurus of English Words and Phrases (2002) Harmondsworth: Penguin.

Rost, M. (1991) *Listening in Action: Activities for Developing Listening in Language Education*, Hemel Hempstead: Prentice Hall International.

Rubdy, R. and Saraceni, M. (2006) *English in the World: Global Rules, Global Roles*, London: Continuum.

Schmitt, N. (2008) Instructed second language vocabulary learning. *Language Teaching Research*, *12*(3), 329–63.

Seedhouse, P. (1997) Combining form and meaning. *ELT Journal*, *51*(4), 336–44.

Seidlhofer, B. (2004) Research perspectives on teaching English as a lingua franca. *Annual Review of Applied Linguistics*, *24*(1), 209–39.

Seidlhofer, B., Breiteneder, A. and Pitzl, M.-L. (2006) English as a lingua franca in Europe: challenges for applied linguistics. *Annual Review of Applied Linguistics*, *26*, 3–34.

Seligson. P. (2007) *Helping Students to Speak*, Slough: Richmond Publishing.

Sharma, P. and Barrett, B. (2007) *Blended Learning*, Oxford: Macmillan.

Sheen, Y. and Ellis, R. (2011) Corrective feedback in language teaching. In E. Hinkel (ed.), *Handbook of Research in Second Language Teaching and Learning* (pp. 593–610), New York: Routledge.

Shemesh, R. and Waller, S. (2000) *Teaching English Spelling*, Cambridge: Cambridge University Press.

Skehan, P. (1998) Task-based instruction. *Annual Review of Applied Linguistics*, *18*, 268–86.

Skinner, B. F. (1957) *Verbal Behavior*, New York: Appleton-Century-Crofts.

Snow, C. and Hoefnagel-hoele, M. (1978) The critical age for language acquisition: evidence from second language learning. *Child Development*, *49*, 1114–28.

Swain, M. (2000) French immersion research in Canada: recent contributions to SLA and applied linguistics. *Annual Review of Applied Linguistics*, *20*, 199–212.

Swan, M. (1994) Design criteria for pedagogic language rules. In M. Bygate, A. Tonkyn and E.Williams (eds.), *Grammar and the Language Teacher* (pp. 45–55), Hemel Hempstead: Prentice Hall International.

Swan, M. (2005) *Practical English Usage* (3rd edn), Oxford: Oxford University Press.

Taylor, E. (2000) *Using Folktales*, Cambridge: Cambridge University Press.

Thornbury, S. (2005) *Beyond the Sentence: Introducing Discourse Analysis*, Oxford: Macmillan Education.

Tomlinson, B. (ed.) (1998) *Materials Development for Language Teaching*, Cambridge: Cambridge University Press.

Truscott, J. (1996) The case against grammar correction in L2 writing classes. *Language Learning*, *46*, 327–69.

Truscott, J. (1999) What's wrong with oral grammar correction? *The Canadian Modern Language Review*, *55*(4), 437–56.

Truss, L. (2003) *Eats, Shoots and Leaves*, London: Profile Books Ltd.

Tsui, A. (2001) Classroom interaction. In R. Carter and D. Nunan (eds.), *The Cambridge Guide to Teaching English to Speakers of Other Languages* (pp. 120–5), Cambridge: Cambridge University Press.

Ur, P. (1981) *Discussions that Work*, Cambridge: Cambridge University Press.

Ur, P. (1984) *Teaching Listening Comprehension*, Cambridge: Cambridge University Press.

Ur, P. (2009) *Grammar Practice Activities* (2nd edn), Cambridge: Cambridge University Press.

Ur, P. (2012) *Vocabulary Activities*, Cambridge: Cambridge University Press.

Ur, P. and Wright, A. (1992) *Five-Minute Activities*, Cambridge: Cambridge University Press.

Wajnryb, R. (1990) *Grammar Dictation*, Oxford: Oxford University Press.

Wajnryb, R. (1993) *Classroom Observation Tasks*, Cambridge: Cambridge University Press.

Wallace, M. (1991) *Training Foreign Language Teachers: A Reflective Approach*, Cambridge: Cambridge University Press.

Warden, C. A. and Hsui, J. L. (2000) Existence of integrative motivation in an Asian EFL setting. *Foreign Language Annals*, *33*(5), 535–45.

Weir, C. and Roberts, J. (1994) *Evaluation in ELT*, Oxford: Blackwell.

Widdowson, H. G. (1978) *Teaching Language as Communication*, Oxford: Oxford University Press.

Wilkins, D. A. (1976) *Notional Syllabuses*, Oxford: Oxford University Press.

Willis, D. (1990) *The Lexical Syllabus: A New Approach to Language Teaching*, London: Collins.

Wilson, J. J. (2008) *How to Teach Listening*, Harlow, Essex: Pearson Longman.

Woodward, T. (2001) *Planning Lessons and Courses*, Cambridge: Cambridge University Press.

Wragg, E. C. (1981) *Classroom Management and Control*, London: Macmillan Education.

Wragg, E. C. and Wood, E. K. (1984) Pupil appraisals of teaching. In E. C. Wragg (ed.), *Classroom Teaching Skills* (pp. 79–96), London/Sydney: Croom Helm.

Wright, A. (1984) *1000 Pictures for Teachers to Copy*, London: Collins.

Wright, A. (1989) *Pictures for Language Learning*, Cambridge: Cambridge University Press.

Wright, A. and Haleem, S. (1991) *Visuals for the Language Classroom*, London: Longman.

Zahar, R., Cobb, T. and Spada, N. (2001) Acquiring vocabulary through reading: effects of frequency and contextual richness. *Canadian Modern Language Review*, *57*(4), 544–72.

Websites

Academic Word List: http://intra.collegebourget.qc.ca/spip/IMG/doc/AWL_complete_list-2.doc

Cambridge Dictionary Online: http://dictionary.cambridge.org/

Classroom observation: www.shambles.net/pages/staff/classroom

CLIL compendium: www.clilcompendium.com/clilcompendium.htm

Common European Framework of Reference for Languages: www.coe.int/t/dg4/linguistic/cadre_en.asp

Creative Commons (pictures): www.Flickr.com/creativecommons

Easy English: www.easyenglish.com/

English Grammar Exercises: www.englisch-hilfen.de/en/exercises_list/alle_grammar.htm

English Profile: http://wordlistspreview.englishprofile.org/staticfiles/about.html

ESLflow: www.eslflow.com/index.html

European Commission: language teaching: CLIL: http://ec.europa.eu/education/languages/language-teaching/doc236_en.htm

ForBetterEnglish: http://forbetterenglish.com/

Guide to Grammar and Writing: http://grammar.ccc.commnet.edu/grammar/index.htm

Hot Potatoes: http://hotpot.uvic.ca/

JustTheWord: www.just-the-word.com/

Learn English kids: http://learnenglishkids.britishcouncil.org/en/

Learn English: http://learnenglish.britishcouncil.org/en/

Learning English – Quizzes: www.bbc.co.uk/worldservice/learningenglish/quizzes/

TESL/TEFL/TESOL/ESL/EFL/ESOL Links – ESL: Reading: http://iteslj.org/links/ESL/Reading/

Merriam-Webster Online: www.merriam-webster.com/

OER Commons (educational material): www.oercommons.org/

Oxford advanced learner's dictionary: www.oxfordadvancedlearnersdictionary.com/

Oxford 3000: http://www.oxfordadvancedlearnersdictionary.com/oxford3000/

Oxford Dictionaries Online: http://oxforddictionaries.com/

ReCall: http://www.eurocall-languages.org/recall/index.html

Roget's Thesaurus of English Words and Phrases: http://poets.notredame.ac.jp/Roget/

Syllabus design links: www.udel.edu/cubillos/622links.htm

Teaching adults: http://writing.colostate.edu/guides/teaching/esl/adults.cfm

TeachingEnglish: www.teachingenglish.org.uk/

Vocabprofile: www.lextutor.ca/vp/bnc/

Word Search Maker: http://puzzles.about.com/od/wordsearches/tp/word-search-makers.htm

Index

Page numbers in italic indicate Glossary items.